The Technique of
GETTING THINGS DONE

The Technique of

GETTING THINGS DONE

*Rules for directing
will power from the lives of
the world's leaders*

by DR. DONALD A. LAIRD
and
ELEANOR C. LAIRD

MCGRAW-HILL BOOK COMPANY, INC.

NEW YORK : LONDON

The Technique of
GETTING THINGS DONE
Copyright, 1947, *by the* McGraw-Hill Book Company, Inc.

XIV

36080

PUBLISHED BY THE MCGRAW HILL BOOK COMPANY, INC.

PRINTED IN THE UNITED STATES OF AMERICA

To

PROF. HERMANN S. FICKE

Inspiring teacher
who has devoted his life
to teaching others to
express themselves and to
appreciate life's richness

Portions of this book have appeared as articles in magazines. We are indebted to the editors of the following for permission to use the material in revised form:

AMERICAN WEEKLY

CORONET

HOUSEHOLD

LADIES' HOME JOURNAL

MAC LEAN'S

YOUR LIFE

Contents

1

How producers are made

THE WORLD has always cried for men—and women—who can get things done, for people who have initiative, who are self-starters, who see a task through to its finish. *It isn't how much you know but what you get done that the world rewards and remembers.*

More people are held back from success because they don't know how to get things done than for any other single reason. A recent survey in 35 states revealed that 40 per cent of all workers, two out of every five, must learn how to get things done if they are to go ahead.

One out of ten is held back because he is not trusted. This one may have the buck-passing habit, take unearned credit, blame others, or be downright dishonest. Ten per cent of all workers are held back for this reason.

One out of four is held back because he lacks the knack of getting along with others. This one irritates when he should win cooperation, criticizes when he should flatter, is sour when he should smile. Twenty-five per cent of all workers are held back for social reasons.

But the big handicap to success, the survey showed, is not lack of brains, not lack of character or willingness. It is weakness in getting things done.

The 40 per cent are the Almosts. They know what to do—and Almost do it on time. They Almost win promotions. They Almost become leaders. They may miss by only a minute or an inch, but they do miss until they learn how to gain that minute or inch for themselves.

There are astonishing differences in what different people accomplish on the same job, using the same equipment and materials. For instance:

One shoe factory worker will trim 1,090 pairs of heels in a typical day, while another worker will trim only 765 pairs.

One laundry worker will iron a shirt in 279 seconds, while another will require only 213, a whole minute less.

One coal miner will turn out twelve times as much coal as another—an enormous difference, but not a unique one.

One silk weaver will produce twice as much silk as another. The weaving machines do not determine the production, but the people who tend them.

One taxi driver will consistently get 60 per cent more passengers than another.

And so it goes in all human activities. Everywhere are frightful wastes of ability and opportunity.

In the present book the authors are interested in cutting down these wastes. They wish to encourage you to use your ability and opportunity. They hope to show you time-guaranteed roads to accomplishment and set you on fire to make them your own.

They want to help the Almosts become Achievers.

A Confession

The Almosts are not lazy. Often they are busier than an old hen with a flock of ducklings. They putter around fussily all day long and half the night, though they fail to accomplish much.

They are held back by indecision, by lack of organization in their work, by overattention to minor details.

They are swirled around in circles, getting nowhere, because they do not chart a straight course and then stick to it.

They don't need to work harder; they need to work more effectively. They must learn how to make their work count.

I used to work hard, but in circles and to little good result. As soon as an idea occurred to me I would start to work on it; other things would be left unfinished. Then I would have another bright idea and leave the first unfinished to work on the new one.

Soon unfinished work so cluttered up my one desk that I had to get a second desk and use a swivel chair between them to run interference on myself. Much of my time was then spent trying to remember in which drawer of which desk I had hidden the work I had started a month before.

It was high-tension work, but it got me nowhere, like eating soup with a fork. What I thought was "efficiency" was more like mania. No wonder I failed to deliver the goods.

Labor-saving gadgets and appliances appealed to me, so I acquired a lot of them to help me get things done. They interested the small boy in me and were heaps of fun. But I tinkered with them, played with them, and altered them so much that soon they were keeping me from producing. I was making work instead of doing work.

I bought a second automobile to speed up my schedule. But that was no more help than the second desk. I was still late.

I removed the pictures and insurance calendars from my walls and put up a prettily framed "Do It Now!" sign, just like a big businessman I had seen. But I did so many things "now" that I was going off half-cocked most of the time. I'd look at that sign and then rush to make a telephone call without planning the conversation, so would have to make additional calls later to explain or justify the first.

I was wasting a lot of other people's time as well as my own.

Blunders? Why, I made so many blunders in my high-speed work that I had to spend hours each night untangling them.

Then one day I read what a five-foot-four-inch redheaded Scotchman, Andrew Carnegie, had said to an office drone. "You must be a poor worker to take ten hours to do a day's work." And I was taking fifteen hours!

That challenged me to take an inventory of my work habits. I found that my frantic speed was making me inaccurate. I needed to plan ahead, to eliminate blind, headlong plunges, to do the hard jobs first.

I needed to simplify.

Too many interesting but unessential side issues were distracting me from the important things.

I was putting off unpleasant tasks when I should have been doing them first.

I was taking too much time over minor decisions.

Unfinished work was worrying me like a politician about to be turned out of office.

Soon I was doing more, earning more, having more fun, and not working a fraction so hard. Principles of accomplishment, gleaned from industrial psychology and the work habits of men who made themselves Achievers, raised my score in getting things done.

After all, I wasn't so badly off as that magnificent putterer, Cervantes. He didn't learn how to get things done until he was fifty-eight. P. T. Barnum, the great showman, another frantic worker, schemed and failed until he was sixty before he finally found how to get things done and started his circus. The artist Goya was still an Almost at past forty.

Sixty years passed before the original J. P. Morgan really got going, but between sixty and seventy he made himself a power in world finance. Abraham Lincoln did not become presidential material until after the age of fifty. And, at the half-century mark, Woodrow Wilson was just a good college professor buried in academic halls. Aristotle did not get down to work until he reached fifty; in the twelve years remaining to him, he produced the work which has made his name permanently famous.

One cannot be too old to get started right.

ALWAYS ON TOP OF THE JOB

While many of us have to learn how to get things done through hard knocks, a lucky few seem to have the knack of producing more than they consume right from the start.

Take Sam Woodley, for instance. The American Association for the Advancement of Science paid tribute to Woodley after he had managed its office affairs for a quarter of a century. Without exception, the scientists admitted their dependence upon him. "A whirlwind for getting things done," one of them said.

Another said—a clue to Woodley's skill in getting things done—"He has an uncanny ability to segregate the essential from the unessential."

Sam Woodley went to work in his small Illinois town at fourteen but took correspondence courses in bookkeeping and evening courses in shorthand. After he was employed by the A.A.A.S., he went to college nights and finally earned a Master of Science degree.

Alexander Legge was another chap who seemed born with the knack of getting things done and keeping on top of his job. Perhaps his boyhood hardships gave him training in this. His immigrant father was fleeced shortly after arriving in this country; he was given counterfeit money in exchange for his life savings. After a few difficult years in Wisconsin, the family again hit financial zero, so moved to Nebraska for a fresh start.

Alexander was ten at the time, but he did his full boyish share to help the family carve a living from the hard soil.

At twenty-five he decided to give up his new career as a cowboy; he figured he could make a better living in business in Omaha. The Omaha branch of the McCormick reaper firm tried him out at their worst job, collecting bad accounts from tough customers.

A few years later McCormick himself began to hear about the abilities of this rangy Scotchman. Legge was promoted to the Chicago branch, ultimately became president of the International Harvester Company.

"He was always on top of his job, always ran his work and never permitted it to run him," McCormick said. That was why this erstwhile cow hand climbed steadily until he was at the desk vacated by McCormick himself.

Companies don't select men; men select themselves, on the basis of their past performance in getting things done.

From boyhood Benjamin Franklin had an eye on how to get things done. At ten he was helping his father salt down the family supply of meat. It took a lot of salt meat to feed that family of sixteen children. It was a slippery, sloppy job. Franklin's sweaty shirt smelled like a fermented pineapple. But he worked willingly enough, thinking ahead as he worked.

When the barrel was nearly filled, young Ben looked at his father. "You could save yourself a lot of work later if you would just say one blessing over the entire batch now, instead of at each meal."

His mother, who wanted Ben to be a minister, tried to appear horrified at his work-saving suggestion.

Years later Franklin applied the same principle to keep himself always on top of his job. "Have you anything to do tomorrow? Do it today!"

Childhood Hardships

Those who have to hustle during their youth seem to acquire habits of effective work early and carry these productive habits through their active lives.

Fuller Callaway was such a man. He was the fourteenth child of a Georgia minister. The family was almost as large as the small congregation. The younger children wore hand-me-downs.

At thirteen young Fuller, seedy as a cucumber, started out for himself. He rented a bit of land and hired a mule to grow cotton. After a year of tough but effective work, he had a net profit of $36.45. Not much for a year of backbreaking toil, but that year gave him practice in the work habits that were to make him a cotton millionaire.

He went to a city store, got a job as porter, and at eighteen borrowed money to start his own variety store. At thirty he had his own chain of cotton mills, which he built into the largest organization of its kind in the South.

His work habits were typified by his favorite quotation.

> Late to bed,
> Early to rise,
> Work like hell
> And economize.

It is a good thing most of us are inconvenienced by having to make a living.

And it is unfortunate that many grow up without having the good training of regular daily chores in childhood to give them the habit of getting things done. Modern labor-saving conveniences and steadily rising standards of living have made children's chores vanish. Nothing has yet been discovered to replace chores for developing hustle early in life.

One of my friends makes an exceptionally good living at a miserable job. For years he helped break in engineering graduates for a large electrical manufacturer. Now he is giving first aid in getting things done to idle sons of the self-made rich. Sounds like easy work, but it is trying, and only an inborn optimist could stick to it.

Two brothers who had built up a sizeable business in the Middle West, for instance, came to realize that their four sons put together could not generate enough gumption to carry on the business that they were running quite effortlessly. So they hired my friend to devote four full years teaching these sons, then grown men with families, how to get things done.

Two of the sons wanted to learn and did. They are now leading the old firm to greater glory.

But the other two sons couldn't understand why a business that furnished employment for the home town should interfere with their fun. They still think it was unfair because they were forced out of the firm; they speak to their successful brothers only when absolutely necessary. They grumble around like horses with empty stomachs. They are teaching their children to hate their uncles. They coddle the children, and make them imagine the world owes them a living without working for it. The children look as if they had been born sneering.

The successful brothers, on the other hand, are following my friend's teachings and training their children to get things done. These lucky boys and girls have regular chores and regular outside work for hourly wages. They take work as a matter of course, as something they owe the world.

Peter F. Collier should have had my friend on his pay roll. Collier came to New York from Ireland as a boy. He started as a carpenter, ended as a millionaire publisher of the classics. He was accepted by the then-haughty Knickerbocker society.

This jolly Irishman, humanly enough, did not want his only son to suffer the youthful hardships that he himself had endured. It had been "root hog, or die" for Peter F. For his son, it was travel and play, with expensive schools sandwiched in between. The only training Robert J. had in getting things done was from his college teachers, and in those days Harvard professors were a bit lenient with sons of the rich.

The immigrant had started a little magazine to advertise his book sets, and he turned this over to his heir. *Collier's Weekly* did well enough for a time, then strange things began to happen to it. Its star writers left for other jobs. Many weeks there was no money to meet the pay roll—because young Rob had taken all the cash for a luxurious vacation. When his decisions were needed, he was nowhere to be found.

He had never learned the rudiments of work. His father had given him everything except experience in getting things done. Half a dozen years after his father's death, Rob Collier lost his magazine, and other hands, not softened by coddling, carried it on to greater heights.

Rob Collier had a brilliant mind. He was charming, honest, handsome. And he knew it. He wasn't exactly lazy, for he worked hard at polo. But he thought things did themselves. Of him it was said, as of so many who have failed to carry on family reputations, "He had every talent except the talent of making use of his talents."

He was poisoned by his father's success.

He did not produce more than he consumed.

Shirkers and sluggards produce less than they consume. So do some capable people who have not trained themselves in effective working methods. It is the producers who raise the world's standard of living. It is the producers who win the big share of the world's rewards.

The world needs producers. Our civilization is young and unfinished. Much needs to be done in every field of endeavor.

The greatest railroad is yet to be operated.

The greatest automobile is still to be designed.

The greatest scientific discoveries are still to be made.

The greatest strides are yet to be made in the conquest of illness.

The greatest of everything is still in the future.

We hope this book will stimulate you toward the future and the work it will afford.

When Napoleon was made emperor he selected bees as the symbol for the new France. *Work.* And to Duroc, his aide, he said, "Work! Work! I have an insatiable appetite for it. Even in my dreams I am at work."

Yet there are those who will do anything to get ahead, except work.

THE WORLD'S MOST FAMOUS STORY OF INITIATIVE

Elbert Hubbard dashed off his famous *A Message to Garcia* in an hour. It was started by a friendly after-supper discussion with his son, Bert, about the Spanish-American War. Bert told him the real hero was Lieutenant Rowan, the man who got a message through despite terrific obstacles. And in the story Fra Elbert immortalized Lieutenant Rowan and all others who get things done despite hell and high water.

The little story was an instant success. It was scarcely in the mails before a railroad president telegraphed for 100,000 extra copies for his employees. Other companies ordered so many that the presses worked day and night but still could not supply the demand.

Nearly a half-century after it was written, it is still being widely issued. The U. S. Naval Academy had special copies printed for midshipmen in the Second World War. It has been translated into twenty-five languages, and more than 85,000,000 copies have been sold.

Why all this lasting popularity?

Because *A Message to Garcia* carries a message the Almosts need—the message of getting things done.

Here is that famous little story in full, reprinted by special arrangement with the copyright owners.

A MESSAGE TO GARCIA

In all this Cuban business there is one man stands out on the horizon of my memory like Mars at perihelion.

When war broke out between Spain and the United States, it was very necessary to communicate quickly with the leader of the Insurgents. Garcia was somewhere in the mountain fastnesses of Cuba—no one knew where. No mail or telegraph message could reach him. The President must secure his co-operation, and quickly.

What to do!

Some one said to the President, "There is a fellow by the name of Rowan will find Garcia for you, if anybody can."

Rowan was sent for and given a letter to be delivered to Garcia. How the "fellow by the name of Rowan" took the letter, sealed it up in an oilskin pouch, strapped it over his heart, in four days landed by night off the coast of Cuba from an open boat, disappeared into the jungle, and in three weeks came out on the other side of the Island, having traversed a hostile country on foot, and delivered his letter to Garcia—are things I have no special desire now to tell in detail. The point that I wish to make is this: McKinley gave Rowan a letter to be delivered to Garcia; Rowan took the letter and did not ask, "Where is he at?"

By the Eternal! there is a man whose form should be cast in deathless bronze and the statue placed in every college of the land. It is not book-learning young men need, nor instruction about this and that, but a stiffening of the vertebrae which will cause them to be loyal to a trust, to act promptly, concentrate their energies: do the thing—"Carry a message to Garcia."

General Garcia is dead now, but there are other Garcias. No one who has endeavored to carry out an enterprise where many hands were needed has not been well-nigh appalled at times by the imbecility of the average man—the inability or unwillingness to concentrate on a thing and do it. Slipshod assistance, foolish inattention, dowdy indifference, and half-hearted work seem the rule; and no man succeeds, unless by hook or crook or threat he forces or bribes other men to assist him; or, mayhap, God in His goodness performs a miracle and sends him an Angel of Light for an assistant.

You, reader, put this matter to a test. You are sitting now in your office—six clerks are within call. Summon any one of them and make this request, "Please look in the encyclopedia and jot down a brief memorandum for me concerning the life of Correggio."

Will the clerk quietly say, "Yes, sir!" and go do the task?

On your life he will not. He will look at you out of a fishy eye and ask one or more of the following questions.

"Who was he?"

"Which encyclopedia?"

"Where is the encyclopedia?"

"Was I hired for that?"

"Don't you mean Bismarck?"

"What's the matter with Charlie doing it?"

"Is he dead?"

"Is there any hurry?"

"Shan't I bring you the book and let you look it up yourself?"

"What do you want to know for?"

And I will lay you ten to one that after you have answered the questions and explained how to find the information and why you want it, the clerk will go off and get one of the other clerks to help him try to find Bismarck—and then come back and tell you there is no such man. Of course I may lose my bet, but according to Law of Average I will not.

Now, if you are wise, you will not bother to explain to your "assistant" that Correggio is indexed under the C's, not under the K's, but you will smile very sweetly and say, "Never mind," and go look it up yourself. And this incapacity for independent action, this moral stupidity, this infirmity of the will, this unwillingness to catch hold and lift—these are the things that put pure Socialism so far into the future. If men will not act for themselves, what will they do when the benefit of their effort is for all?

A first mate with a knotted club seems necessary; and the dread of getting "the bounce" Saturday night holds many a worker to his place. Advertise for a stenographer, and nine out of ten who apply can neither spell nor punctuate—and do not think it necessary to.

Can such a one write a letter to Garcia?

"You see that bookkeeper," said the foreman to me in a large factory.

"Yes. What about him?"

"Well, he's a fine accountant, but if I'd send him up town on an errand he might accomplish the errand all right, and, on the other hand, he might stop at four saloons on the way and when he got to Main Street forget what he had been sent for."

Can such a man be entrusted to carry a message to Garcia?

We have recently been hearing much maudlin sympathy expressed for the "downtrodden denizens of the sweatshop" and the "homeless wanderer searching for honest employment," and with it all often go many hard words for men in power.

Nothing is said about the employer who grows old before his time in a vain attempt to get frowsy ne'er-do-wells to do intelligent work or about his long, patient striving after "help" that does nothing but loaf when his back is turned. In every store and factory there is a constant weeding-out process going on. The employer is constantly sending away "help" that has shown its incapacity to further the interests of the business, and other "help" is being taken on. No matter how good times are, this sorting continues; only, if times are hard and work is scarce, the sorting is done finer, but out and forever out the incompetent and unworthy go. It is the survival of the fittest. Self-interest prompts every employer to keep his best men—those who can carry a message to Garcia.

I know one man of really brilliant parts who has not the ability to manage a business of his own and yet who is absolutely worthless to anyone else, because he carries with him constantly the insane suspicion that his employer is oppressing or intending to oppress him. He cannot give orders, and he will not receive them. Should a message be given him to take Garcia, his answer would probably be, "Take it yourself!"

Tonight this man walks the streets looking for work, the wind whistling through his threadbare coat. No one who knows him dare employ him, for he is a regular firebrand of discontent. He is impervious to reason, and the only thing that can impress him is the toe of a thick-soled number 9 boot.

Of course I know that one so morally deformed is no less to be pitied than a physical cripple; but in our pitying let us drop a tear, too, for the employer who is striving to carry on a great enterprise, whose working hours are not limited by the whistle, and whose hair is fast turning white through his struggle to hold in line dowdy indifference, slipshod imbecility, and the heartless ingratitude that, but for his enterprise, would be both hungry and homeless.

Have I put the matter too strongly? Possibly I have. But when all the world has gone a-slumming I wish to speak a word of sympathy for the man who succeeds—the man who, against great odds, has directed the efforts of others and, having succeeded, finds there's nothing in it, nothing but bare board and clothes. I have carried a dinner pail and worked for day's wages, and I have also been an employer of labor, and I know there is something to be said on both sides. There is no excellence, per se, in poverty; rags are no recommendation; and all employers are not rapacious and high-handed any more than all poor men are virtuous.

My heart goes out to the man who does his work when the boss is away as well as when he is at home; and the man who, when given a letter for Garcia, quietly takes the missive, without asking any idiotic questions, and with no lurking intention of chucking it into the nearest sewer or of doing aught else but deliver it, who never gets laid off, never has to go on strike for higher wages. Civilization is one long, anxious search for individuals of just this sort. Anything such a man asks will be granted. He is wanted in every city, town, and village, in every office, shop, store, and factory. The world cries out for him; he is needed and needed badly—the man who can "carry a message to Garcia."

Seest thou a man diligent in his business? He shall stand before kings.

—PROVERBS 22:29

Progress is not an accident, but a necessity.

—HERBERT SPENCER

A man is a worker. If he is not that, then he is nothing.

—JOSEPH CONRAD

There are two kinds of men who never amount to much: Those who cannot do what they are told, and those who can do nothing else.

—CYRUS H. K. CURTIS

2

Producers in spite of everything

So you think luck has been against you? Listen to these stories. John Kepler was one of the world's most successful men. He produced far more than he consumed. Though he was always poverty-ridden and died a pauper, he left the world infinitely richer than he found it.

He did this in a quiet, plodding way, working against a lifetime of obstacles that would have made disgruntled failures of other men. But frail John Kepler had something within him that made him get things done.

Life gave him a bad start from the outset. He was born two days after Christmas, two months early. That was the era when a premature baby had scarcely a chance in a million. Kepler just pulled through a sickly childhood to become a frail youth, a semi-invalid adult.

Both his parents were peculiar; eventually both lost their minds.

His first wife, an older woman who had been married twice before, was as nagging and quarrelsome as her relatives; they all seemed bent on making Kepler's life miserable.

His second wife was an old maid who pouted because her husband was not paid his back wages and she could not buy the trinkets for which she longed.

As if that were not enough, his employer, bachelor King Rudolph of Bohemia, was nine-tenths lunatic. He wanted Kepler to look at the stars as an astrologer and forecast the most favorable times for starting wars and hunting expeditions. Kepler's self-trained, mathematical mind told him astrology was rubbish. He guessed there were real secrets in the stars and was determined to wrest some of these secrets from them.

He humored the paranoid king and his wife, but not his own weak eyes and frail body.

Kepler would sit up most of the night, holding his myopic eyes so close to his sheets of figures that his eyebrows were nearly singed in the smelly candle. Bundled up against his chronic chills, the sickly man would fill sheet after sheet in the flickering light, while his wife pouted from her neglected bed.

His blurred sight found more attractive visions in his tables of the stars and planets. Kepler saw not only figures on his pages but the keys to the universe.

Kepler was not strong, but he had determination. Week after week, year after year, he worked on. The hours passed unnoticed. He filled oceans of paper with his observations and computations.

Smallpox struck his family, took his favorite son. Soon Kepler was back beside his sputtering candle.

The plague came. Kepler wrapped his fraying cloak around his shoulders and hurried his family away—taking along stacks of paper and a supply of greasy candles.

Neither pestilence nor chronic illness nor empty pockets kept him from getting things done.

He stuck to his tasks, and, from the stacks of foolscap that were covered with the figuring of years of nights, he prepared accurate tables of 1,000 stars by which mariners were to navigate safely for centuries.

He discovered the use of two convex lenses and measuring wires that gave the basis for the modern astronomical telescope.

He discovered the three laws of motion of the heavenly

planets, this half-invalid who became the Lawmaker of the Heavens.

He laid the foundation for the new mathematics of calculus, harassed as he was by annoyances and obstacles.

When I begin to feel sorry for myself, when I am inclined to leave things unfinished because of obstacles or difficulty, Kepler's voice rises from the past to my mind. It whispers his Virgilian motto, the motto that helped him get things done, "Things live by moving, and gain strength as they go."

Verily, John Kepler was one of the world's greatest successes, though he was buried at fifty-nine in threadbare clothes in Ratisbon's cheapest coffin. Nothing stopped him from getting things done.

Chopin

The thin, tubercular voice of Frederic Chopin also speaks from the past. He, too, knew that it is not outward circumstances but the inner man which determines how much we may accomplish.

At twenty, women felt sorry for him because he was so undersized. He was shattered by lung disease, the smell of tobacco smoke turned his stomach, and his French father, a tobacco merchant married to a Polish girl, was bankrupt.

Trouble was brewing in Poland. His friends rushed to arms, but this pale, physical wreck was too sick to join them. He fled to Vienna, taking a cup of Polish soil with him.

Then he went to Paris, spitting blood and drinking nothing but milk. On the Island of Majorca, for his health, the health authorities ordered him away and fumigated his house; Chopin had to pay for the fumigation, too.

"My dear corpse," George Sand addressed him.

And Chopin summed up his various doctors' reports, "One

said I would die, the second said I was about to die, the third said I was already dead."

Newspapers several times carried false reports of his death before he was forty.

Dying by inches and joking about it, yet working feverishly to compose fifty-four mazurkas, eleven polonaises, and seventeen Polish songs, Chopin perpetuated his fame and nourished the spirit of Polish nationalism. Fantasies, waltzes, preludes, and ballads flowed from this pale young man as he struggled against time and watched his life ebb away.

He was far from his native land, yet his nationalistic compositions helped to unite and glorify the Polish spirit. And, at forty, the goblet of Polish soil was sprinkled on his casket. He had forced himself, against handicaps, to get things done, making his genius the greater.

SCHILLER

Another Frederic—Schiller, the poet—lost his health at thirty and during his remaining fifteen years jam packed his life with more intellectual achievement than any other man of his time. Weak, in pain, one lung adhering to his chest wall, no more shoulders than a banana, he worked fourteen or more hours a day.

His constant companions were his wife, Charlotte, and suffering. Yet he wrote not merely reams of poetry but reams of happy poetry. No one who reads his "Hymn to Joy" can imagine that it was written by a man in agony. The agony was of his body, not of his spirit.

He stayed up late nights to do his writing, stealing from his sleep because well-wishing friends and admirers interrupted him during the day. This made his health worse, but he was determined to get things done regardless of the consequences.

The Sage of Chelsea

Thomas Carlyle, like Schiller, worked against physical suffering; unlike the poet, his work was filled with almost unparalleled bitterness. Carlyle scolded and bickered with his wife. His breath drew flies. He had a picklish disposition and point of view but was heroic in the way he got things done against chronic ill health and indigestion. His habitual fault-finding may have been a cause of his ill health. But give the Sage of Chelsea full credit for the more than twenty large octavo-sized volumes he produced.

He produced more than he consumed, though we may not like the bitter spirit which permeated his labors. Perhaps his sense of humor was upside down.

"H.M.S. Pinafore"

The lilting music of "Pinafore" must have been written by a happy, carefree man; or so it would seem.

It was written by Sir Arthur Sullivan while he was in torment from kidney stones. His pain, day and night, did not keep him from getting things done. He made the pain more endurable by creating frolicsome music, not a dirge.

The Archbishop of Friendly Satire

Alexander Pope was a gnome of a hunchback, so crippled he had to be laced in stiff canvas to stand up and had to be helped in and out of bed. His teeth were like a decayed waterfront piling, his eyes like pink ping-pong balls.

He laid out a plan of work when he was only twelve and followed the plan during the balance of his life, drinking gallons of coffee daily to relieve the pressure of his constant headaches.

Repulsive to the eye, Pope charmed thousands by his elfin work and became the unofficial Archbishop of Friendly Satire. The constant gnawing and grating inside his head did not keep him from getting things done—and he did pleasant things.

Samuel Gridley Howe, like Pope, had headaches which completely incapacitated him at times. In addition, he suffered recurrent attacks of fever, which he had contracted while taking part in the War for Greek Independence. Knocked out at unexpected times by this fever and by his migraine headaches, Dr. Howe, nevertheless, managed to make himself the world's foremost educator and trainer of the deaf and blind as well as reformer in the care of the insane.

Dwight Morrow, Julius Caesar, Max Muller, Hendrik Willem van Loon, William Pitt, and William of Orange are others who endured the excruciating agony of migraine headaches yet produced more than they consumed. Charles Darwin had this handicap, could work only a half day at a time most of his life, but his "Origin of Species" revolutionized biological science. Gustav Mahler, another victim, conducted symphony orchestras while deathly pale and biting his lips to keep from screaming at the pain.

Metchnikoff, who discovered the phagocytes in human blood, worked against recurrent attacks of headaches. Timid James Watt, inventor of the steam engine, was kept in bed for days at a time by the same malady.

Sir Walter Scott, too, was headachy through life. The headaches started in his early manhood, were ever present to plague him. Yet this pug-nosed lawyer—who had no sense of smell—made himself get up at five mornings and start his work. He answered his letters the same day they were received. Added to his headaches was a crippled right leg, the result of infantile paralysis before he was two years old. Despite these obstacles he got a great thrill from just being alive—and producing. He swore only four times in his life.

NOBEL AND DORSET

Alfred Nobel was sent to a sanitarium at twenty, where his rheumatic heart was relieved but not cured. It is an irony of fate that the man who invented ways of making nitroglycerin safe to handle had to use it for years as a drug to steady his ailing heart.

Despite his sickly life, this self-educated man got many things done, including 355 patented inventions.

Marion Dorset had rheumatics, too—and $600 from his father's estate. Dorset's rheumatics hit the muscles of his legs and back. Yet for months he limped painfully through the hog-country wallows and barnyards. His muscles tingling with pain, he wrestled with young pigs and big hogs, extracting blood samples and trying experimental injections.

Those were the days when farmland hillsides were dotted with fires like Indian signals—pyres of hogs that had been killed by the dread cholera. Suddenly a pig would stagger, turn red, then purple, and die, all within a couple hours. One out of every eight hogs was struck with the disease.

The remedy the government recommended was useless. Yet here was an appalling loss; struggling farmers were wiped out in a few days. Dorset worked for a cure and discovered one indirectly. Shrunk to a mere five feet four inches by the tightening of his rheumatic muscles, he worked on, hope in his brown eyes, determination in his soul. This crippled invalid eventually found the serum that immunizes against hog cholera.

IF THE SICKLY AND FEEBLE

CAN GET SO MUCH DONE,

WHAT CAN LIMIT THE

HEALTHY PERSON EXCEPT

HIMSELF?

Hog cholera was conquered by a man who would not let his handicaps keep him from getting things done.

WITHERING—LAENNEC—HOOKE

Many human plagues have also been lessened by men who got things done despite the handicaps of personal weakness and ill health.

William Withering, an Englishman who studied botany because fresh air and sunshine helped his tuberculosis, discovered digitalis, the heart remedy, said to be the most valuable drug discovered since quinine. As his consumption advanced, another scientist coined the poor pun, "The flower of physicians is indeed Withering."

René Laennec's mother was a consumptive, and from childhood so was René. Later he developed chronic asthma and breathed like a squeaky hinge. But the sawed-off Frenchman fought against his frail body, took medical courses, became the leading pathologist of his day. He invented the indispensable stethoscope which, through its snakelike listening tubes, gives physicians inside information about your body.

Robert Hooke, too frail to study for the ministry as his parents wished, educated himself in science. A hunchback with an ashen face and teeth like yellow icicles, he got things done, made half the scientific discoveries of his time. He invented the balance spring that is on your watch.

TUBERCULOSIS

Dread consumption, once one of mankind's most fatal diseases, has given many determined spirits an opportunity to get things done.

Cecil Rhodes left the humid British Isles as a young man to get the benefits of South Africa's dry air for his infected lungs. There his work in the open laid the foundation for his development of the world's richest diamond and gold mines.

Eugene O'Neill was flat on his back in bed, fighting tuberculosis, when he wrote his first play.

"Treasure Island," "Dr. Jekyll and Mr. Hyde," "Kidnapped," and most of Robert Louis Stevenson's charming stories were written, a few hours at a time, while he was painfully wasting away. Everything about him drooped except his spirit. An attack of diphtheria speeded up his tuberculosis, but he continued getting things done.

Nina Wilcox Putnam, at twenty-five, had been given two years to live. She spent the winter—fourteen hours a day—bundled up on the roof of an apartment in the soot of New York City, smoke playing peekaboo with her features. She wore woolen mittens over her gloves and, without removing them, wrote her first novel, "In Search of Arcady." The novel was successful enough, it solved her financial problems temporarily, and her cure was complete. Most successful was her proof that she could get things done.

Other Thoroughbreds

That picturesque leader of American lawyers, Rufus Choate, with his mackerel-like complexion, was ill most of his life with symptoms which were not understood in his time but which were probably due to Bright's disease. The strongest thing about him was his heavy watch chain; it was strong enough to hold a bull.

His friends, noting his weakened condition, urged him to take a vacation to rebuild his constitution. "The constitution was destroyed long ago," Choate responded, "I am now living under the bylaws."

Francis Parkman, the Boston Brahmin, was born to wealth and could have lived the life of a sick man about town. But he made himself an outstanding historian of early America. For forty years he worked, in a darkened room, on his bed or in a wheel chair, so threatened with blindness that others had to read to him.

Insomnia and ill health plagued Elizabeth Phelps, yet in her small college town she wrote a book a year for thirty years. Twenty editions of her first book were sold the first year, but neither this early triumph nor her chronic invalidism kept her from doing things for a third of a century more.

Marcel Proust's father was Health Commissioner of Paris, but the son was about the unhealthiest citizen in the Republic. Asthma plagued him from childhood, made every breath an effort. His last six years were spent in bed, in a cork-lined room protected from draughts, lighted by a glaring bulb. Drinking tank cars of coffee, Proust scribbled away, writing against time, to complete his masterpiece, "Remembrance of Things Past."

Hounded by persecution, slight, and weak, John Calvin always had the body of an old man, but the Ten Commandments were stamped on his face. He spat blood, rheumatism tied him in knots, and his head split with headaches. But his iron determination made him a leader in the Reformation and, for nearly quarter of a century, he ruled Geneva as well as himself. "You must submit to supreme suffering," he said, "in order to discover whether you are destined for joy."

The wealthy parents of Florence Nightingale objected to her study of nursing. But she wanted to get things done, became a nurse, raised the profession's low standards, reformed the British Army's medical service. Her long days and nights of work in the field during the Crimean War left her health broken. But, to the age of ninety, she worked to establish new hospitals and training schools for nurses.

Catherine Mumford developed spinal trouble and had to leave school at fourteen. At twenty-two she became engaged to William Booth, devoted the rest of her life to organizing the Salvation Army. Catherine Booth was a semi-invalid, forced to spend much of her time in bed. She had scarcely a day that was free from pain. Yet she was constantly in the field organizing, speaking at religious meetings, or at home doing paper work, as she and her energetic husband worked hand-in-hand to establish their new group of religious welfare workers. Daily pain did not keep Kate Booth from getting things done.

Many of the world's great producers have had excuses for not getting things done. But they have ignored the excuses and produced. They have not had an easy-chair state of mind.

They have had ailments galore, but they have been spared that combination which is fatal to producing, dropsy and heart trouble—dropping into an easy chair and not having the heart to get up from it.

They have produced! Regardless!

A man may have brains and many admirable traits, but unless he's got BACKBONE, too, he doesn't accomplish things. In times of stress he wilts like a cut blade of grass in the sun.
                    —HUDSON MAXIM

Pulcherrimum genus victoriae seipsum vincere. (The fairest kind of victory is self-conquest.)
                    —*Latin motto on the fireplace of*
                    SIR RICHARD TEMPLE

A lost battle is a battle one believes lost.
                    —MARSHAL FERDINAND FOCH

3

Be dissatisfied first

THERE IS magic in a goal.

"What were you working for on your last job?" prospective employers ask applicants.

Ninety-nine out of a hundred applicants give their last salary as an answer. They often hopefully name a higher rate, if they think they can get by with a little stretching.

But the hundredth says he was working for some specific goal —he wanted to learn the business, to buy a house, to get married, to lay by for independence by the time he was fifty.

Keep your eye on that hundredth man. He is working for a goal. He is the one who will get things done. Pull up your chair, and we will tell you about him.

THE RICHEST MAN OF HIS TIME

Everyone in little Burslem, England, seemed to be working for a wage rather than a goal. It was a pittance of a wage, too, for Burslem was one of the most disreputable places in the world. It offended the eye and smelled like a zoo.

It was a pottery town. Every backyard had its own small pottery beside the outhouse, when there was an outhouse.

Waking hours were devoted to making cheap stoneware, drinking, and fighting. On Sundays a few folk attended church, mostly for the fun of interrupting the traveling preachers.

Thomas Wedgwood had a little pottery in his backyard and

28

thirteen children. But, even with the labor of all thirteen children, he could not pay off his mortgage.

When Thomas died his eldest son inherited the place, including the durable mortgage. The other children worked for their brother, except those who had attained the age of independence.

The youngest, Josiah, was nine when his brother took over the backyard establishment. For ten years Josiah worked for his brother in the mud of the pottery.

Josiah had a painful limp; his right knee had been crippled by smallpox. Later he was to have the leg amputated, but that is getting ahead of the story.

Squire Wedgwood, a dignified cousin of the Burslem family, drove over from Cheshire one day with his motherless daughter, Sarah, to inspect his poor relations. The squire owned three times as many horses as the entire town of Burslem.

Sarah was a traveled young lady, but she felt sorry for the nineteen-year-old cousin who sat with his lame leg in front of him, his face yellow from years of child labor in the pottery shed.

She gave him the book she had been reading.

Josiah could read, though most of his brothers and sisters could not.

He memorized the book before returning it to Sarah, with a grateful letter. She sent him another book. He could not send her books, but he made a porcelain box in a beautiful new shade of green which he had developed.

The ugly, pock-marked potter and the tall, slender girl who played the harpsichord were in love; and Wedgwood now had a goal for which to work.

The goal seemed impossible. A rich attorney had already spoken to Sarah's father about marriage. The squire harrumphed to his lame cousin; no Burslem potter could marry his daughter. She would have a dowry of several thousand pounds, and the man who married her would have to match it, shilling for shilling.

They must not see each other for a year, the squire commanded.

"I'm sorry the dowry is so much," Sarah told Josiah as he left, "but you can match it, I know you can!"

The timid lad went to Sheffield, where he made pottery ornaments for knife handles. He was no longer an ordinary potter. His ornaments were beautiful and were fired to be harder and more durable than others.

He worked toward his goal for five years, laid away a thousand pounds. Then back to dirty Burslem he went to start his own business.

He wrote Sarah, "Burslem shall yet be a symbol of all that is beautiful, honest, and true; and I'll be the best potter England has ever seen."

More goals for him! He was now out not only to marry Sarah but also to remove the odium from the expression "a common Burslem potter."

He started a flower garden, something new in dirty Burslem. He bought a horse so he could ride the forty miles to visit Sarah. The squire grumpily chaperoned every single minute they were together.

Burslem potters had been working four days out of the week, drinking two, and hectoring the preacher on the seventh. They had been satisfied with their low condition and miserable living. That is the pathetic aspect of poverty; people get used to low conditions and are satisfied.

The young man with the limp and a goal gradually changed that. His flower garden was the start. He interested some of the villagers in new kinds of pottery, though many remained more interested in the two-days drunk. He hired a young artist to teach them color harmony and design.

He changed Burslem. Instead of the old, coarse, brown pickle jars, the potters now made vases and dinner sets of exquisite lightness and glaze, which the nobility bought at fancy prices.

At thirty Josiah invited the squire to Burslem, to take another look at the potters' town which his lame cousin had improved. The squire harrumphed and wiped his brow. He inventoried Josiah's property and regretted that it did not quite equal his daughter's dowry; the squire's investments had increased the dowry.

So Josiah worked toward his goal for four years more, when the inventory more than matched the dowry. He and Sarah were married. One goal had been reached. But Josiah had other goals now. He was determined to remove the village and the potter's trade from the disrespect that had always been their lot.

Sarah and Josiah labored together toward these goals. Burslem became an art center and was recognized the world over as the home of Queensware; Wedgwood had been appointed Potter to the Queen.

He extended his goals as he continued to do more things, became the richest man of his time.

He gave goals to others, too. He awoke the decrepit, satisfied town by making the people dissatisfied and then showing them how to improve their products and themselves. Burslem became a show place.

Satisfied people do not get things done. The satisfied person has reached his goal, if any, and works only for the necessary wages to keep him from starving and freezing.

The dissatisfied person has the urge to get things done. That is why many apparently ordinary people do extraordinary things.

DALEN

Wedgwood was not the first—nor will he be the last—to be stimulated to get more things done in order to get married. Occasionally a lover's rejection gives the incentive to do things.

Gustaf Dalen, for example, had made a few trifling inventions as a boy in Sweden, but he remained on the farm to help his parents. He liked farm life and seemed satisfied. Love changed that. His fifteen-year-old sweetheart was eager enough to marry him but had wisdom beyond her years; she refused to marry him if he remained a farmer. She knew he could be a real inventor. So the young Swede left the farm and enrolled in an engineering school at twenty-three.

He graduated, they married, and he started a series of inventions which revolutionized the lighthouses of the world, inventions that Edison said were impossible.

First came the automatic beacon, then a flashing attachment, then a valve which shut it off during the daytime. He applied the same genius, now trained and educated, to acetylene and to a stove that cooked twenty-four hours on eight pounds of coal.

Winner of a Nobel prize in physics, Dalen had a sweetheart who gave him his goal for getting things done; she was dissatisfied with a farmer-husband.

He kept on getting things done long after he might have retired, for a full quarter-century. He was blinded throughout those last twenty-five years as the result of an explosion during an invention.

GIBBON

There was a woman in the case of Edward Gibbon, too. By the time he had finished college his parents had almost given up hope for him. The short, fat boy would never amount to anything; he was addicted to a luxurious existence. The only thing that seemed to dissatisfy him was his own religion. He changed first to this church and then to that.

But he was positive he had found something to cherish when he met Suzanne Churchod, at twenty-one. The fat young man whose face was so comical, with its puffy cheeks and tiny, upturned nose, became engaged to straight-faced, blue-eyed Suzanne, a minister's daughter.

Still he didn't settle down to work. When his father objected to the match, this youth like an overstuffed chair wrote his fiancée asking for a release from their engagement. He did not want to risk losing his allowance.

Suzanne received this caddish letter and gave him his release. She wrote him, "I can assure you that you will one day regret the irreparable loss you have suffered in alienating forever the too tender open heart of S.C." In a year she was married, on the rebound, to a wealthy, elderly banker and trundled off to Paris to live in a style Gibbon envied.

So he would regret breaking their engagement, would he?

He'd show her—and the world—that he was a better man than the boiled shirt of a banker she had married to spite him! Gibbon at last went to work. He was determined to make her regret her cutting words.

He plunged into study, into a lifetime of study, and made himself one of the world's outstanding historians. It was not to drown his unhappiness but to show Suzanne, now the famous Madame Necker, that it was she who should regret their broken engagement.

When he had an incentive to work he eagerly put his pug nose to the grindstone.

THE KING OF IRELAND

Charles Parnell had had an American mother. As a tall young man with brown hair he fell in love at first sight with

an American heiress. They became engaged. Suddenly she returned to Newport, sending him a cold note that her family
disapproved of the match.

He followed her to America, only to be told that Miss
Woods did not intend to marry him since he was an unknown.

This jilting shocked him into making something more of
himself than an unknown country gentleman. He fought against
his natural shyness, entered the field of political reform, originated boycotting, served prison terms for his convictions, became the Uncrowned King of Ireland to show the haughty
heiress he could be famous.

Years later the heiress exclaimed, "Oh! Why didn't I marry
him!"

Perhaps it is better she did not, for her jilting gave him a
divine discontent. He was dissatisfied with himself but not discouraged.

Hard Luck

Family misfortunes have given many people git-up-and-git.
The Hastings family had been notable for generations, then
lost their property. Young Warren arrived in the world when
the family had nothing. At seven, lying on the bank of a brook
that his relatives had once owned, he daydreamed about their
plight and resolved to win back their lost lands.

He had a goal as a seven-year-old, a goal that took him far
beyond his original goal as it expanded. Remember Wedgwood? Goals are that way; they keep giving momentum to get
still more things done.

The Hastings orphan not only regained the family fortunes,
but the momentum of getting things done made him Governor
General over fifty million people in India.

James L. Kraft's thrifty Mennonite parents had bad luck,
too, and their farm was saddled with a $4,000 mortgage. With
$65 and an old horse, James started peddling cheese to pay off

the mortgage. He reached his goal of clearing off the load of debt, and the momentum carried him along to build up the nationwide Kraft Cheese Company.

JANE ADDAMS

Dissatisfaction over the lot of others gives some a goal. Jane Addams's mother died when she was two; then came typhoid fever, and she had scarcely recovered before the physicians discovered tuberculosis, which left her with a crooked back and her head drawn to one side.

One Sunday afternoon her father took the frail, crippled girl for a ride through Freeport, Illinois. As they passed through a slum section Jane's sympathies were aroused; it was her first view of how the other half lived.

She tugged at her father's sleeve, pulled close to his side.

"When I'm grown up, I want to live right next door to poor people, and the children can play in my yard." A goal, and Jane never forgot it.

Until she was thirty she spent many months in hospitals, in a plaster cast or steel-framed canvas jacket. Then, with a friend, she started Hull House in Chicago's slums and for nearly half a century worked toward her goal.

The momentum for getting things done won her a Nobel prize and a place at the head of America's greatest women.

ANTHONY COOPER

Anthony Cooper lived in luxury. But his childhood was unhappy. His father was busy with petty politics; his mother was more interested in society than in her children.

At fifteen the unhappy rich boy was on a side street in a small city when he came upon some ragged drunks carrying an unpainted coffin. They staggered with their load, singing

---

BLESSED ARE

THE DISSATISFIED WHEN

THEY HAVE A GOAL

---

off-color tavern songs. In their unsteadiness the coffin slipped, struck the ground, and split open. Their dead comrade tumbled out.

Right there curly-haired Anthony Cooper found a goal. He would devote his energies and wealth to bettering the conditions of the poor.

For seventeen years he fought to get a bill through Parliament that would provide for the mentally sick; he worked for twenty years to break the system that sold pauper children to mill owners; he became the first president of the Y.M.C.A. and held this position for twenty-one years.

Those are just a few of the accomplishments of Anthony Cooper, the seventh Earl of Shaftesbury, who got his goal from a funeral procession of drunken paupers. As a youth he was unhappy; as an adult, happy, because then he knew exactly what he did not want.

THE WIZARD OF FARM CHEMISTRY

The Carver boy found his goal earlier in life and on a more personal basis.

He did not know his family, so picked the name of George

Washington Carver to please himself. As a child, wandering about the South, he saw a mob beat out a Negro's brains and burn his body in the public square.

He had no permanent home, just slept in barns, until a laundress in Joplin, Missouri, took him in to help her. He taught himself between schools and was finally accepted at Highland University—he had sent his high-school grades there—but when the president saw him after he arrived on the campus, he abruptly remarked, "We don't take niggers." Highland University is now defunct, but not so George Washington Carver's fame.

At Simpson College he lived in a shack on the edge of town, where he did washing for other students. Scholastically he led his class, this tall Negro with the falsetto voice and meek manner.

His paintings of flowers won prizes at the World's Columbian Exposition; his musical skill won him a scholarship to the Boston Conservatory of Music. But he went to graduate school to specialize in agricultural chemistry.

"I can be of more service to my race in agriculture," he said. "I want to help the man furthest down—the Negro—by teaching him how to help himself."

Iowa State College offered him a teaching position, but Dr. Carver packed his battered suitcases and went to Tuskegee Institute, where he gave his people new goals by making them dissatisfied with the primitive way in which they were growing their thin crops.

He worked long hours in his ramshackle laboratory, found out how to make plastics from soybeans, rubber from peanuts, flour from sweet potatoes. Edison offered him a salary in six figures; a rubber company and a chemical firm offered him blank-check fees to work for them. But he stuck by his goal and stayed at Tuskegee for $1,500 a year.

George Washington Carver could have been a millionaire, but he never deviated from his goal. He got things done; he made himself the Wizard of Farm Chemistry, this son of slave parents who was one of the few Americans ever chosen to a fellowship by the Royal Society.

He inspired his people to do new things by making them *dissatisfied with the old*. He knew that the surest way to be a dub is to be satisfied with yourself.

Get a Goal

Dissatisfaction is a powerful incentive to get things done, especially when it is tied to some goal.

Easy success in early life becomes a handicap when it brings self-satisfaction. That is why many child prodigies become has-beens in their twenties.

Getting what one wants is sometimes worse for later production than not getting it. That is why new crops of self-made men are always coming to the top, why old family businesses pass into new hands.

Without dissatisfaction one is like a watch without a mainspring. The works are all there, but it takes the spring struggling to release itself to make the watch run. Bernard Baruch's mother wound him up by telling him, "No one is any better than you, but you are no better than anyone else until you do something to prove it."

Men and women who go through life without definite goals to strive for are like tired children—they don't know what they want and will not stop whining unless they get it.

Sudden Riches

What would you do if you unexpectedly received $200,000? Psychologists asked that question to a large group of intelligent people. Most of them said they would put part of it into an annuity to provide a sure income, then spend the rest of their lives in travel and play.

Practically no one thought of using the sudden wealth to further his life goal, probably because few had goals.

The sudden wealth would have taken most of them out of the producers' ranks and left them mere consumers of others' efforts.

Several New England communities tell the story of two bitter rivals. A couple of young lawyers had harsh words, then blows in the courtroom. Their feud continued throughout the lives of both. One lawyer remained a bachelor, the other was early left a widower with one son.

The town's wealthy spinster, a gospel-soaked religious recluse whose nose looked like a rudder, died when the widower's son was eighteen. The community turned out when the bachelor attorney brought her will to probate. Bets were made that most of her wealth would go to this or that religious group.

All were aghast when they learned that her fortune had been left to the widower's son.

The bachelor attorney diligently minded his own business and settled the estate.

The widower's teen-age boy began to receive deferential treatment, and a few pleasure lovers toadied to him. He entertained more and more in the taverns.

Time passed. A nephew whom the bachelor had educated became his law partner. Together they became the leading attorneys of the section. Old-timers said the nephew had a barrel of brains in his head and used them.

The widower struggled along alone as he grew older. His son was never around, and he had no serious interests when he did stop in between pleasure jaunts. He had all the bad traits of an aristocrat and none of the saving graces.

The bachelor's business prospered; the widower's declined.

The bachelor was proud of his proficient nephew; the widower was ashamed of his son who thought every woman had her price.

When the bachelor died the town had another flurry of excitement. A yellowed document, with an attached note, was found among his papers. The document was the spinster's true will. The one he had probated was a forgery to which he had carefully traced her signature.

"I did this," the attached note read, "to humiliate my rival. I poisoned his son's initiative. My conscience is free, since I am leaving more than enough property to fulfill the terms of her true will."

Legendary as this story may be, it is all too true in essence. For instance:

Thomas Masco, of Chelsea, Massachusetts, found $1,450 in an old mattress he had bought. The ragpicker went on a protracted drunk, spent the windfall, and died from the effects of his spree.

In England, Horace King won $84,000 on a sweepstake ticket for which he had paid $2.50. Said his employer, "As soon as he got the money his whole nature changed. He had been a jolly man, but the money made him suspicious of everybody, and he took to drink." King drank up his $84,000 in four years and died from the effects of excessive drinking.

A bootblack in Minneapolis, Minnesota, won $3,200 on a horse race. He quit his job at once, had his shoes shined, and gave the shiner a $5 tip. The man who got the big tip quit his job, too.

Frank Greges, mouse-poor all his life, found $42,000 worth of bonds in a snow pile on Wall Street. The seventy-six-year-old man could not stand the sudden prosperity of the reward he received. In a few days he was saying, "I am God! Nothing is too good for me. The hat I wear is worth fifteen dollars. I have ten-dollar shoes. I can kill anybody who looks at me." The suddenly rich man was locked up in the psychopathic ward at Bellevue Hospital.

MINING MILLIONAIRES

James Marshall was building a millrace for a saw mill near Sacramento in 1849. He saw gold in the stream. This was the fabulous discovery that started the California gold rush. He found a fortune, stopped work, died filthy, drunk, and without enough money to feed a fly.

And look at the fate of the Silver Millionaires of Colorado. H. A. W. Tabor got his millions but had no other goal, lost his wealth, family, self-respect, and went back to pick-and-shovel prospecting.

August Rische got 262 thousand-dollar bills for his share in the Little Pittsburgh Mine, became a saloon-keeper, and spent his declining years as a humble night watchman at the state capitol.

The Little Chief Mine, discovered by the Dillon brothers, had a vein of silver eighty feet thick. One brother died from alcoholism; the other became a rooming-house janitor.

Jack Morrisey's millions were lavished in triumphant world tours and displays of high spending. He died in the Denver poorhouse.

Jack McCombe, who owned the Maid of Erin Mine, also died broke.

Nat Creede built himself a regal mansion, willed his property to a Los Angeles waif, and shot himself through the head.

Those picturesque Leadville millionaires couldn't stand prosperity because they had no goal but finding money.

Pedro Alvarado's father had a small diggings for gold and silver in Mexico. Pedro worked it hard, developed it into a real mine, took in a fortune. He spent a million to build a palace, furnished it with importations from Paris. There was not a single bath tub in the village, but he installed a dozen. Fifteen grand pianos were scattered around his spacious rooms. Sundays he gave local paupers baskets of silver pieces.

He offered to pay the national debt of Mexico but was ignored so made a will providing to pay the national debt of the United States. He disinherited the United States only after he received the bill for the twelve bath tubs.

Pedro was having such a grand time that he neglected his mine. He stopped getting productive things done. The mine flooded, could no longer be worked. Pedro was left with nothing but his white-elephant palace. He lived in a couple rooms, which soon became furry with old dirt.

Recall, too, some of the famous prize fighters. Each made hundreds of thousands of dollars. All earned it. They went through long periods of rigorous training and bruising sparring to prepare for their matches. Their goal was to win. But for most of them the goal ended right there, with the closing rounds. They made their fortunes, then passed into disgrace and ended in poverty.

When they had a goal—fights to win—they got things done. But they lacked long-range goals that would keep them doing things after they tasted the fruits of victory.

Arthur Ryley was the first American dentist in Berlin. He was waiting for his first patient when a disheveled man rushed into his office without knocking. Dr. Ryley was puzzled by the man's accent. He spoke English tolerably well but did not seem to be a German. The man looked vaguely familiar, but the dentist could not place him.

A tooth needed filling. The dentist looked at the man's cheap clothes and suggested a cheap, silver filling. Then he added, "Of course, platinum would be better, but it is very expensive."

"Make it platinum," the patient said, with a queer laugh.

When the work was completed the patient became embarrassed, for his pocketbook was empty. Dr. Ryley muttered under his breath—he should have known better than to use expensive platinum on such a shoddy-looking person.

Several hours later two elderly gentlemen appeared at the dentist's office. They presented an impressive document to Dr. Ryley. It was signed by Czar Alexander III and gave him outright an Imperial platinum mine in the Ural Mountains. The same day Dr. Ryley sold the mine for six million dollars and quit dentistry.

Kalifala Sidibe's ship came in when a planter on the Niger River saw the pictures he was painting on wrapping cloth with ordinary house paint. Soon the designs of this African native were on exhibition in the galleries of Paris, Berlin, and Stockholm. They became the rage and sold for large sums.

As the money poured in the primitive artist, who had no goal, bought an accordion, a bicycle, and a talking machine. Then he bought a second wife, forgot his first wife and his painting. Then he bought a third wife, started for metropolitan Dakar for the lively time he felt befitted his new wealth. He brawled, was robbed by the gay girls, remained steeped in liquor, and died after barely a year of fame, at the age of thirty-two.

Such true incidents of sudden wealth reflect the hazards that may befall those who are not working toward some life goal. People need the incentive and stabilizing influence of a goal in order to keep on getting things done; they need lifelong goals for constructive accomplishment.

This holds true even for the highly honored professions.

The ranks of physicians, accountants, lawyers, engineers, teachers are crowded with the dead wood of those who have reached a degree of financial independence and have ceased to do their best. They have made their needed money, then slumped into lack-luck mediocrity. They wilt their laurels by resting on them.

All in all, it may be a good thing that so few of us have to face the perils of prosperity.

FINANCIAL DEPRESSIONS

Many psychologists think that good times help bring on bad times.

The prosperity of good times removes the incentive to do more than one has been doing. Those who have short-term goals manage, during prosperity, to get the few luxuries for which they work. They become satisfied and quite pleased with themselves. Their motivation for work vanishes as soon as they accumulate a few extra comforts. They ease up on effort, increase their play and recreation. They begin to consume more than they produce. They begin to imagine they are worth money because they have plenty.

When the money depression hits, they try to become producers again, but it isn't always easy to shift back from the new habits that have softened them.

A key task of education, of self-management, of raising children is to develop a lifelong goal that will continue to lead one on to produce and keep on producing. Hand-to-mouth living goes with a week-to-week goal.

People can do, but don't do, without motives to keep going.

You can easily set up definite goals to help get more things— and more important things—done.

BE DISSATISFIED but not discouraged.

The great difference between men, the feeble and the powerful, the great and the insignificant, is energy and invincible determination—a purpose once fixed and then death or victory.

—T. FOLWELL BUXTON

My desires are limited only by my imagination.

—GEORGE EASTMAN

Give me neither poverty nor riches.

—SOLOMON

I look upon indolence as a sort of suicide.

—LORD CHESTERFIELD

An hour's industry will do more to produce cheerfulness than a month's moaning.

—BARROW

Man must be disappointed with the lesser things of life before he can comprehend the full power of the greater.

—BULWER-LYTTON

4

Detours that mislay initiative

'TIS NOT ENOUGH to work diligently. We must work at the right things and in the right direction, *keep on the main roads and off the detours.*

A gangling redheaded schoolboy was entered in a relay race at Providence. His hair was bright enough to light a candle. He was nervous; it was his first public race.

His turn came. He seized the baton from the breathless runner, started off full tilt, tipsy with excitement.

A murmur arose from the spectators, grew into hysterical yelling. The harder the redhead ran, the louder the crowd yelled. When he reached the finish line, wrong side to, Nelson Eddy realized that the wild yelling had been for him; he had run the race in the wrong direction.

But Nelson Eddy quickly learned to go in the right direction, to avoid the detours, and reached the top as a radio and concert singer.

General Lafayette, who helped win our War for American Independence, was in a prison at Olmutz, Austria. Dr. Eric Bollman and a young American, Francis Huger, planned to liberate him. Dr. Bollman bribed the prison physician and made arrangements with Lafayette for his rescue.

All went according to schedule; the adventurous pair overpowered Lafayette's guards and started to flee with the General.

But, in the excitement, they raced their horses in the wrong direction and ran smack into the guns of their pursuers.

46

The best-laid plans, the most heroic efforts, lead nowhere unless we keep going in the right direction. Folks who wonder why they do not get more done are amazed, when they take an inventory of their detours, to discover how much of their abilities they have dissipated on things that got them nowhere.

Many who appear to be stalled are not in a rut, just on a detour.

They are on a wild goose chase.

Business Detours

As firms grow larger they take on many detours. Governments do this, too, although government detours are called red tape.

One railroad system had a committee study the multitudinous printed forms that had to be filled in daily, weekly, and monthly for the reports along its lines. There were hundreds of these forms, and the committee discovered few of them had any except nuisance value. The committee eliminated enough unessential forms to save the system twenty thousand dollars a year in the cost of printing alone.

The biggest saving, however, was in the release of employees' time; now they could tend to running the railroad, not detour with needless reports. Any employee of a large corporation will know what a relief this was for them.

When a firm has that common complaint of form-itis, it usually means it has set up a lot of detours.

John J. Carty grew up with the telephone business from its crude, young days. As chief engineer he looked back with a humorous memory to some of the early detours that had sent him and his fellows on wild goose chases.

"At first we invariably tackled every problem from the wrong end," he reminisced. "If we had been told to load cattle on a steamer we would have hired an animal trainer to train the cattle for a couple years, so they would learn how to walk up a gangplank. But today, if we have to load cattle, we know enough to make a greased chute and slide them aboard in a jiffy."

Many of our larger firms keep special groups of experts to dig out the detours that gradually develop in their methods. "Can't a lot of it be eliminated?" is their motto. Their goal is to simplify, to throw out the detours.

Big firms can hire experts to simplify and keep them off detours. The individual has to be his own detour detector. He has to check on his own ways frequently and block off the unproductive activities. I'll explain shortly how I do this for myself.

Emil Rathenau had done nothing but odd jobs for ten years when, in a moment of optimism, he bought the German rights to Edison's light patents on borrowed money. In those early days there was a multiplicity of current varieties, of claims and counterclaims. The industry had growing pains.

Rathenau was of medium height, medium weight, and medium brains. No intellectual giant, he was just a hard-working, average man who changed his luck.

Problems which presented many pros and cons to men with better heads seemed simple to Rathenau, because he could not understand complicated things. He worked directly on the simple things he could comprehend, kept off the involved detours, and built up one of the first "horizontal trusts" in the world, the giant European A.E.G. electrical company.

"He never touched anything which did not fit in with what he was planning," a business historian said of him; "he avoided frittering away his energies."

Chain stores close out unprofitable lines of merchandise, sell their stores when they are in unpopular locations. They stick to the goods and locations that get results.

And so must ordinary people concentrate on the things that produce results.

Stanford White was commissioned to design a magazine cover. After days of work he brought the editor a design, classical and simple. His bill was $500.

"Isn't that a steep price for such a plain design?" the editor asked.

"The price is for knowing what to leave out!"

STRAIGHT THINKING AND INVENTIONS

Slender John E. Sweet, one of the founders of the American Society of Mechanical Engineers and the Engineering College at Cornell University, made many improvements in the design of high-speed steam engines. For his work on high-speed engines he was awarded the Fritz medal, with which we will be better acquainted later in this book.

On the main entrance to his factory a large sign proclaimed, "Visitors Always Welcome." And what an assortment of visitors he had! Among them were many impractical inventors, but the grand old man of engineering always examined their notions patiently.

To many of these would-be inventors he said, "Well, it seems to be a mighty good way to do a thing that doesn't need to be done."

At an A.S.M.E. dinner in his honor, one speaker said of him, "His mind is built on the straight-line model. With him, a straight line is the shortest distance between two points. While the rest of us are laboriously thinking our way around Robin Hood's barn, he thinks straight to the point."

Concentrate on the Things That Count

The quality that is called "executive judgment" is largely the ability to concentrate on what counts, to spot detours and keep off them.

Mary Dillon was one of a post-office clerk's eleven children. She started working in a garment shop on West Broadway when she was eleven. In her senior year at high school she was offered a job with the Brooklyn Borough Gas Company, jumped at the chance, and quit school. In thirteen years this short woman with the golden-brown hair and soft voice was acting general manager. In eleven more years she was president and chairman of the board.

Asked for the formula of her success, she said, "It must have been that I liked working at essentials rather than at trivialities."

That's the executive approach to getting things done—work at essentials, keep off the detours!

John Ruskin, whom we shall meet again, kept his initiative from being mislaid by pretending to be dead when he wanted to work. He had circulars printed and used them to reply to invitations and letters. These unusual correspondence notes read:

> Mr. J. Ruskin is about to begin a work of great importance and there-fore begs that in reference to calls and correspondence you will consider him dead for the next two months.

The dark-skinned Brandeis boy wanted to be a lawyer. With $200 borrowed from his brother he entered Harvard Law School to compete with the rich young men in its classes. He studied so much his eyes began to hurt, so he had friends read the lessons aloud to him to save his eyes.

He quit smoking, quit playing the violin to save time and money to concentrate on the thing he wanted, a law education. Soon he was tutoring rich young men who had mislaid their initiative. When commencement came around, blue-eyed Louis Brandeis, with his Southern accent, was at the head of his class, had paid back the borrowed money, and had $1,500 of his own.

He was offered an assistant professorship at Harvard but turned it down. "I want more practical experience," he said, keeping off that detour.

When he was thirty this slim young man from Louisville had made a million by keeping on the tracks that led somewhere. At forty-two he was a justice of the United States Supreme Court.

"Nothing must deflect the magnetic needle," he often told others during his life. This phrase, practiced in his own life and works, gave him an initiative of steel.

Charles Goodyear

Back in the days when India rubber was a novelty, an inventive Yankee, Charles Goodyear, noticed a store window in New York City that was filled with rubber life preservers. The thirty-four-year-old Jack-of-all-trades bought one out of curiosity. At home he discovered the valve leaked air, so devised an improved valve.

When he was next in the city he took his improved valve to the store and demonstrated it to the branch manager.

"Sure, that's a better valve, but it's no use to us," said Arthur Lowenstern. "Come, look in our back storeroom."

The storeroom floor was covered with inches of gooey, gray paste—the remains of the life preservers. The India gum could not hold together under the heat of summer, had reverted to its original state, and gave off an odor that would have put even a camel to shame.

"Your improvement of the valve shows you are clever, Goodyear. Apply your ingenuity to making rubber keep during hot weather. The Roxbury Company will pay you almost anything for such a process."

The thin inventor, who knew debtor's prison from the inside, looked at Lowenstern eagerly.

"I think it is worth looking into," said Goodyear, extending his bony hand.

And Lowenstern's rich, throaty parting remark followed Goodyear, "Don't waste your time on little things. Stick to the big thing."

Don't waste your time on little things! That was exactly what the puttering inventor had been doing. But Lowenstern's parting remark awoke Goodyear, kept him off the detours, and for ten years he concentrated on the big thing—to make India gum durable and heatproof.

He pursued the goal relentlessly. He sold his furniture, pawned the gold watch his father gave him, worked on rubber in the kitchen, parlor, and again in debtor's prison. Discouragement clouded his haggard, bony face, but he did not waste time on other things.

Ten years, and he had discovered how to vulcanize rubber!

They Thought Marriage a Detour

Long-nosed Mary Lyon had a goal. Except for that vital difference, she was just another conscientious New England school teacher. But she had a burning goal, a desire to establish a school where young women would have as good an opportunity for higher education as had men.

She quit teaching and spent three years visiting many cities and villages, talking up her plan, asking from house to house for financial support of her dream school. As she whipped up enthusiasm and saw her dream for Mount Holyoke College nearing reality, she paused to analyze the detours that might lead her astray from her chosen work.

She turned down an offer of marriage and sold her hope chest. That was a real sacrifice, but the proceeds of the sale went into her building fund without a tear being shed, at least not shed in public.

She analyzed her work habits and commanded herself to get off the detour of daydreaming, to quit hesitating, to avoid the detour of worry. Mary Lyon intentionally steered herself straight and succeeded in establishing a great educational institution, despite ridicule, masculine opposition, and the sale of her hope chest.

By shunning the detours she marched ahead boldly instead of stumbling along. She avoided the blind alleys, kept on the direct route. Mary Lyon is now in the American Hall of Fame —for getting things done that counted.

Evangeline with the dark-red hair also had numerous proposals of marriage. One was from a millionaire. And a royal prince trailed her for months, offering his hand. But Evangeline Booth refused marriage. She considered it would be a detour from her goal of carrying on and extending the work, started by her parents, of establishing the Salvation Army. She spread the band of social uplifters over the world.

Were these live-wire women right in believing that marriage would have been a detour from their goals?

IMMIGRANT TO INVENTOR

"Michael the Serbian," they called the raw freshman at Columbia University. His clothes were odd, his English amus-

---

DON'T

MISLAY YOUR INITIATIVE—

CONCENTRATE ON THINGS

THAT COUNT!

---

ing. His physical strength drew attention during the freshman-sophomore "cane rush." He had been hardened physically by farm work and lumberjack work during his few years in America. More important was the fact that he had also hardened the inside of his head.

"We need you to row on our crew," the captain of the freshman team said to Michael.

That tempted the Serbian. He enjoyed physical exercise, would have appreciated the cheers given the crew. But he thought of his life savings of $311. They had to take him through college. He had planned to increase his funds by winning academic prizes, and he had some other ideas. So he kept off the detour of going out for the crew.

No cheers for the big Serbian at the regatta that spring! The cheers came at the end of the school year; he won two prizes, each of $100. They were dividends for keeping off the detours. More dividends were to follow.

Before he finished college he was coaching weak sisters who were in danger of flunking out. This earned him more than some of his instructors were paid.

Michael Pupin's march of progress was not circular. He did not run the wrong way. He knew what he wanted and aimed directly for it.

He invented a system of multiplex telegraphy, the Pupin coil, which made long-distance telephone conversations possible, and many other important devices. He became a millionaire. His autobiography, "From Immigrant to Inventor," won a Pulitzer prize.

He simplified and concentrated on the things that counted, got more things done by keeping off detours.

A Detour Inventory

Einstein claims that using two kinds of soap would complicate life needlessly. He uses the same soap for both washing and shaving.

Henry Ford put it mildly when he observed, "The number of needless tasks that are performed daily by thousands of people is amazing."

They use time and energy on things that do not count.

They make too many telephone calls.

They visit too often and stay too long on each visit.

They write letters that are three times as long as necessary.

They work on little things, neglect big ones.

They read things that neither inform nor inspire them.

They have too much fun, too often.

They spend hours with people who cannot stimulate them.

They read every word of advertising circulars.

They pause to explain why they did what they did, when they should be working on the next thing.

They hurry to the movies when they should be going to night school.

They take trips to the country when they would get more things done if they spent the week end in a public library.

They daydream at work when they should be planning ahead for their jobs.

They do hosts of things which, while not venial sins, are certainly not worth the time they take.

They are going to beat the band—but in circles.

On my birthday and on Christmas day, which fall approximately half a year apart, I take inventory of my detours, then get off them.

One birthday I decided to get off the detour of shaving. Frank Gilbreth, the industrial engineer, learned to shave himself with two straightedged razors at once, but he was a better man than I am. It took courage to grow whiskers, however, since I was at the time employed by a university that enjoyed the financial support of a shaving-cream family. Shaving is a minor detour, and I do not recommend whiskers wholesale, but my whiskers keep reminding me to avoid more serious detours.

On those rare occasions when you see a set of whiskers, let them remind you, too, to inventory your detours.

I work in my shirt sleeves most of the time. Rolling them up was an annoying little detour. So now all my shirts have eleven-inch-long sleeves, including the yellowing dress shirt I reluctantly wear about once in five years.

I found too many invitations were detours, much as I enjoyed people. So I decided to say a cordial no to all except one invitation a month. And if someone leaves the party before I do, I know I am on the detour of staying too long.

I belonged to many organizations, resigned from most of them, much as I disliked to break away.

I keep off the detour of writing long letters by using many

post cards, with an occasional half-size letterhead. And when I use a post card I don't write things I may regret later, for it may be read by more people than it is intended for. (Gladstone, Shaw, Steinbeck, Osler, and many others were and are post-card addicts, too, thanks to the little card invented in 1870 by a professor of economics. Why, even the American Viscose Corporation was started by a post card, written by Samuel A. Salvage.)

Henry Ford avoided the detour of unnecessary letters by simply not answering those sent to him. Probably he received many more unexpected letters than I receive, but I am still a conscientious slave and answer all of mine, and promptly. If the automobile maker had used post cards he might have been able to answer some of his letters. (William Pitt, who lived before the era of post cards, never did.)

I listen to the radio for news only, and from only one station. An automatic clock switch turns the news on at breakfast, lunch, and dinner, so I don't have to think about it beforehand.

Detective stories have always thrilled me, but I have given them up entirely as detours. They were keeping me from working at things that counted. So were cameras and guns, so I sold my hobby equipment.

I have lived in the country, in a small town, in a small city, and in the heart of a great city. The bigger the place, the more detours for me. So now I am located for keeps in the country. It is flattering to see that big corporations are slowly following my example and decentralizing their plants, setting up small units in small places.

The biggest detour I avoided by quitting a nice, easy job. I was teaching, doing consulting work, writing, lecturing, and researching. As many irons in the fire as hairs on top my balding head. One Christmas when I reviewed my progress I decided I was scattering my big shots. My goals had become hazy, so I cleared them up.

I quit individual consulting work. I also did the unconventional thing and quit a university job in the middle of the year, gave up a long vacation every summer, a pension, and all that, after twenty years as a professor. I cast away from a sure-pay job to stake my future on the gamble that I could get things done.

The soft job had really been a brake on getting things done. I bounded ahead as soon as I got off the detour and could concentrate on getting done those things I felt I should do.

So, you understand now, one reason I am preaching my little sermon about the pitfalls of detours is that I have long practiced the sermon. No one knows better than I how attractive a detour can be and that getting off detours helps powerfully to get more things done.

TENDING TO BUSINESS

A word about that perennial detour, minding the other fellow's business and neglecting one's own. It keeps many persons on long detours and sets some organizations on needles and pins.

Alanson D. Brown knew this. Early in his work of building up the gigantic Brown Shoe Company, he adopted Benjamin Franklin's motto, "Speak ill of no one, and attend to your own business."

At one of the company's annual meetings much time was spent disparaging its competitors. A. D. Brown put up with this as long as he could, then sprang to his feet.

"I always find it pays me best to attend to my own business," he said, "and if I do this properly I do not have time to waste talking about the other fellow's. To each of you who will sign a promise that you will attend strictly to your own business, I will give a new hat."

He had to buy eighty-one hats.

Timothy Eaton, a ninth child, was born after his father's death. At thirteen he went to work in a dry-goods establishment, sleeping under the counter. He tended to business, built up the chain of large department stores that carries his name to the remotest corners of Canada.

One day in his Toronto store he noticed a big Irishman who was a new employee. "How long have you been here?" Eaton asked him.

"None of your business."

"What are you doing here?"

"Minding my own business. And I recommend you to mind your own; you are blocking the passageway."

Was the Irishman fired? "The man was quite right," Eaton said. "I wish I could find 500 such who would mind their own business and make everybody else mind theirs."

The chap who is all business is off the detours. He produces.

When you have an enterprise on hand concentrate upon it wholly; forget that anything else in the world exists.

—NAPOLEON

Never leave to chance what can be achieved by calculations.

—DISRAELI

Let not sleep fall upon thy eyes till thou hast thrice reviewed the transactions of the past day. What have I been doing? What have I left undone?

—PYTHAGORAS

5

Reading that helps get things done

ONE OF THE best ways to make money during the first thirty years of life is to invest it in reading that counts. Saved money may be lost, but *hoarded knowledge sticks and multiplies at an illegal rate of interest.*

Henry Ford is speaking in his slow, deliberate way. "Saving money as it has been schooled in young people gives money altogether too high a place. The young person's job is not to accumulate dollars, but to use them to prepare himself with training, knowledge, and experience every leader needs.

"Boys have been told to save money so they might not go to the poorhouse in their old age. No boy who learns how to spend money lands there.

"So I say: Boys, spend your money. Be sure to spend it for things that put you ahead of where you were yesterday. It is time enough to save when you earn more than you can spend wisely."

Just after his voice changed, Ford himself ran away to work in a machine shop for $2.50 a week. He practiced then what he preached above and spent a few dimes each week buying mechanics' trade journals.

When he married Clara Bryant they started housekeeping with little more than bundles of these journals, which were educating and inspiring him. The young couple went to live on a forty-acre plot his father turned over to them, and Henry Ford might have remained a farmer but for those machine and engineering magazines. They lured him away from the farm and back to machines.

We can also be thankful that Edison could say of the days when he was an expert telegraph operator, "I never was much for saving money, *as* money. I devoted every cent, regardless of future needs, to scientific books and materials for experiments."

The Escape Artist

Ehrich Weiss wanted to act in a circus, so this nine-year-old practiced in a shed behind his home in Appleton, Wisconsin, until he could hang by his knees from a trapeze and pick needles from the floor with his eyelids. At twelve he ran away from home.

In a secondhand book store, when he was sixteen, he picked up a book on magic by Robert Houdin that was to change his life. He paid a dime for the book, started to read it after supper. He could not leave it. He thought about magic tricks while cutting neckties, while running in amateur races. He got more secondhand books on magic, worked up a few tricks of his own, and changed his name to Houdini.

He was a lifelong habitué of secondhand book stores, gathered more than 5,000 volumes on magic and spiritualism which are now in the Library of Congress.

The Atomic-bomb Reporter

A neighbor in Lithuania loaned the twelve-year-old Siew boy a book that speculated about life on Mars. The book fired him to learn more about science. At seventeen he landed in the United States, with 50 cents in his pocket. He worked his way through Harvard in seven years, changed his name to that of the street on which he lived—Laurence.

As William L. Laurence, science writer for the *New York Times*, he was appointed by the government to have charge of reporting on the atomic bomb, flew with the bomb that was dropped on Nagasaki.

In such unexpected ways does reading give many a goal in life.

And to many others it gives a fresh start.

THE SUBMARINE INVENTOR

A redhead of ten read Jules Verne's fanciful story, "Twenty Thousand Leagues Under the Sea." Why couldn't it be made true, the lad asked himself, in a voice that barely rustled? That is how a Welsh stripling was launched on his life's goal, building boats that would travel safely under water. Simon Lake, the redheaded boy, was inspired for more than sixty-five years to build and continually improve submarine and deep-sea salvage equipment.

THE ALLIED SUPREME COMMANDER

In Abilene, Kansas, a tallish high-school boy from across the tracks wondered what to do when he graduated. He was tired of working in the creamery. He visited the weekly-newspaper office; famed editor J. W. Howe loaned him a book that had just come in. The book told the story of that amazing military leader, Hannibal. Young Dwight Eisenhower was fascinated. It was the turning point in his life. Reading the right book started "Ike" Eisenhower on the way to West Point Military Academy to become Allied Supreme Commander in history's greatest war.

Even that ponderous and dull collection "The Congressional Record" has turned some from detours to a goal. Young Jonathan Dolliver found a discarded volume of the "Record," read it through, memorized some of the speeches, and resolved to become a senator. At forty he was United States Senator from Iowa.

DISCOVERER OF THE NORTH POLE

Robert E. Peary, a dreamy boy from Cresson, Pennsylvania, was inspired by Elisha Kane's book on "Arctic Exploration" (a dreary tome, if you ask me). Robert's dreamy eyes narrowed, he could already see visions of the frozen Northlands. "I will help the world understand the mysteries of those places," he decided.

That book gave him a goal. At thirty he made his first voyage of exploration to Greenland. At forty-seven he tried to reach the North Pole and failed. But he still had his goal, born of boyhood reading.

Heroically, he tried again and six years later did reach the Pole, the first person to capture this goal which men had been trying to reach for four hundred years. Scientific societies and governments the world over honored the boy who had gotten his start from reading, reading that gave him a wrought-iron determination.

NATURAL SELECTION

Alfred Russel Wallace lived in poverty near the Bristol Channel with an impractical father who called their hens peacocks. Alfred went to work with a surveying gang at fourteen. Four years later he happened to buy a secondhand book on botany. Soon, while he carried the surveyor's chain, he thought of botany, and at twenty-two he began to work toward his new goal in earnest; he would become a natural scientist.

At thirty-three he originated the theory of natural selection, the same theory as Darwin's, but discovered independently of Darwin, who announced his theory the same year, at the age of forty-nine. Later in this book we will have the story of the unusual circumstances under which Wallace hit upon his theory of natural selection.

Forel—Pennington—Cuvier

Someone gave the Forel family a book on ants. Like many gift books, it remained unread until one rainy day when ten-year-old Auguste was looking for something to do. The story of the ants caught his fancy, and he could scarcely put the book down to eat supper. He became a world authority on the puzzling life of ants—and that gift book was carefully preserved by him until his death.

Mary Pennington, at twelve, found a book on medical chemistry that started her on the road to becoming one of the greatest authorities on the refrigeration of perishable foods.

Georges Cuvier was a frail infant, miraculously raised by his mother, who had only a widow's pension to support them. She taught him Latin, history, and literature. One day he found a beautifully illustrated book on nature study that almost hypnotized him. He copied the illustrations, borrowed other books on natural science and, before his teen years, was a well-read naturalist. Later he became Baron Cuvier, founder of the science of comparative anatomy and probably the greatest scientist of his day.

Keep a supply of worth-while books around where children can see them. Select books that cover a variety of subjects. *Expose young people to the stimulation of reading.* There is no telling where it may lead.

Inventor of the Microphone

Emile Berliner had ten brothers and sisters; before he thought of shaving he went to work as clerk in a store. He landed in the United States at nineteen, haggard from two weeks of seasickness. Here he peddled men's clothing, then found a job washing bottles for a chemist. While visiting with August Engel, a druggist around the corner, Berliner borrowed a copy of Mueller's "Synopsis of Physics and Meteorology."

The chapters on electricity and acoustics he read and reread.

With a small soap box, the head from a toy drum, a sewing needle, a steel dress button, and a piece of guitar string, he made the first practical telephone transmitter—at twenty-six. His invention has not been superseded; you still talk into it on your telephone.

His original soap-box transmitter is exhibited in the United States National Museum, a monument to reading that counted.

BAYARD TAYLOR

Bayard Taylor was a devil in a printer's shop at Kennett Square, Pennsylvania. One day he saw a small book which had been sent to the office. The boy, who was too young to grow even a timid moustache, read this "Tourist Guide to Europe," by George P. Putnam. It was more exciting than setting type and scrubbing presses. He used the tourist guide as a plan for more and more reading and, in two years, aged nineteen, with $140, he set out to be a world traveler. World travel became his career. He wrote books, newspaper and magazine articles about his travels; finally he became United States Minister to Germany.

FATHER OF THE WEATHER REPORTS

Joseph Henry was apprenticed to a watchmaker in Albany and hated the trade. He was inclined to throw in his lot as an actor when he happened upon a book left by one of his mother's roomers.

"Lectures on Experimental Philosophy, Astronomy, and

Chemistry" was its formidable title. It sounds deadly, but to the stage-struck Scotch boy it opened a new world, far more alluring than that of the theater. He decided to become a scientist.

The unit for measuring induced electrical current, the *henry*, is named for him; it is one of his discoveries. As pioneer director of the Smithsonian Institution, he started the first weather-report system.

The book with the frightful title he preserved until his death. On its flyleaf he wrote, "This book exerted a remarkable influence upon my life. It opened a new world when I was sixteen, and caused me to resolve, at the time of reading it, that I would immediately commence to devote my life to the acquisition of knowledge."

John Masefield ran away to sea at fourteen, was assistant bartender in New York for a while. At eighteen he read Chaucer's "The Parlement of Foules." That decided him; he would be a poet. And in fifteen years his poetry had won everlasting fame. He became Poet Laureate.

The right reading—often accidental—wakes up slumberers and gives needed goals to those who still have none. The right book or article has started many on the main road and off the detours.

A LIBRARIAN, your BOSS, a BOOK DEALER, a TEACHER can help you pick the reading that will count. Often we just stumble across the right reading; that's why it is wise to read many things. I accidentally stumbled into psychology. I was halfway through college, majoring in chemistry, and an assistant in the physics laboratory. Then one Christmas vacation I started to read a four-volume manual on experimental psychology by E. B. Titchener. At the end of the vacation I knew I was changing my vocation. My chemistry professor was disgusted. But the halfhearted chemistry student became an enthusiastic psychology student.

Great Lives Remind Us

Do you have a hero? "Tell me whom you admire," said Sainte-Beuve, "and I will tell you what you are."

The lives of great men have aroused sleeping abilities in thousands of people who were once stumbling along. Reading such lives has given many an irresistible determination to get more things done.

There was Havelock Ellis, for instance. He was born at St. John's Grove with an abnormally large head and a weakness that kept him frail into his twenties. He went with his seafaring father to Australia, where he was left behind because his father did not think he could stand the climate of Calcutta, the next stop. Ellis taught in a lonely little Australian school and wondered what to do with himself.

One evening he was lying on his back, reading "The Life and Letters of James Hinton." The nineteen-year-old read Hinton's description of how he came to be a great ear surgeon and philosopher.

In a flash Ellis leaped up. There was his answer; he would become a physician! So back to London, where he entered medical school, to begin his rapid climb as international authority on sociological medicine.

Rudyard Kipling

Rudyard Kipling went to Bombay at seventeen wearing real whiskers. In the heat and sickness he toiled on a newspaper, apparently his lifework. Alone in the house one hot evening he picked up a book by Walter Besant, "All in a Garden Fair." The book told the story of a young man who wanted to write and who did in spite of great obstacles.

That selfsame evening Kipling resolved that he, too, would write, whatever the obstacles. He started at last to save money. At twenty-four he returned to England with his savings, settled in a room over a sausage shop, and began the writing that was to make his name world-famous.

Plutarch's "Lives"

S. F. B. Morse was one of eleven children. He was ten when he read Plutarch's famous "Lives of Illustrious Men," those stories of ancient Greek leaders and noble Romans. The book fired the young man; he, too, was going to accomplish something. Within a quarter-century he won recognition as a portrait painter, and a short time later invented the telegraph. Plutarch's "Lives" started him on the road to the American Hall of Fame.

Plutarch's work has given many young men the stimulus to get things done. Napoleon carried a copy of it for twenty years. Oliver Hazard Perry, hero of the War of 1812, read and reread Plutarch, starting in his youth. So did Robert Brookings, who established the famous Brookings Institute in Washington.

The Quaker, Benjamin West, America's first noteworthy artist, was inspired by Plutarch to paint historical subjects. He tried to do with his paints, which the Indians taught him to mix, what Plutarch had done with words.

And the very un-Quakerlike Madame Roland read Plutarch surreptitiously during religious services.

Edward A. Ross, an orphan, was raised by his aunt in Iowa; she did not permit him to play or read on Sundays. In the attic of her farmhouse he discovered an old copy of Plutarch's

"Lives," quietly hid away Sunday after Sunday to pore over its pages. It inspired him to carve out his career of world's pioneer in scientific sociology.

FRANKLIN'S "AUTOBIOGRAPHY"

Benjamin Franklin's "Autobiography" decided a crosseyed Irish immigrant to become a printer and editor—James Gordon Bennett, founder of the *New York Herald*.

Henry Morgenthau, another immigrant who made a fortune, was worried for fear his own wealth would sap his son's initiative. He had Henry, Jr., read Franklin's book. Henry Morgenthau, Jr., was United States Secretary of the Treasury for a dozen years.

Franklin attributed his own zeal for getting things done to reading "Essays to Do Good," by Cotton Mather. He was about sixteen, working in his brother's print shop, when he seriously began to read to improve himself. He says in his "Autobiography":

. . . I then proposed to my brother that if he would give me, weekly, half the money he paid for my board, I would board myself. He instantly agreed to it, and I presently found that I could save half what he paid me. This was an additional fund for buying books.

But I had another advantage in it. My brother and the rest going from the printing-house to their meals, I remained there alone, and, dispatching presently my light repast, had the rest of the time till their return for study.

OLDER—PRESCOTT—LOYOLA

Fremont Older, a boy on a farm in Wisconsin, read a biography of Horace Greeley. He decided to become a crusading editor, and carried the well-worn book with him for years.

Older, a fearless, vigilant editor, cleaned up the political corruption in California and let nothing stop his crusading, not even kidnappers.

William Prescott, at twenty, was slowly going blind. What could his lifework be? When the autobiography of Gibbon was read to him, he knew he was going to be a historian, too. We will learn later how, with ever-dimming eyesight, Prescott made himself a world-famous historian.

Loyola was thirty and a common Spanish soldier when he was laid low with a leg wound. While convalescing he read "The Lives of the Saints," which inspired him to become a religious worker. He founded the Jesuit order, was consecrated a saint by Pope Gregory XV.

"Study a great man," said Louis Pasteur.

Great men who have done things, who are still doing things, can become our inspiring lifetime friends through their biographies and autobiographies. Get a hero—and get better acquainted with him by reading about him.

Some rich man who wanted to make the world hum could put more books about people who have done things within reach of the minds of the generation which is yet to do things.

Everyone can find new friends who count by reading books about people who count. Try reading a biography a month for several months.

EVENING EDUCATIONS

Education is within easy reach of people who have the gumption to get it—in reading of the right sort. And there is no tuition charge.

"The best part of every man's education is that which he gives to himself," said Sir Walter Scott, the lawyer who had infantile paralysis and turned writer.

"In the long run, he learns most who studies much and is taught little," John Cotton Dana observed.

Charles Darwin, the Cambridge University and Edinburgh University man, said, "All I have learned of any value has been self-taught."

Thomas Midgley, Jr., taught himself chemistry, not an easy subject to learn. He used this self-taught knowledge to invent ethyl gasoline, freon for electric refrigeration and air conditioning, and to help in extracting bromine from sea water.

Fifteen-year-old Edward W. Berry went to work for a cotton firm, later became a traveling salesman. At thirty-two, with no college education, he was elected to the faculty of Johns Hopkins University. He had educated himself to become an authority in paleontology. Later this noncollege man was elevated to the deanship.

"It isn't what we learn at an institution that is of value to us, so much as the attitude we develop toward all learning," Dean Berry said.

Hot-tempered James J. Hill left school at fourteen, started educating himself at eighteen, and kept at it through life. Living in the cabin of an icebound boat, with his one good eye he read things that counted.

His self-education made it possible for rusty-headed Hill to build up the Great Northern Railroad and an agricultural empire in the Northwest, in direct competition with larger and older railroads that enjoyed government subsidies. Without any government aid, but with his self-education, Hill's line marched forward while the competitors went into receivership.

"I guess the only thing is to read things that count, notice things that count, and remember them," Hill said.

Read for keeps. Read books to remember and later to use.

One can get an education at college, of course. A few actually do. But nothing excels the education one picks up systematically for oneself.

Planning Reading

Rufus Choate, a lifelong reader, once remarked, "Desultory reading is a waste to life; read by system."

This brings to mind a childhood experience of James Martineau, who was to become a preeminent religious teacher. His mother left him one evening with instructions to read the Bible while she was gone. On her return young James reported he had read the entire book of Isaiah.

"Why, you couldn't have read all of Isaiah in this short time," he was admonished.

"Yes, I did," he replied, "but I had to skip the nonsense."

Edison had been at school only three months when a teacher told him not to return because he was too dumb to learn. His mother taught him reading, writing, and some figuring.

He went to a Detroit library, took the first book on the shelf, and read it. When it was finished, he took the next book on the shelf. One day the librarian asked him how many he had read.

"Fifteen feet!"

He had been reading without guidance, with no plan, just reading one shelf after another. The librarian showed him how to plan his reading, gave him assistance which helped make the boy, who had less than a term of schooling, one of the best informed scientists of his time.

Ask a librarian to help you plan your reading.

Get suggestions, too, from some SPECIALIST in the profession or field in which you are interested.

Read your TRADE JOURNALS to keep informed of new developments.

Borrow books.

Buy some books. Buy them to keep on hand for future reference. I buy from 250 to 300 books each year. Nine out of ten I read and keep; the tenth may be a detour that I throw away. Most of these books are bought in secondhand book stores. *A good secondhand book costs no more than a poor movie.*

The father of the famous Mayo brothers made his sons promise to spend at least an hour a day in medical reading. Dr. Will Mayo, to the end of his life, kept a record of the hours and minutes he read. Otto H. Kahn followed an inflexible rule of reading something worth while for at least one hour each night before going to bed.

Reading vs. Working

Some ambitious persons try to advance themselves by doing two jobs a day. They work eight hours on their regular job, then four more hours on another paying job. This increases their incomes by half or more, and doubles their fatigue so they are worth less on their regular jobs.

It seldom advances them one inch.

If those four hours after the regular workday were spent in reading things that counted, such folk would soon be qualified for doing work that was really worth more.

Their second job is likely a detour in getting things done.

But the right reading is never a detour.

"An extraordinary ordinary man" is the way people described Benjamin Lamme, the Ohio farm boy who designed electrical generators for harnessing the power of Niagara Falls. He made himself extraordinary, not by working at two paying jobs, but by concentrating on things he needed to know in his spare and evening hours.

He started this early in life, as a schoolboy, when he noticed he had difficulty remembering. So he made himself learn the multiplication table up to thirty-six times thirty-six!

After he got a job with Westinghouse he continued to do extra work at home, but not unfinished office work. "I early adopted the practice," he said, "of not taking any routine work home with me. My evening work at home was entirely on new problems, or something radically different from my day's work, and which would, therefore, constitute a change and a challenge. For about fifteen years I averaged from twelve to fifteen hours a week at such work."

Inevitably, he went ahead made himself an uncommon engineer.

We call some folks common laborers; they are common because they do not concentrate on new things that count.

There are also common bankers, common doctors, common engineers, common executives, common businessmen. They may put in more than an eight-hour day, but their production remains common because they have not given themselves background and know-how for doing something uncommon.

Otto Kahn was no common banker. The Mayos were not common doctors. Lamme was not a common chief electrical engineer. Daniel Guggenheim, who studiously read an hour each evening, was not a common industrialist.

Do today's work in eight hours; work for next year by reading helpful books in the hours remaining.

That's a secret for becoming UNcommon.

Books have changed the course of nations as well as of individuals.

François Arouet, who wrote under the pen name of Voltaire, satirized social and political shams. His books laid the foundation for the French Revolution.

PUT LESS EMPHASIS ON

INCREASING THIS WEEK'S PAY,

MORE EMPHASIS ON INCREAS-

ING YOUR EARNING POWER

BY THE RIGHT READING

Small Harriet Beecher Stowe wrote a book which was read the world over. "Uncle Tom's Cabin" inflamed opinions and helped precipitate the War Between the States.

"Mein Kampf," which Adolph Hitler wrote in jail, aroused the Nazis to embroil the whole world in chaos.

Reading has made nations—and individuals—rise or fall.

It can be waste power or power applied.

They Read the Dictionary

The dictionary can be used to keep the door from blowing shut or to make a dining chair high enough for visiting children. It gives a learned air to the home. Some people even win puzzle contests by finding strange words within its covers.

And there are still others who find the dictionary fascinating reading, page by page.

There was Polly Richards' second child, for instance. Not much is known about Polly. She was a second-rate actress. Her second child's father was a stranger with whom she spent a few evenings after her husband was lost at sea.

The child, Dick Freeman, was adopted at two by a hoarse-voiced fish peddler. Dick played hooky from school to sell newspapers. Then he worked as a printer's devil, then in a shoe shop, then in a smelly rubber factory, then on a smellier fishing ship as cook.

None of these seemed the vocation he wanted, so he tried a milkman's job, a plasterer's, a roadmaker's—all by the time he was eighteen.

Then he solved his vocational problem by enlisting in the Army for seven years. He was thin as a shad and barely tall enough to pass the physical requirements.

At twenty-one he found himself an orderly in a post hospital in South Africa. It was a soft Army berth—a little scrubbing to do, some records to keep, and on Fridays a walk along the avenue of fragrant eucalyptus trees to buy vegetables and supplies. But for the red ants and the heat his Army life was a cinch.

Then he met Marion Caldecott, a Scotch missionary's wife. She was middle-aged, mother of ten children. There was, of course, an eighteen-year-old daughter who made orderly Dick's visits to the mission take on the regularity of sundown. Daughter Ivy awakened his heart, but it was her gray-haired mother who awakened his mind.

So this medical orderly, who ran away from school to peddle papers, bought a small pocket dictionary. Midst the jumble of medical aromas in the quiet orderly room he studied this dictionary from cover to cover. When he had "exhausted" it he presented it to his sergeant, who spent the boiling afternoons on his bunk, smoking and staring at the ceiling.

Private Dick Freeman garnered extra money by going on a diet; he pocketed the extra ration allowance. He got more money for brief stories he began to write for newspapers near the camp. After six of his seven years' enlistment, he bought his way out of the Army and started a fresh life in which he was to make a new name resound around the world. That new name was Edgar Wallace.

As Edgar Wallace he became the best-selling author of all time, grinding out story after story as intensely as he had once read the pocket dictionary. Nor did he slow down with age. During the ten years from fifty to sixty, he wrote forty-six books, more than four books a year. And the public still clamored for more.

The amazing speed was easy for him because his dictionary reading those hot afternoons in South Africa had equipped him so well he was seldom at a loss for the right word to express his ideas.

THE FIRST LIBRARY IN THE WHITE HOUSE

No one knows the month the Fillmore boy was born. His father was too busy trying to make a living out of a clayey farm to record such minor details as births. At fifteen the boy was apprenticed to learn wool carding and dressing with the firm of Cheney & Kellogg. Three years later a new schoolmistress came to the small backwoods New York village where he was working. Miss Abigail Powers, with her luxuriant curls, was destined to have a profound influence on tall Millard Fillmore.

She was only two years older than the wool carder. But she had enjoyed a cultured home life, though her family had been hard-pressed ever since her father had died soon after she was born. She was the first educated person Millard Fillmore had met—and those black curls!

So he saved his small wages and bought a dictionary, which

he propped open in front of him on the carding machine. In the short moments between jumps to keep the machine filled, he would study a word and its definition, working systematically through each letter of the alphabet.

He was intent upon narrowing the cultural gap that separated him from the schoolteacher. In eight years they were married, the bride continuing to teach school and the groom continuing his new work of teaching himself law.

When Millard Fillmore became President of the United States, almost the first thing he asked from Congress was an appropriation to start the first library in the White House.

LAWRENCE BARRETT

Lawrence Barrett's Irish father was a Detroit tailor who wore a dignified pair of Galway side whiskers. The immigrant was a steady worker, but the children's home advantages were skimpy. They got lots of love, mixed generously with firm discipline, and that was about all.

Young Larry, whose face had a monklike intenseness, found for his first treasure a dog-eared dictionary. To the tempestuous youth the book was filled with magic. He stretched out flat on the floor to read it, his deep, burning eyes eagerly hurrying on as new worlds opened, line after line. That was the start of his path to fame as actor, then as director and producer.

"America owes more to Lawrence Barrett for his production of high-class dramas than to any other of the tragedians of his day," said Otis Skinner.

And Larry Barrett owed his start in life to his prized dictionary.

Up to the time of his sudden death, years later, he could recite page after page of that dictionary from memory, giving the spelling, pronunciation, and definition of each consecutive word. His memory was unusual, to be sure, but so was the object of his study.

THE SEED KING

Peter Henderson was a Scotchman, raised by his sister. His first work was in a liquor store; he became a teetotaler. Still in his teens, he obtained work as gardener's assistant at Melville Castle. This ruddy, gray-eyed six-footer ate his meals with one hand while slowly turning the pages of the dictionary with the other. Oblivious to the chatter of his fellow apprentices, he concentrated on studying the dictionary from *A* to *Z*.

The other young men thought this a peculiar thing to do. It was. But it enabled him to come to the United States, begin at scratch, and build up one of the most successful seed businesses in the world. His mealtime study gave him a command of words that made his catalogues more effective than those of his competitors and equipped him to write articles for horticultural journals that revolutionized garden and nursery work.

HOMER CROY

None of the Croys had more than a grade-school education, so when young Homer announced his intention of going to high school at the county seat it was a momentous occasion for the whole family. The youth was shy and self-conscious. It hurt him to put up with the jibes the city children gave him for wearing his father's Sunday trousers to high school and for riding an old plow horse to and from town. He rode on roundabout side streets to avoid meeting the city children he envied.

The old horse was smart as a milk-wagon horse and soon knew every turn to be made. Homer had nothing to do but sit and ride. That gave him lots of time to think each morning and afternoon—to think about the city students who slyly laughed at his rustic ways and clothes.

The idea came to him that, instead of envying the city children, he might excel them. He would make use of the time the horse carried him to and from school. He bought a dictionary with a red back and gold index tabs.

He read that dictionary through on horseback, wearying his eyes as the horse jolted him along. And the city youngsters? They soon had to get help from the farm lad who seemed to know so much. Their sly laughter turned into open respect. Homer Croy turned into a man of culture who made a trip around the world taking motion pictures. He wrote a famous novel, "West of the Water Tower," several other books, and talking pictures for Will Rogers—all started by an envious lad studying the dictionary on horseback.

A REAL POT OF GOLD

Edwin Markham was born in Oregon, where his mother ran a little store stocked with general merchandise. When the rangy lad was five his mother moved to greener pastures, in central California, to try to improve her fortunes raising sheep. Edwin was an uneducated farm boy. At fifteen he had been in school exactly fifteen months.

But he wanted a dictionary and some other books. He plowed stony land for neighbors to earn enough money to buy a Webster's "Unabridged." He carried the bulky volume in his saddle pack, reading it in every possible odd moment. He was getting an education for himself from its pages, and he wanted more.

He heard of the State Teachers College at San José and decided he must go there. But there was no money. His mother saved, and Edwin worked for others in his spare time.

Then one summer day he was digging beside a path in the

yard when his shovel hit something that made a metallic sound. He uncovered a rusted tin can, inside of which was a rotted canvas bag. In the remnants of the bag he found a number of firm, round gold pieces—$900 in coins that someone had hidden there years before.

Here was sudden wealth for him! But it did not ruin him, as it had the Silver Millionaires described in an earlier chapter. Tall Edwin Markham had a goal; he had started to reach that goal by reading the big dictionary; and now he could advance further along the way toward it by going to college.

He graduated from college, taught country school in places where there had never before been schools. He progressed, became a professor in the state university, then superintendent of schools at San Francisco. He crowned his career by writing the famous poem "The Man with a Hoe," which has been translated into thirty-seven languages.

Wanamaker—Webster—Pitt

Self-made John Wanamaker, several times a millionaire, spent many evenings in his ample library reading just one book. Even at seventy he would read the dictionary while his less successful competitors were reading detective stories.

Daniel Webster, too, read the dictionary seriously from cover to cover. He wanted to improve his use of words; that he did so was undoubtedly a factor in his becoming the leading orator of his age.

Ironically, another Webster—Noah—made himself the most famous of dictionary makers.

The illustrious English orator, William Pitt, who became the Earl of Chatham, is reported to have read Bailey's dictionary through twice.

Sidney Porter's Review

Shy Sidney Porter was clerking in his uncle's North Carolina drugstore and becoming more tubercular by the week. His father, a dreamy physician, was more interested in a perpetual-motion invention than in his son's health, so the eighteen-year-old was in a dangerous condition before it was realized that he needed a change of climate. He was sent to Texas, where he lived outdoors herding sheep on a lonely ranch.

Sheepherding is said to be as lonely as living at the bottom of the sea. But the Porter boy found it an interesting job. During his two years on the Hall Brothers' Ranch his constant companion was a large Webster's "Unabridged" dictionary.

It was some ten years later, when he was becoming known as a columnist and short-story writer, that he wrote the following review of the dictionary:

There is not a dull line between the covers of the book. The range of subjects is wide, and the treatment light and easy without being flippant. A valuable feature of the work is the arranging of the articles in alphabetical order, thus facilitating the finding of any particular word desired. Mr. Webster's vocabulary is large, and he always uses the right word in the right place. Mr. Webster's work is thorough, and we predict that he will be heard from again.

Sidney Porter is better known by his pen name of O. Henry.

Encyclopedia Readers

If a dictionary seems like a lot of dull reading, consider this story.

Habakkuk Bowditch—his real name—was a drunkard who quoted the Bible in a rumbling voice through his rust-colored beard. A cooper by trade, he spent much of his time at sea, away from Salem, because he could not stand the babies around his house.

His fourth child, Nathaniel, was frail and stooped, with a squeaky voice and large and protruding ears. He wanted to go to sea, too, lied about his age to ship captains, but they refused to take the high-cheekboned boy because he seemed too weak.

So, at twelve, Nat turned to work in a waterfront store. There he could still hear and smell his beloved ocean while he kept the store's accounts. He liked figures almost as well as he did ships.

Judge Ropes, one of the proprietors of the store, loaned the young bookkeeper his four-volume set of "Chambers' Cyclopedia." Nathaniel Bowditch read every word of the bulky book, using slack minutes in the store and getting up two hours before daybreak in winter.

The "Cyclopedia" stimulated his contemplative mind, especially the sections that dealt with weather phenomena, astronomy, and navigation. Though barely in his teens, Nat wondered why his father and the other Salem sailors still navigated their ships by guesswork and dead reckoning; they could use the stars and be really certain of their courses.

He worked out new star tables and simpler mathematical ways for navigating ships. These he taught to common sailors and convinced captains and shipowners that they could save weeks in their voyages if they set their courses by his methods.

His books on navigation have safely guided thousands and thousands of ships through the trackless seas. His boyhood reading of the "Cyclopedia" started him on the road to becoming "the best-informed mathematician in America."

BOTANY—SHIPS—MICROSCOPES

From tiny Sauquoit, New York, Asa Gray's father, the village tanner, sent his teen-age lad away to learn medicine. The boy finished his courses in medicine well enough, but with his tongue in his cheek. After all, his heart was not in medicine. He had read through Brewster's "Encyclopedia;" he had conned the section on botany so many times he could almost repeat it from memory. It had turned all his thoughts toward botany. He received the degree of Doctor of Medicine but did not become a practicing physician. For seven years he eked out a living by part-time work, devoting every possible minute to the study of plants; then a position opened by which he could make a living as a botanist. For more than half a century he was our living leader of botanical sciences.

William Jackson, seventh son of a fatherless family of eleven children, went to work as laborer in a shipyard when only twelve, working from six in the morning until nine in the evening. In the shipyard office he found a set of the "Encyclopaedia Britannica," which he studied from *A* to *Z*. He later became a large shipowner.

Charles A. Spencer, a child on a small upstate New York farm, read a broken-backed encyclopedia he found in the attic. The section on optics caught his fancy; he read it until he knew it by heart. Then this slightly-built boy, not yet twelve, pushed back his brown hair and started to make an optical lens. At twenty-five he had his own factory for making lenses—in a barn. He made the first American microscopes, took the laurels away from European optical manufacturers.

Verily, there are more than words and facts in dictionaries and encyclopedias. I know there is romance, inspiration, and education, for I have read through a six-volume encyclopedia and a sixteen-hundred-page dictionary. That is how I learned, among other things, about many of the stimulating people whose stories are being told in this book.

Down in southeastern Massachusetts, near the Rhode Island border, is a small town called Franklin. It was named for Benjamin Franklin, and thereby hangs an interesting tale.

The organizing selectmen who established the town, with true New England thriftiness, wrote to Franklin and suggested that he repay the honor by donating a bell for their new white church.

Franklin repaid the honor by sending them 115 books instead. He told them that "sense was preferable to sound."

That gift was the start of what is claimed to be the first free public library in the United States.

Franklin, the self-taught genius who got things done, knew from personal experience the power of reading that counted. He called the man most deserving of pity "a lonesome man on a rainy day who does not know how to read."

Books and magazines can be friends that help you get things done—or they can get you off on detours.

You may need to work less and read more.

Leaders are readers.

It is better to get wisdom than gold.
                                        —PROVERBS 16:16
It is the struggle toward a goal that makes a man happy.
                                        —FRIDTJOF NANSEN

6

How to get friends who help

OUR FRIENDS are like our reading. They can stimulate and inspire us to do something—or they can sidetrack us onto detours that make accomplishment a gamble.

It is easier to make the acquaintance, even win the friendship of important people than most of us realize. Young folk have discovered this to their advantage by nonchalantly making the acquaintance of great men whose names have frightened away their more restrained elders.

Listen to the story of Arthur Farquhar, a Quaker lad of eighteen who lived in a small Maryland town a dozen miles from a railroad. He read in a magazine about some big-business leaders and decided he would like to know more about them. He also thought they could give him some advice before he started work as a machinist.

So the raw country boy arrived in New York City one morning. At seven o'clock, ignorant of city office hours, he went directly to William B. Astor's office. A round-shouldered clerk was already at work in the outer office.

In the adjoining room young Farquhar saw a heavy-set, bushy-browed man he recognized instantly from Mr. Astor's photographs. The big man tried to be gruff when he asked what the boy wanted.

"I want to know how to make a million dollars."

Mr. Astor smiled and softened up at once. They talked for

an hour, chiefly about real estate, and Mr. Astor gave him a list of other men of affairs to visit.

Farquhar called upon leading merchants, editors, bankers—even sat in on a bank-directors' meeting, this boy who lived in a log house in a backwoods town.

The advice he received on how to make money did not help him much. But the acquaintanceship he formed with men who were getting things done gave him more than confidence; it gave him models to imitate.

No longer would the small timers of Montgomery county, the satisfied failures, be the ones he unconsciously copied. After his unusual visit to the seat of the mighty he began to adopt the work habits that had made them mighty.

Two more years, and this twenty-year-old boy was partner in the shop where he had started as an apprentice. At twenty-four he was sole proprietor of a farm-machinery business from which he in time made more than his million dollars, although his plant was twice wiped out by disastrous fires.

During his sixty-seven years of active business life he continued to practice the basic lesson he learned on that early trip to New York—get acquainted with people who count. He often said that meeting those older men who were doing things was the turning point in his life.

THE BOK BOY

The Bok family met financial reverses, so emigrated from Holland when Edward was six. He did the usual boyhood jobs to earn money in Brooklyn—washed windows, peddled papers.

He wanted to get acquainted with people who counted, wanted to learn their methods and secrets of work. When newspapers reported that distinguished people were in New York City, young Edward used to pay them unexpected visits.

> ## FRIENDS MAY NOT BE ABLE
> ## TO GIVE YOU PULL, BUT THE
> ## RIGHT FRIENDS CAN HELP
> ## YOU GET SOME PUSH

He went to the Fifth Avenue Hotel to call on General U. S. Grant, and the General invited Bok to have dinner with him. Big men are not merely friendly; often, too, they are lonesome and esteem pleasant company.

When Abraham Lincoln's widow was taken to Dr. Holbrook's sanitarium with a mental disease, young Bok visited her.

He went to Boston, this sixteen-year-old boy, and had breakfast with Oliver Wendell Holmes. He helped white-haired Longfellow read his mail and went to the theater with him, where he met other famous men.

The offices of the brass hats held no terror for this boy. When he had an idea he thought would interest a company, he would call on its president without hesitation or embarrassment.

He started an almost make-believe newspaper at nineteen and induced famous people to write for it. At twenty-three he branched out to form one of the world's first newspaper syndicates; he had gained momentum from associating with big people.

This momentum helped him become one of the leaders of the United States and the donor of the American Peace and Harvard Advertising awards.

Edward Bok, in his search for self-education, discovered not only that successful personages will give of their time and friendship to a sincere and eager young man but also that one of the best forms of self-training is to understudy great men and women.

Youngsters are usually frank about their hero worship. Oldsters, unfortunately, seem to feel they should conceal it.

Don't conceal it. Put it to work by making the personal acquaintance of your heroes. It will flatter and please the hero and stimulate and encourage you.

TELEGRAPHER TO RAILROAD PRESIDENT

Roy B. White started to get somewhere at sixteen, as a beginner in the railroad-telegraph office of a small Indiana town. At twenty-seven he was division superintendent. Later he became president of the Western Union Telegraph Company, then of the Baltimore & Ohio Railroad.

When his son went away to school his father advised him, "Associate with the campus leaders, for men who lead anywhere lead everywhere."

This does not mean one should try to be a snob or a social climber. Snobs are not always getting things done. The most some of them can do is look haughtily down their noses and consume rather than produce. And social climbers are often just plain obnoxious.

But associate with the producers, with those who set examples that are worth following. Like books, our friends can also be teachers.

Live where you will have neighbors who get things done, who don't waste their resources trying to keep up with the Joneses.

Work with a company where you will have big men around you.

Join a club or organization that is doing things in the community, whose members are at the front of the procession. Work actively in that club.

Work actively, too, in your trade or professional associations.

Keep your old friends; don't go high-hat. But **make new friends—steadily—from among the ranks of the doers.**

THE FRIENDLY GREAT

One's first important friendships with doers, like one's first million dollars, are the hardest to make. This is not because the doers are aloof, but rather because of one's own hesitancy.

Isaac F. Marcosson, of Louisville, Kentucky, probably knew more living great people than any other man of his time. His business was to interview world leaders for the *Saturday Evening Post*.

"The busiest men in the world are the men who find time to do everything," Marcosson said. "The busier some men are the more time they have to do what they want to. No one discovers this more readily than the interviewer."

Nineteen-year-old Ernest Thompson Seton, just recovered from tuberculosis, was intensely interested in natural science and wanted to use the famed British Museum Library in London. This boy from far-off America was living mostly on bread and a so-called coffee he made from bran, beans, and molasses. His physical diet was meager, but he wanted to get a good mental diet. The Museum attendants told him coldly that no one under twenty-one years old could use the Library.

"But someone can give me special permission," the youth pleaded.

"To be sure," the attendants smiled. "The Prime Minister, the Prince of Wales, or the Archbishop of Canterbury."

Did those big names frighten young Seton? Perhaps. But he

saw the august three and received a life ticket to the Library. That was his start toward becoming one of the world's great naturalists, author of a shelf of more than forty nature-study books. He started at the very top when making the acquaintance of people who counted. Though he won a favor at the first visit, he knew, too, that acquaintanceship with people who count gives more than favors—or pull.

Of this something plus we obtain, Carlyle said, "We cannot look, however imperfectly, upon a great man without gaining something from him."

"One mistake of young men is their failure to cultivate their seniors," commented Ferdinand Foch, marshal of France during the First World War. "Every young man should know well at least one old man to whom he can go when he wants the teachings of experience rather than mere sympathy."

And Thackeray said, in the same vein, "Might I give counsel to any young man, I would say to him, try to frequent the company of your betters. In books and in life, that is the most wholesome society; learn to admire rightly; the great pleasure of life is that. Note what great men admired; they admired great things; narrow spirits admire basely, and worship meanly."

There is a too-human tendency to make friends among those who are not quite up to our own par. This is a comforting thing to do, since it enables us to feel superior to our associates. But it handicaps us, since we can learn nothing from those who produce less than we do. Friends who are doers, whose accomplishments are superior to our own, can challenge us away from the detours.

That is one reason why the first important friendships are the hardest to make. We like to be comforted by inferior friends and need to force ourselves to win the stimulation of superior friends.

Most friends are acquired accidentally. We just happened to

live near them or became acquainted in some casual way. But friends exert too much influence on personal progress to be left so largely to chance. They are vital enough to be sought deliberately.

Make the right friends and you are making good luck for yourself.

"I want to reform, but I don't know how to give up my undesirable friends," a young man told Dwight L. Moody.

"That is easy," the evangelist replied. "Just live a desirable life and your undesirable friends will give you up."

Artemus Ward

As a Cleveland printer, Charles F. Browne led a gay, Bohemian life. Then he moved to New York City where opportunity beckoned. He made the most of the opportunity by turning over a new leaf. He wrote back to a friend in Cleveland, "I am making influential friends fast. I have altered my views on some things and have courted the friendship of men whose friendship is worth having."

This was the serious young man who was better known by his professional name of Artemus Ward. He made himself world-famous during the few years before his untimely death. He died of tuberculosis in London at the age of thirty-three.

Nikola Tesla

Nikola Tesla invented the first practical and reversible electric motor. He came to America from Budapest, thin as a mummy, and sold the rights to the Westinghouse firm. The impetuous inventor was now a rich man.

In his little laboratory on Grand Street he produced wireless light, high-frequency alternators, and other spectacular inventions in quick succession. His demonstrations became the talk of the town. Sportsmen and society playgirls took him up as a glittering new toy.

Tesla could soon afford to return their entertaining, and he did, in a lavish fashion and with an imagination that delighted the butterflies.

After two years as a social lion, Tesla took stock of himself. His money was disappearing. He was making no more inventions. His friends were just hangers-on. And he was getting completely bored with it all.

"What have I accomplished in the last twenty-four months?" he asked himself. He shouted the answer. "Nothing!"

So he quit his society life right there. He became aloof to the social climbers and gadflies and turned to those friends who were doing things, who could stimulate him to produce again. Remember this amazing man, for we shall have more stories about him in later chapters.

DAVID SARNOFF

David Sarnoff came to the United States as a boy, made himself head of the Radio Corporation of America before his fortieth birthday. His quick rise to success naturally brought him many invitations. But he remained successful because he knew how to choose friends who kept him getting things done.

When a millionaire playboy invited Sarnoff to a sumptuous week-end party on his Long Island estate, the self-taught radio chief replied, "I don't play golf. I don't drink. I don't play cards. I don't tell stories. So I could add nothing to the party."

People who get things done keep improving themselves by making friends with those who are better than they are. They don't fritter their time away with those who can give them nothing but entertainment.

Lord Collingwood, who took command of the English Navy when Nelson died at Trafalgar, told his men, "You had better be alone than in mean company."

You can easily get acquainted with more people who count. Make a list of the worth-while people in your town. Make another list of similar people in the business or profession in which you are interested. Get acquainted with one of these people each week.

Great people have great friends.

—ELBERT HUBBARD

We gain nothing by being with such as ourselves: we encourage each other in mediocrity.

—LAMB

People seldom improve when they have no other model but themselves to copy after.

—GOLDSMITH

7

How to plan to produce

PLANFUL WORKERS accomplish more than those who are merely diligent workers.

Hudson Maxim was raised on a one-hundred-fifty-dollar Maine farm. He had his first pair of shoes when he was thirteen. His grandmother was insane. Not much of a start for any man.

When he was forty and experimenting with a fulminate compound, an explosion blew his left hand off at the wrist. Weeks of discouragement followed. Then one night he was accosted on the street by a drunkard. Maxim lost his temper and let fly. The drunkard fell down unconscious.

Maxim's artificial hand came off, and he lost his hat. But that hasty blow made Maxim think. An artificial hand was not so much of a handicap to getting things done after all. He began to depend upon his wits, to plan his work for one natural and one artificial hand.

"By having to depend more on my brains," he said later, "I found they were better than hands. Now I planned more, and got more done."

Maxim invented smokeless powder, the high-explosive maximite, torpedo boats, methods of making carbide, and, for thirty years after he lost his hand, he was a valued consultant of the Du Pont firm.

He had only one hand, but he used both sides of his brain.

He thought twice before the other fellow had started to think.

THE 2-CENT NOTE PAD

"You taught me one of the most useful things I ever learned," a former student, now vice-president of a nation-wide corporation, told me.

I preened as I waited for him to return some of my own pearls of wisdom.

"I learned it by watching you," he continued, pulling a 2-cent pad from his vest pocket. "We noticed that you often wrote something on one of these pads, then tore off the little sheet and filed it in a stack clipped to the back of the pad. Occasionally you would remove the top sheet, crumple it, and toss it into the wastebasket.

"The class was making bets about that pad. Someone even suggested you were writing poetry on it. I snooped in the wastebasket and found that the slips contained businesslike orders to yourself about things you had to do.

"I had forgotten about your pad until a few years ago. I was behind in my work and forgetting a lot of small but important things. So I bought a 2-cent pad and tried your scheme. I made notes the instant I found something needed to be done. Used a separate sheet for each thing and arranged them in the order in which they could be done quickest.

"Then I started getting things done."

There is nothing original about this little arrangement, but it is extremely effective, for it is a written plan of one's own activities.

DEVOTEES OF THE PAD

Young Harry Heinz, of Pittsburgh, carried a pocket pad as he peddled his homemade horse-radish. His ideas, his orders to himself, were jotted down as he went and organized later in the day. This planning was the backbone of his self-supervision; it enabled him to build up the food-packing business which became famous under the slogan "57 Varieties." He had jotted that slogan down while riding on a New York City elevated train.

A canal-toll collector in Dayton knew the use of planning, too. He even kept a pad beside his bed. This young fellow, John H. Patterson, was one of the "gettingest-done" men of all time. He called his sheaf of notes "Things to Do Today." He built up the gigantic National Cash Register Company from scratch.

Victor Hugo always supervised himself by a little pad of notes. He kept the pad beside him night and day.

Leonardo da Vinci started the note-pad habit in his youth and kept it up through his old age. He carried his pad in his belt.

Bismarck used blank sheets and kept them between the leaves of his prayer book.

Lord Bacon called his paper plans "Sudden Thoughts Set Down for Use."

Beethoven was never without a planning pad; it was almost the only systematic thing about his life.

Henry B. Hyde planned the Equitable Life Assurance Company and kept it going on a pocket note pad.

John Hays Hammond, the mining engineer, saw that he did the things he had to do by the same system.

John Hunter, a carpenter, could barely read and write when he was twenty, but he became one of the world's leading surgeons and anatomists. He used a note pad to plan his work, to jog himself into getting things done.

"My rule," Hunter said, "is deliberately to consider, before I commence, whether it is practicable. If it be practicable, I can accomplish it if I give sufficient pains to it; and having begun, I never stop until it is done."

William Osler, another great physician, carried a work-planning pad with him wherever he went.

Use a pocket pad to write down the things you should do. Make a note the instant an idea hits you or an order is given. Organize your notes so that one job will logically follow another. Then you will not lose time wondering what to do next or waiting to be told.

SCHEDULING TIME

Cyrus W. Field was ready to retire in luxury at forty. But he had the habit of getting things done and could not stand the inactivity of doing nothing. So he started anew, to do what others said was impossible, to lay a cable across the ocean. After heartbreaking failures, he succeeded in laying the Atlantic cable. Field planned his daily work in detail. At six o'clock each morning he wrote down the things he wished to do that day—then did them.

Charles Evans Hughes, the Baptist minister's son who became Chief Justice of the Supreme Court, planned each day's work in similar fashion. Hughes allowed himself exactly nineteen minutes for lunch. The waiters in the Capitol Restaurant could set their watches by him.

Dwight Morrow was a small, sickly Irish boy who wore his brother-in-law's castoff clothes. He planned his day's work the night before. He became a Morgan partner, turned down the presidency of Yale University.

Jacob Gould Schurman was a Canadian lad who became president of Cornell University, later Ambassador to Greece, China, and Germany. He laid out detailed plans, minute by minute, of the things to be done each day and stuck to them.

Frank Gannett took a correspondence course while tending bar, taught himself shorthand. Then he became Dr. Schurman's secretary. He quickly adopted the boss's plan of scheduling his day's work. This teetotaler won the nickname of "Can-do" for his adeptness in getting things done. He made himself a newspaper magnate with a string of more than twenty daily newspapers.

Gamaliel Bradford was frail, battled with the effects of tuberculosis most of his life. He, too, scheduled each activity of the day, made permanent fame by the excellent biographies he wrote.

Nearsighted Herman Schneider went to work in a Pennsylvania coal mine when he was fifteen. At thirty he was teaching at the University of Cincinnati. He reorganized their school of engineering and later became president of the university. This man who revolutionized the teaching of engineering had the lifelong habit of scheduling his time for days in advance. In this schedule he did not overlook time for play and recreation. This is important. Planning by schedule does not imply all work and no play: it merely provides that neither is overlooked and that each is in the right proportion.

Gladstone lived by a timetable and rarely made a deviation from it.

William Rainey Harper was an infant prodigy who could read when he was three, graduated from college at fourteen, and orated in Hebrew at his graduation. This stocky youth was not content, however, merely to have lots of ability. He wanted to make good use of it as well. Each week of his adult life he made out a definite list of how he would use his hours. From week to week he changed his programs, since he had a horror of getting in a rut.

He had barely turned thirty when he was offered the presidencies of Brown University, the University of Iowa, and the

University of South Dakota respectively. He rejected these offers and continued to schedule his hours and to produce. When he was not yet thirty-five, John D. Rockefeller heard of him and gave him the opportunity for which he had been waiting—the chance to start a great new university incorporating the ideals he envisioned. William Rainey Harper, who scheduled each hour in advance and stuck to his schedule, organized and led the University of Chicago until his early death from cancer.

Rules for Everyday Planning

Plan your day "tight." Schedule enough things to keep you on the jump. Don't be easy on yourself; you will understand why better when you have read a later chapter.

But be reasonable with yourself, after all. Plan enough to keep you sprinting, but not so much that you will get discouraged or that you can't possibly finish it. As Sir Francis Bacon quaintly said, "Young men embrace more than they can do, fly to the end without consideration of the means and degree."

Said John Wesley, "Though I am always in haste I am never in a hurry because I never undertake more work than I can go through with calmness of spirit."

Plan enough to keep you hustling but not so much as to make you unhappy.

Schedule your outgoing telephone calls in a bunch, all at one sitting. There is less chance of finding busy lines early in the morning or late in the afternoon.

Plan conferences near the beginning or close of the day, not in the midst of work periods. And write out a list of things to discuss in each conference.

Plan things you can work on or think about while you are in transit or waiting around. Have reading or other constructive work handy for the odd moments that inevitably crop up.

Plan tomorrow, tonight; don't wait for tomorrow morning.

Julia Ward Howe lived an active life, crammed full of accomplishments. In her ninetieth year, she told how she had been able to do so much. "Cultivate systematic employment and learn to estimate correctly the time required to accomplish whatever you undertake."

This sort of clock watching helps get things done.

The best way to stop marking time is to schedule your time.

THE START OF FORESIGHT

Most of us can see. But it is the few who can foresee who achieve great things. Any horse trader can figure out how to make a dollar today, but it is more helpful to figure out how to make ten dollars next year.

Tall, spindling Arthur Morgan had this important lesson driven home to him, unwittingly, by his shiftless father, who lived from day to day. The boy left home early to make his own way in the world. His worldly possessions were wrapped in a compact bundle, which contained a small cyclopedia of universal knowledge and a diary.

At nineteen he wrote in that diary, "a destination is a fine thing to have. It makes all the difference between a man and a tramp. There are mental tramps, men who labor from day to day laying up nothing on earth or in heart, living just because they have a physical impulse to live. The worst kind are the moral tramps. They have no moral destination. They see only their immediate gains and will lose a friend or a reputation for slight personal advantage."

In view of such foresight, we are not disappointed to learn that in five years Morgan had taught himself surveying and was well on his way to becoming one of the world's outstanding drainage, flood, and reclamation engineers. This man, who had

---

PLANNING FAR AHEAD

HELPS ONE GET AHEAD

---

no college education, made himself president of Antioch College and chairman of the Tennessee Valley Authority, which developed the gigantic hydroelectric power system in the South.

He worked for more than today or tomorrow.

People who get things done plan further ahead than from day to day. They plan for next month, next year, and for twenty years hence.

Many life plans do not work out because they are weighed only against short-term gains. **Immediate opportunities count for less in getting things done than does some long-range goal.**

The Joliet Boy Who Became Sir William

William Van Horne was an eighteen-year-old telegraph operator at Joliet, Illinois. The youth's eyes popped one morning when the general superintendent arrived in his private car to inspect the station. Van Horne decided right then that he would be general superintendent someday and ride in his private car.

"I imagined that a general superintendent must know everything about a railway—so my working hours were no longer governed by the clock. I gladly took up the work of others who took holidays. I became acquainted with all sorts of things I could not otherwise have known—even opportunities to drive engines and conduct trains."

His brothers teased him for this "unnecessary" work, but dark-haired William, with his high forehead, had a long-range plan in view and kept right on working.

At twenty-nine he became a railroad superintendent, moved steadily upward to become president of the Canadian Pacific, founded the city of Vancouver, and at forty-eight was made a baron for the things he had got done.

His plan was not to gain the immediate advantage of a dollar-a-week raise, but—a long-range idea—to learn how to be a big railroader in the future.

Forster—Pope—Wells

William Forster's Quaker parents were poor as church mice, but from boyhood William planned to enter Parliament; there were some reforms he wished to bring about and he figured, correctly, that he could bring them about quickest as an M.P. He could not study law, for he had to stand up twelve hours a day in a factory. But in what little spare time he had he picked up some knowledge of legal affairs. Even as a young lad employed in a woolen mill he practiced for the career at which he aimed by writing long memoranda, full of statistics and logic, to various government officers who paid them not the slightest attention.

This prepared him, and at forty-three he got elected to the House of Commons. He worked nine more years to get through a bill providing for free public education. He fought to put over a bill for the secret ballot. He helped pass legislation to relieve the distress of Ireland's tenant farmers. The Honorable William Forster got important things done, for he had planned and practiced as a boy, not just for tomorrow, but for a lifetime job.

Piteously crippled Alexander Pope—he looked more like a spider than a human—at twelve set himself a systematic plan of study and work enough to last a lifetime. The long-range plan of this poor, deformed boy made him one of the famous men of his era; his household and business epigrams are still widely quoted.

Always keep that distant goal in view. It is not enough merely to be active; do definite things which fit in with your life plan. Have a clear idea from the beginning of where you want to end up.

H. G. Wells often wrote the last chapter of a novel first to keep the plot from going astray. Make a life plot for yourself— the way you want the last chapter to turn out.

A single move on the checkerboard is not the end of the game.

Children May Do More Than Parents Plan

A horse can be led to water, but he can't be made to drink.

A young person may be started off on an ambitious career by his well-intentioned parents, but this does not mean his own heart and soul will be in it. The life plans that parents want for their children are often miles apart from the life plans that the children work out later for themselves.

The world has been fortunate because some children have rebelled at the plans made for them by their parents and started on other careers for which *they had talent and hopes their parents did not suspect.*

For example:

John Quincy Adams was a short, roly-poly boy, with no interest in girls. His father, second President of the United States, wanted son Quincy to be a minister and sent him to college to be trained for that purpose. But, after his graduation, young Quincy shifted to the law of his own accord and against the advice of his father. He did so well in his self-chosen legal career that he became the sixth President of the United States.

Michelangelo's father whipped him for wanting to be an artist and sculptor.

The Swiss parents of Louis Agassiz wanted him to be a businessman and objected strongly to his interest in natural science. Yet he became one of the world's leading naturalists and founded the Harvard Museum of Comparative Zoology. We will be meeting him again in later pages of this book.

William Booth's father tried to get his black-haired, headstrong son to become a pawnbroker—an easy way to make lots of money. But the son, after a try at being a pawnbroker, became the militant founder of the Salvation Army.

Fanny Burney's parents tried to "stop her scribbling"; she had to sneak into the attic to write. She became a famous novelist.

The father of William Cowper insisted that his son become a lawyer. Shortly after William was admitted to the bar he began to show signs of mental disorder. He recovered his reason and shifted from the law to writing poetry; among his works is the famous ballad about John Gilpin. The fact that he was forced into an uncongenial occupation may have had something to do with the melancholy of his nature and the mental breakdowns in which it cropped out.

Lee DeForest's missionary father insisted that the thin, shabby son follow in his steps. But Lee invented the radio tube and three hundred more electrical inventions. He is called the father of radio.

Knut Hamsun was raised by a clergyman uncle who tried to make a shoemaker out of the boy. The lad finally ran away and wandered about the world for years, working at assorted un-skilled jobs. He had always wanted to write, even as a teen-age boy at the cobbler's bench. His "Growth of the Soil" won him a Nobel prize in literature.

Henrik Ibsen was another Scandinavian boy who was given the wrong life plan by his elders. His father tried to make a druggist out of him, apprenticed him to an apothecary in a dreary seacoast village for six years. Later Ibsen made himself world-famous as a playwright.

Frank Lahey's bridge-building Irish father wanted his son to become an engineer, but the son rebelled and studied medi-cine instead. He became a famous American surgeon and chief of the Lahey Clinic in Boston.

The father of Carolus Linnaeus tried to make his son a min-ister like himself. The son failed the theological course at Uppsala, was introduced to science by Dr. Olaf Celsius, and devoted the rest of his life to becoming a leader in botany. He was made a noble by Gustavus III.

Vincent Lopez was intended for the priesthood by his devout and stern parents. Instead he found his niche as a preeminent orchestra director.

Martin Luther's father wanted him to be a lawyer and marry a rich woman. He disowned Martin when the latter became a monk.

Papa Mascagni wanted son Pietro to be a lawyer, refused to let him practice music. The son took lessons secretly and, when they were discovered by his father, fled in terror to live with an uncle. Mascagni's opera "Cavalleria Rusticana" is now a perennial favorite. It, together with his other compositions, won him the royal decoration of the Order of the Crown before he was thirty, after which his father let him come home.

Elisabet Ney had to go on hunger strikes before her parents would permit her to study sculpture. They even asked a bishop to talk their determined, redheaded daughter out of entering the career in which she was to win international renown.

Isaac Newton's father died before his famous son was born. His mother vainly tried to make Isaac into a farmer. He did so poorly on the farm that she sent him to school. He invented differential calculus and was the first to hit upon the idea of universal gravitation.

Florence Nightingale's well-born parents objected when she became a nurse; it was a menial task, they said. But she revolutionized the nursing profession and was the first woman to win the Order of Merit.

James Polk's father, a farmer and surveyor, wanted his son to become a merchant. Instead, the sickly youth made himself a lawyer, was elected President of the United States.

Jean Baptiste Poquelin's father tried to push his son into the family upholstering and furniture business. All his relatives endeavored to stop this boy with the big nose and thick lips from writing plays but, under the name of Molière, he became one of the world's greatest playwrights.

Joshua Reynolds' minister father attempted to inveigle his son into a career of medicine but was wise enough to alter his plans when the son strongly objected to his medical courses and showed some promise as an artist. Sir Joshua painted continuously and famously until blindness stopped him at sixty-seven.

James Whitcomb Riley's father had his boy visit all the courts in the Indiana circuit to win him over to the legal profession. But the son became one of the world's best-known dialect poets and the Poet Laureate of Democracy.

Rubens's mother wanted him to be a lawyer, too, not suspecting his great abilities as an artist.

Robert Schumann's mother made her fatherless lad prepare for a legal career. The son wanted to be a musician and did develop into one of the world's greatest song writers, despite a mental breakdown which halted his work when he was forty-four.

Ignaz Semmelweis's merchant father forced him into law school. The son switched to medicine on his own responsibility, discovered the cause of countless needless deaths during childbirth.

Richard Sheridan's penniless father insisted upon the law for his son. The son deceived the father into thinking he was attending law school when, in fact, he was working in a theatre. Richard Sheridan became one of England's greatest dramatists.

Edward A. Sothern's parents wanted him to be a minister. So, to spare the family feelings, the son used an assumed name when he went on the stage. After he became the foremost actor of his day the family was proud to have him use his real name.

Spallanzani's father wanted him to be a lawyer. The son pretended to follow his wishes but became a priest and teacher instead. He was the first to discover how microbes multiply.

Jan Swammerdam refused to study for the ministry. His father, a druggist, retaliated in hatred. When the son went to medical school his father would not ship his clothes to him or send him money. The younger Swammerdam was the first person to describe the red blood cells and the valves of the lymph vessels of the human body.

William W. Story studied the law to please his father, a Supreme Court justice. When he gave it up to become a sculptor, his mother said, "William, you are a fool!" She did not realize he was to become one of America's most famous sculptors.

Nikola Tesla was ordered to the priesthood by his Serbian father. After a stormy youth of revolt against his parent's insistence, he invented the first practical electrical motor, became one of the world's outstanding electrical inventors.

Albert Payson Terhune's mother wanted him to be a Congressman; his father wanted him to be a clergyman. The six-foot-two-inch son became a popular novelist, especially noted for his dog stories.

Vincent Youmans outraged his father, who ran a prosperous hat store, by becoming a songwriter. "Why don't you become a bootlegger and be done with it," his father scoffed. Vincent composed "Tea for Two" and many other well-hummed songs.

Richard Wagner's stepfather, a second-rate actor and painter, wanted his stepson to be a writer. Instead he became the world's best composer of operas and tone poems.

David Wilkie's father opposed his painting and tried in every way to get his son to become a minister. The boy became Sir David, Scotland's best-known painter.

This list could be made longer than a giant's arm. Innumerable people, misdirected by their elders, have become successes because they made their own long-range plans which kept them getting things done. They had abilities their parents did not suspect.

No one can estimate adequately the hordes of people who have been kept in lackluster mediocrity because they let someone else do their important long-range planning for them.

Do your long-range planning for YOURSELF. Get advice and information from others, to be sure, but make your own final plans—then follow them through with day-after-day effort toward your goal.

And with your children, stimulate them to make long-range plans; give them information, help, encouragement; but let them reach decisions for themselves.

When people decide for themselves, they have an obligation to make good.

When someone else does their deciding, they just half-heartedly go through the motions.

Planning Later in Life

How about changing one's long-range plans after working in a single direction for years?

Horatio Alger, Jr., became a minister to please his father. At thirty-five he dropped that long-range plan to write "Ragged Dick" and other immensely popular stories about the struggles of poor boys.

Hannah Brown was a foundling, raised in an orphanage. She worked as a maternity nurse until she was fifty. Then she turned to writing, produced a best seller. At sixty-three she took up painting; her landscapes were hung in the Royal Academy, and she became a popular book illustrator. She shifted her long-range plans late in life, but she shifted them to higher achievements, not to lower ones.

Robert Winston was a Southern gentleman, a superior-court judge in North Carolina. At sixty he replanned his work, entered the field of historical biography, and was given honorary membership in Phi Beta Kappa, scholastic honor society.

Emile Herzog was a French textile manufacturer. At fifty he quit business, turned to writing, gained fame under his pen name of André Maurois.

James F. Rhodes was in the coal and iron business in Ohio until the same age. Then this self-schooled man gave up business and made himself an authority on American history.

Edward Harriman was an office boy who became a dilettante broker, later devoted himself to railroad problems and reorganization. His wealth and fame as a railroad genius were made after he had shifted his long-range plans at the half-century mark.

Sir Henry Spelman did not start his scientific work until he was past fifty.

It is better to shift one's plan late in life than to run around in circles with the wrong plan.

IT IS NEVER TOO LATE TO PLAN.

IDEALS ARE IMPELLING

One must be wholeheartedly enthusiastic about one's long-range plan. There must be ideals involved in it, not just selfish aims for success.

A plan without ideals makes ambition seem insincere and repulsive.

His long-range plan reveals a person's philosophy of life and his true character. Many people's plans are weak and difficult of attainment because they are weak on ideals. A plan may be strong on dollars but weak on sense.

One should always consider lasting value, human worth, and the proper relationship of all things. This is the framework on which to hang the details of a plan, the day-after-day activities of getting things done to reach one's goal.

The plan without basis in vigorous ideals is just a scheme. That is why many "jackpot" ideas turn out to be "crackpot" ideas.

The plan built on ideals provides foresight, maintains enthusiasm to get things done no matter how rough the going.

And such a plan brings the highest compensation, the respect of one's fellow men.

In all your doing, DO FOR AN IDEAL.

The most interesting thing in life is to plan some big piece of work that everybody says can't possibly be done, and then jump in with both feet and do it!

—EDWARD H. HARRIMAN

The work of the engineer calls first for a correct ideal. While, as in other human affairs, it is not often that he attains an ideal solution of his problem, he understands the value of a correct ideal toward which he works.

—JOHN J. CARTY

He that does good for good's sake, seeks neither praise nor reward, but he is sure of both in the end.

—WILLIAM PENN

It is by attempting to reach the top in a single leap, that so much misery is caused in the world.

—WILLIAM COBBETT

8

How to say no to yourself

LIKE APPLES, some people ripen as they grow older, while others turn soft and rot in spots.

People who get things done have to be TOUGH-MINDED, have to say no to tempting short-term gains and stick to their long-range goals.

Neighbors said John Sutter was not practical. He was somewhat of a visionary, to be sure, as are many men who get things done. But he had a long-range plan and was practical enough to establish a vast personal empire in the rich heart of north-central California only a few years after leaving Switzerland.

California was almost without inhabitants then. San Francisco consisted of a dozen cabins. Inland, up the river, Captain Sutter, recently of the Swiss army, started his feudal estate of thousands upon thousands of virgin acres.

His long-range plan was to make this a productive agricultural empire. A producer at heart, he started a store in his fort, fought and treated with the Indians, turned the untouched soil, grew its first cultivated crops, built grist mills, established a ferry down the river to rapidly growing Yerba Buena, which was to become San Francisco.

Surely this was the work of a practical man, of a man with enough imagination to see what could be done and enough initiative to do it.

Sutter started a sawmill. While digging a channel to the

mill wheel, one of his workmen saw shining particles, nuggets of real gold. That was the discovery that precipitated the California Gold Rush to Sutter's private empire on the Sacramento.

Swarms of adventurers and rascals poured into Sutter's domain. The mild, tender-minded Sutter lacked the spunk to say no to them. The interlopers ran up big bills at his store, but kindly Sutter lacked the gumption to cry, "No more credit for you, sourdough." They squatted on big chunks of his land and scampered away with bags heavy with his gold. They burned his house.

In a few years Sutter's dream of a productive empire was shattered. Sutter, a mumbling, broken old man, died in a humid room in Washington, where he was trying to persuade Congress to repay him for the loss of his lands.

Sutter was practical, but not quite practical enough; he couldn't say a strong enough no.

LOUIS NAPOLEON

Charles Louis Napoleon Bonaparte also had an empire within his grasp. He spoke three or four languages but could not say no in any of them, so forfeited his opportunities.

Louis Napoleon, as he was called, had the imagination and initiative to get things done. After the 1848 French Revolution this nephew of the first Napoleon became President of France. In three years he made himself dictator and was planning another French empire in Mexico.

But when he should have said no he twirled his moustache, smiled blandly, and gave in. His wife, sensing his weakness, threatened to cut off the moustache to see if that would make him say no.

When imperious Bismarck talked about state affairs with this

Napoleon II, he learned plenty, for Bonaparte twirled his moustache and talked too much about things he should have kept to himself. As a result, the Germans overran France in the Franco-Prussian War.

PRESIDENTS HARDING AND COOLIDGE

Warren G. Harding, affable, small-city newspaper publisher, became President of the United States at a time when everything seemed favorable for an unusually successful administration. But Harding could not say no to others, so there was a series of unprecedented scandals among his officials and friends.

Harding could not say no to himself, either. He got mixed up in a deplorable affair with a young woman, spent many long nights playing poker and drinking. He died suddenly under strange circumstances that have never been explained.

Had he been able to say no the history books would not pass him by with only an apologetic word.

Of course, yes is an easy way out, but it is usually more helpful to say no and mean it.

Calvin Coolidge was perhaps not so brilliant as Harding, but he knew how to say no and had a better record for getting things done. Coolidge was raised in a frugal Vermont community where it was necessary to practice self-denial or starve.

Coolidge learned from the cradle that present pleasures have to be sacrificed to future goals. At college he said no to fraternity bids, waited for three years to receive an invitation from the fraternity he preferred. He said no to another presidential campaign, although his exact words were not so abrupt. "I do not choose to run."

Coolidge was no easy mark; he made himself say no.

How They Learned to Say No

Theodore Vail was no genius, but after many failures he learned to say no. As a young man he was impulsive and made no progress. His parents were beginning to give up hope for him. Vail himself finally began to despair, perhaps because his unusually big ears had overheard what others were saying about him.

At twenty, when he was away from home trying to make a living, he wrote to himself, "Staying up late nights playing billiards and drinking lager is not what young men should be doing and for one I am determined to stop it. But what am I saying 'Determined to stop it.' Yes, But how many times have you said the same before and are you stopping it now." (The punctuation and capitalization are Vail's.)

At this time young Vail's greatest ambition was to own a fur coat and a ruby ring—not very long-range objectives, but no one could see any chance of his getting these, either.

It took half a dozen years of effort before Vail finally had the upper hand over himself and was no longer an easy mark for his own impulses. That conquest marked the turning point in his triumphant march from railway mail clerk to superintendent of the railway mail service and thence to organizer of the American Telephone and Telegraph Company.

He had learned to say no to himself and to others. In founding the giant telephone system, he also said no and based it on sensible, long-range policies, avoiding the blind alleys of impulsive expedients for temporary gains.

But there was one thing to which Vail could never learn to say no. He could never inhibit his impulse to remodel and alter his home. He kept a crew busy most of the time tearing down and adding to the house. We can overlook this in a man who

simply had to be doing something, who was a builder at heart.
He was never satisfied, though he had long since forgotten his
youthful yearning for a fur coat and a ruby ring.

Peter Cooper

Peter Cooper was a born tinkerer with sufficient horse sense
to become remarkably successful. Horse sense, it seems, is little
more than the ability to say no to the things that do not count
in making one's way. Cooper acquired his horse sense before he
reached his teens, from an experience that had painful consequences.

He had built a small wagon for himself at his home in Peeks-
kill, New York. The cart's bright red paint attracted a neighbor,
who paid him $6 for it. This was the future big businessman's
first transaction, and he did not keep the $6 long.

He put most of it into a lottery ticket, the rest into a long,
black cigar. He lost the lottery, and the cigar knocked him out
for a couple days. As soon as his stomach was back on an even
keel, he swore off speculation and dissipation for life, kept the
vow, and lived to be ninety-two. Part of the fortune he accumulated by saying no he put to work for coming generations who
were learning to say no to themselves by founding Cooper
Union, a technical school.

When dedicating this institute for free education short
Cooper, who was born on Lincoln's birthday, said, "Feeling,
as I always have, my own lack of education, I have been led, in
deep sympathy for those whom I knew would be subject to the
same wants and inconveniences that I had encountered, to provide here an Institute where the courses of instruction would
be open and free to all who felt the want of scientific knowledge
as applicable to any of the useful arts of life. Having started in
life with naked hands and an honest purpose, I persevered

through long years of trial and effort to obtain the means to erect this building, which is now devoted with all its rents and revenues to the advancement of science and art."

Nicholas Longworth

"Old Nick" Longworth was a self-made millionaire before the Astor and Vanderbilt fortunes were established. He got his start from a copper still that was given him in place of cash as payment for his first legal fee. He traded the still for thirty acres of land—"not worth shucks"—on the Ohio River.

Natural science was his hobby. He discovered how the wild strawberry could be domesticated. He adapted foreign grapes to American farming conditions.

And he often said no to himself.

He made himself quit playing cards. "I used to win a great deal," he said with a chuckle, "but it did me no good, for the chief loser always borrowed money from me to settle up. So, finding how expensive it was to be the winner, I was afraid to try what losing might cost."

On his golden-wedding anniversary, pioneer Cincinnatians gave a sumptuous dinner and reception to honor the arch-nosed man who had done so much to build up their city. Sociable as "Old Nick" was, he could still say no to himself; he left his own reception early because "he had the incorrigible habit of keeping good hours."

Fannie Hurst

A dark-haired, buxom girl came to New York from St. Louis. To help support herself while doing graduate study, she worked as waitress, nursemaid, and wardrobe woman with a burlesque troupe. During spare moments she wrote and, for more than two years, tried without success to sell her stories. Fannie Hurst knew how to keep herself plugging away by saying no to useless diversion.

When she had taught herself to write, she broke down the barriers to editorial sanctums and became a phenomenal success. Money rolled in from the two dozen books she wrote, most of which were best sellers.

Success did not undermine her ability to say no. She still got up at 6 A.M. for a brisk hour's walk, then set to work. No smoking, no drinking. She said no, also, to the attractive trinkets and baubles that women usually like but that would have complicated her life.

"I own some things, of course," she said, "but there are so many which I do not own. No houses in the country, no cars. I won't let myself be buried under bracelets and shields."

Possessions, temptations, and invitations seldom receive a firm enough no.

THE GENERAL AND THE LADY

The whole course of the War for American Independence was influenced because General Howe could not say no to an invitation from an attractive lady. Mary Murray, who had been a Quaker belle in her youth, lived in a big, square house on a hill near the center of Manhattan Island.

On September 15, 1776, she saw five ships loaded with redcoats sailing up the East River, half a mile away. Howe's forces were coming to trap General Washington, four miles to the north.

Quick-witted Mrs. Murray hurried an invitation to General Howe, bidding the leader and his staff to dinner. As course followed course and the dinner was prolonged, Washington and Putnam hastily marched their four thousand volunteers out of the trap, thanks to Mrs. Murray's invitation.

Though few know that story, her family name is perpetuated in the Murray Hill section of New York City.

"Duty must take the precedence of pleasure," said John Paul Jones, father of the United States Navy.

CONTROLLING IMPULSES

Children are creatures of impulse. They shift from one thing to another like quicksilver. They start many things, finish few. Their attention is distracted by every passing sight or sound. They are perpetually doing things but, since they do not direct and control their impulses, they get nothing done.

Growing up is largely a matter of getting random impulses under control and coordinating hit-or-miss activities. Harum-scarum activities are avoided as one grows up; activities that count are followed through to completion.

Children scatter their activities; adults direct and coordinate theirs. Young folks become grownups when they get the habit of saying no to activities that are uncoordinated.

It takes brains to say no. The feebleminded can't control their impulses. They are distracted every moment, get into one predicament after another because they lack the mature brain cells to say no.

On the other hand, geniuses get things done, not only because they get bright ideas, but also because they can discriminate between the bright ideas that are worth following through and the bright ideas that had better be dropped. The man of genius finds it relatively easy to say no; if he doesn't, he is merely brilliant but erratic.

PEOPLE WHO GET THINGS

DONE HAVE TO LEARN TO

SAY NO—TO OTHERS

AND TO THEMSELVES

Everyone knows that the brain is composed of several layers of nerve cells. Man's innermost layers are not much different from those of four-footed animals. His outer layers are much more highly developed. These outer layers are known as the brain cortex.

The chief purpose of the cortex of the brain is to coordinate impulses, to say no to most impulses while giving a few priority. The cortex functions, not to generate bright ideas, but to inhibit random, useless, and unproductive actions. To inhibit means to say no.

So, when someone tells you to use your head, what he means is for you to say no.

THE DINNER-TABLE TEST

Thrifty farmers in Maine will refuse to hire a fat man to work for them, or so the story goes. These farmers maintain that a hard worker does not get fat. Perhaps, in addition, the thrifty bosses do not relish having such a heavy eater to feed.

Frank A. Munsey came from the poorest farming section in Maine. At twenty-three this sandy-haired, freckle-faced young man went to work in a telegraph office. In the next forty years he made forty millions.

He was an austere man who said no to himself perhaps more often than was necessary. As he built up his business empire he was cautious to hire others who could also say no to themselves.

A newspaper executive in Chicago was recommended to him, and Munsey wired the man to come East for an interview. When the man arrived, Munsey peeked through a crack in the door and saw he was fat. He took a second peek, could not tell whether the man was sitting down or standing up—he was that fat.

"Give him his expenses and send him back West," Munsey said, "I won't hire a man that fat."

Inspecting the New York *Press* which he had just purchased, he saw a three-hundred pounder, huge jowls quivering like jelly. "Fire him—he's too fat." This fat man happened to be essential to the paper, so he was kept on the pay roll under a fictitious name and hastily hidden in a large closet whenever Munsey entered the building. Such fat employees as he had to retain he sent to a health farm where they had their surplus poundage reduced and were given a start in the habit of saying no to too much food.

It was not down-east stinginess but the business of getting things done that prejudiced Munsey against people who ate themselves out of shape. When he saw someone surrounding a dessert that resembled a spring hat, he concluded the person could not say no, and he did not intend to hire people who were in danger of lowering their figures to half-mast.

His attitude toward fatness was almost a phobia. But many employers who are looking for people to get things done have the same prejudice. Arthur Brisbane, another great editor, avoided fat men and kept a complete set of encyclopedias in his automobile.

There are many who could start using their brain cortex by saying no at the table.

Men who can control themselves and their own appetites can control circumstances and other men.

THE POCKETBOOK TEST

Whenever you enjoy a dish of soup, remind yourself that the severest test of one's no ability may be the pocketbook test. Here is the connection.

John T. Dorrance was a Bristol, Pennsylvania, boy who specialized in chemistry at college. After two years of graduate study he became Dr. Dorrance and was offered teaching positions in one foreign and three American universities. The offers were flattering to a young chemist, but he turned them all down without a qualm. His father was furious and said the upstart son could consider himself dropped from the family.

Dr. Dorrance—he was twenty-four—had a goal in view and did not feel that a sinecure teaching chemistry would lead him any nearer toward it. He passed up the academic enticements and went to work with a Camden, New Jersey, company that was packing two hundred kinds of canned foods and losing sixty thousand dollars a year. His first week's pay envelope contained just $7.50.

The low pay did not bother him, for Dr. Dorrance was applying his chemistry to a new thing—canning the world's first concentrated soups. He reached his goal, made canned soups an American habit, and revolutionized the nation's eating. The mammoth Campbell Soup Company was started by this young chemist who said no to a better-paying job because he had plans for something he was convinced was more important.

THE BLANK CHECK

Imagine a hard-dealing magazine editor sending an author a blank check to be filled in for any amount. That amazing contract was offered to Edna Ferber. She had written some short stories about an energetic traveling saleswoman named Emma McChesney, and the editor wanted more, regardless of cost.

Here was temptation indeed for the young woman with the alert eyes, high-bridged nose, and crooked mouth. She had started at seventeen as a small town reporter. Her father, an impractical man who was always looking for a sure thing, had failed steadily and repeatedly in business. Money was a scarce commodity with her, and here was a treasure-chest lid opening wide.

Forward-thinking Edna Ferber returned tne contract without signing it. She said later that it was no hardship to say no to it. She wanted to write novels, not short stories about an amusing woman. If she had accepted that offer she would have been a short-story writer for life. Her no to financial temptation cleared the way for her record-breaking novels, among them "Show Boat," "Cimarron," and "So Big."

THE GIRL FROM SLABTOWN

Slabtown is the real name of a place in Tennessee. It was Grace Moore's birthplace. This Scotch-Irish girl had a God-given voice and had to run away from home to use it. A Greenwich Village cabaret hired her after her singing met with an ovation one amateur night. From there she jumped several steps up the musical ladder and became a star in musical comedies.

She wanted to go higher. She tried out for the Metropolitan Opera. The audition committee listened to her sing and gave her a polite thank you.

She quit musical comedy after failing to impress the committee. She was going to train her voice for opera. Producers imagined she was angling for bigger pay and increased their offers to her. Still she said no and continued to train for opera, which had turned her down.

She tried out at the Metropolitan a second time, got a second thank you, and kept on turning down musical-comedy opportunities.

A third tryout at the Metropolitan. "Come down," the committee said, "for we have good news." A new opera star was born through Grace Moore's determination and her ability to say no to a sure thing, to work for something higher.

She Knew When to Quit

While still in her teens a New England girl with a golden voice knew how to say no to what might have been a blind alley. Geraldine Farrar had many offers to sing in cabarets but unhesitatingly turned them down because she was "seeking more enduring laurels." She, too, was bitten by the grand-opera bug. With borrowed money she went to Paris on a cattle boat to study opera.

Asked to sing in Covent Garden, she rejected the offer because the management did not also offer her roles in which she would shine. She needed the money, but she wanted to sing, not only in the best circles, but also at her best.

She was only a girl, too, when she said an important no long in advance; she pledged herself to quit opera at forty and enter concert singing. She had seen the pathetic performances of others who had continued in strenuous opera after their voices had passed their prime.

Her long-range planning and her long-headed nos, begun in her youth, helped make Geraldine Farrar the idol of two continents, not a washed-out Boston cabaret hostess with a cracked voice.

You have been saying no to some things. All you may need to get more done is to SAY NO TO MORE THINGS.

YES and NO are, for good or evil, the giants of life.
                                        —DOUGLAS JERROLD

One loses all the time which he might employ to a better purpose.
                                        —ROUSSEAU

Most powerful is he who has himself in his power.
                                        —SENECA

There never will exist anything permanently noble and excellent in the character which is a stranger to resolute self-denial.
                                        —SIR WALTER SCOTT

9

Doing the thing you hate most

THE DOER likes his work because he has no unpleasant jobs
hanging fire. He has already cleaned them up. He does not
dread the next task, for the unpleasant task is behind him.

Two schoolteachers asked me to stay for an impromptu Sunday supper. Looking forward to a return invitation, I offered
to wash the dishes. I'm rather proud of my dishwashing, too.
The offer was a mistake that evening.

It took only a few minutes to finish the dishes from our
little supper. As I started to scour the sink, Ruth feigned surprise and said, "I just happened to remember those dishes in
the pantry."

So she hauled out Saturday's dishes, then Friday's—enough
chinaware to stock a bargain basement.

Friday's dishes were about done when the water ran cold.

Then Katharine gave a sidelong glance. "Oh, yes!" she said.
Sure enough, she produced Thursday's dishes, from under the
icebox, really. And they had eaten lamb on Thursday—the
greasiest, stickiest substance of all to cleanse, even with my
great skill. And no hot water by this time!

The kitchen soap had disappeared as the dirty dishes appeared, and I was using a perfumed toilet soap and lots of elbow
grease. My spirits began to rise as the last of Thursday's plates
rested shining in the scalding rack, ready to be doused with the
now-lukewarm water.

"Should we?" Ruth asked, as she dragged out from behind the stove a roaster, thick with Thursday's lamb grease.

Did you ever try to wash three-day-old lamb grease from a roaster with chilly water and scented complexion soap? It can't be done. I cut the grease with gasoline on the back steps, but the perfumed soap did not completely cover the gasoline odor in the roaster.

But I had, at last, cleaned up the unpleasant tasks they had been putting off. Come to think of it now, perhaps they were smarter than I was, for I worked hard for that free Sunday supper.

Someone always has to work hard when the unpleasant tasks are put off. Usually the hard work has to be done, with heavy interest paid, by the person who put it off.

He Was Against Whiskers

Get acquainted with Peter; he had a great record for getting things done—a person who never pushed the unpleasant lamb roasters out of sight.

Peter lacked only four inches of being seven feet tall. Not only was he head and shoulders above other men in height but also in getting things done. His active mind sought for the unpleasant tasks that other men put off. He tackled the difficult jobs first, with a roguish twinkle in his eye.

Czar Peter Alekseyevich of Russia probably did more to civilize more people, against their own inertia, than any other figure in history.

Hard work was his fun. While his young nobles played at the easy games and weary intrigues of the capital, Peter distinguished himself as a workman; he studied blacksmithing, ship-building, and worked incognito in foreign countries to learn better ways of doing things firsthand. Back home, the Russian people laughed at the innovations the curly-headed giant suggested for them.

But unpleasant tasks were his meat. Opposition did not keep him from doing things. He tackled first the jobs that were opposed most and got them out of the way. No shilly-shallying for him.

There was the question of whiskers, for instance. Long beards were a source of great personal pride in Russia. But Peter knew that most luxuriant beards concealed a variety of insect life. So he forcibly sheared the hair off the faces of his nobles, then put a prohibitive tax on growing it back. There was more uproar over this interference with personal liberty than over his secret construction of the first Russian shipyard, the start of the Muscovite Navy.

The traditional long cloaks of his time dragged the ground—good dirt catchers, Peter said. He had them chopped off to a more sanitary length. And the long sleeves that drooped over Russian hands were snipped to the wrist for the same reason. What yowling and complaining about these headlong efforts to modernize a people!

Peter introduced many other innovations and many more important ones. But he started with those that would cause him most difficulty. He had found he could get things done better if he cleaned up the unpleasant tasks first. Then, with nothing distasteful left to hang over him, he could throw his energies without restraint into the bigger and more likeable labors.

He started Russia's first factories, changed her money system, introduced the European calendar, began a postal system, started town councils for local government. He built a new city, St. Petersburg—on a marsh, it is true—but where it would be close to Europe, stimulate trade, and furnish Russia with a seaport of sorts for the first time.

This Peter the Great, against the open opposition of nobles

and the lethargic inertia of peasants, singlehandedly raised his country to a recognized place among the world powers. He had great physical energy to help him and a fearless determination to do what he knew should be done.

He didn't gnaw his fingernails, worrying about the nasty jobs. He went ahead and DID THEM FIRST.

HE RAN A ONE-BOY FERRY INTO MILLIONS

At sixteen Cornelius could barely read and write, but he could figure like lightning. He already knew the merits of tackling the hard job first. In those days he spelled his name Vander Bilt.

He borrowed $100 which his mother had saved, copper by copper, in an old earthenware bowl. This sixteen year old was starting a ferry, and the power for propelling the boat was to be his own strong arms on the oars.

"Connie, if you're dead set on running a ferryboat," his mother advised, as she handed over her savings, "why don't you start where there ain't so many others to fight with for business?"

But Connie had decided in his thick Dutch head that he could get more done if he worked where the competition was hottest. He was no innovator. He did not look for a new business opportunity. Simply, all his life he got things done by sticking his head into the toughest competition. And he increased that borrowed $100 to two hundred millions.

His one-boy ferryboat grew into a steam-ferry line.

"Well, Vander Bilt made a pile of money on his ferry," they said along the waterfront, "but he'll lose it all when he sets up his line of boats on the Hudson. Don't that fool Dutchman know there are too many Hudson lines already for any of them to make money?"

DO FIRST THE THING YOU

HATE MOST

But the spunky Commodore won out on the Hudson, on the Connecticut, on Long Island Sound, wherever the competition was toughest. His ventures in railroading, too, were begun the hard way.

He was not looking for an easy start. **The smooth sailing came after he had finished the hard jobs.**

His father, in contrast, put off unpleasant jobs. He always took easy work, the sure things. The father would have died a pauper but for the financial assistance of his son.

The way to get things done is to **tackle the hard jobs first.**

The Alaska Purchase

William H. Seward put new vigor into the American diplomatic service and got difficult things done by clearing his unpleasant jobs out of the way as quickly as possible. This Welsh-Irishman from Auburn, New York, worked his way up to become Secretary of State. While holding this office, he made a verbal agreement with the Russian Minister in Washington to buy Alaska for seven million dollars. The Russian Minister seemed satisfied and said he would return the following day to draw up the formal treaty of purchase.

Secretary Seward, with his firm mouth, knew that, when it came to putting the agreement in writing, there would be bickering and unpleasantness. His policy was not to delay the unpleasant.

"Why wait until tomorrow, Mr. Stoeckl? Let us make the treaty tonight," he said, rubbing his big nose.

He sent messengers to summon members of the Senate Committee on Foreign Affairs and kept the Russian Minister under his eagle eye so the latter could not connive behind his back. By four o'clock that morning the treaty was drafted and signed. Thus the United States got Alaska cheaply, easily, and without the usual delay and complications of diplomatic quibbling and double-crossing.

The mention of Alaska brings to mind the vigorous ballads and verse of Robert W. Service. He was a clerk for a system of chain banks, shipped by luck to a remote branch in the Yukon. It was there that, after hours, he wrote "The Shooting of Dan McGrew." (And he paid to have this classic of the north country printed—an investment that started him on the way to fame and fortune.) From his boyhood in Scotland he had always seemed to have to do things he didn't like to do. As he looked back on life he observed, "I got more joy from doing things for which I was not suited than from others which might bring me success with little effort." That is another reward of doing first the thing you hate the most.

Cause and Cure of Puttering

Putterers are usually putting off doing something unpleasant. They putter over easy, little things, trying to keep busy so they have a pseudo excuse for not doing the job that worries them.

Frank Phillips was no putterer. He was born in a Nebraska log cabin. He ran a small-town barber shop in Iowa and made a fortune half again as big as Vanderbilt's.

At fourteen Phillips decided to be a barber because he wanted to wear striped trousers. At thirty he was drilling for oil in Oklahoma and not wearing striped trousers. He drilled his first two wells in proved, producing oil fields, but the wells brought in nothing but dust.

His third well was started in a location experts did not think worth testing, and they laughed at the barber turned oilman. But he brought in a gusher this time.

He drilled other wells, became a large oil producer. Then Phillips decided he would like to sell gasoline direct to the motorists.

"I move," he said to a meeting of his directors, "that we build the dangdest string of filling stations you ever saw. If it's all right, let's make it unanimous."

By now he knew a great deal about producing petroleum products. But selling them retail was something else again. Phillips had seen from experience that the way to learn a job was to tackle the hardest part of it first. So he had some men locate the worst place in the country in which to try to sell gasoline. They picked Wichita, Kansas, and it was here he started.

In a few years he had built a 681-mile gasoline pipe line, the first in the country for gasoline, to connect his refineries with his enormous chain of filling stations. Engineers advised against a gasoline pipe line, said it would be impossible to prevent evaporation through the joints. But Phillips by this time knew how to get any mean job done, and the joints were securely welded.

"The king of the independents," oil men call Frank Phillips. Tackling the difficult part of each job first enabled him to get things done and earned him that title.

Men who say their jobs have too many headaches are usually confessing they put off the unpleasant things while they putter around at others.

In front of his desk, Sir Thomas Lipton, the butcher's boy

who made himself the world's tea baron, had this motto, "Work is my fun." He made it his fun because he did not let the distasteful tasks accumulate. A cheerful Irishman and a good loser, Sir Thomas was no putterer.

Putter-offers are putterers.

THE LESSON OF THE MULTIPLICATION TABLES

What is two times nine?

That was easy. Now, what is seven times nine?

Why was the second one harder? Simply because the higher figures have not been practiced so much. **It is a human weakness to practice the easy things and neglect the difficult ones.** But individual progress comes from practicing what is difficult.

In the Second World War, for instance, the usual method of learning the international radio code was reversed. Beginners were taught the most difficult dot-dash combinations first. The easy-to-learn letters were taught after the confusing ones. The work became easier as it went along. In this way, many days were cut from the time previously needed to learn the code signals.

Arthur Balfour mastered golf late in life, and he studied the difficult shots first. He practiced on uncertain sand before he tried shots from firm sod. He practiced holing for days. After three months on hard strokes, he played his first game and beat friends who had been playing for years; they had been getting most of their practice on the easy ones.

PARALYSIS OF THE WILL

The unpleasant job that is put off is likely never to get done. This is because of the human tendency to forget unpleasant things.

But there is a more serious aspect to the putting off of disliked duties. An accumulation of unpleasantness may cause *abulia,* or paralysis of the will. Apprehension over delayed unpleasantness may so preoccupy one that other things cannot be done effectively.

Thus putting off an unpleasant task handicaps other work.

It also means that we do the unpleasant task many times in worry, instead of actually doing it once in fact. **Dreading a task can be more tiring than doing it.**

Put the jobs you dislike at the top of each day's schedule. You will be pleasantly surprised to discover how much easier this makes the rest of your day's work.

Don't file unpleasant tasks away in a drawer labeled "For Future Attention." Keep them right at your fingertips until they are finished.

Brusque John H. Patterson, founder of the National Cash Register Company, was concerned because a good man in his outfit was beginning to slip; he was not getting things done. One evening Mr. Patterson emptied the man's desk drawers and piled the contents on top of the desk. He left this scribbled note on top of the pile of unfinished work, "Clean up the unpleasant jobs you have stored in your desk; we are running a business, NOT a morgue."

Busy Sir Walter Scott disliked answering letters, and the popular author of the Waverley novels had many to answer. But he did not let this unpleasant work make him a putterer; he answered his letters the same day he received them.

Any dead fish can float downstream, but it takes a LIVE ONE to swim upstream.

There are amusing aspects to putting off disliked tasks. A woman in the Southland, for instance, heard me make the above point in a public lecture. Later she wrote me a letter of thanks; it seems my lecture had had a long-desired effect upon her husband. After my reminder of the importance of not putting off unpleasant tasks he went home and, at long last, trimmed his toenails!

On the serious side, people are killing themselves daily by putting off such unpleasant tasks as seeing their doctor or dentist. Others, like the philosopher Kant, are forced to remain single because they delay proposing too long. His ladylove became tired of being dangled on a string, married another.

There is nothing new about doing the unpleasant job first. It is one of those old-fashioned virtues of which we need to be reminded time and again. When John Quincy Adams was President of the United States, for example, he had a secretary who was always behind in his work. Adams told him, "When you have a number of duties to perform, do the most disagreeable first."

Nothing is too small to know, and nothing is too difficult to attempt.

—SIR WILLIAM VAN HORNE

The man who understands his own powers and aptitudes, forms purposes in accord with them, and pursues these purposes steadily, is the man of success.

—FRANCIS PARKMAN

The purest pleasures lie within the circle of useful occupation.

—HENRY WARD BEECHER

Difficulties show men what they are.

—EPICTETUS

10

How to make yourself do it

ONE OF THE mightiest forces for getting things done is the human will, your own will. The trick is to release the will for action. And that trick is astonishingly simple—**make yourself do it.**

Roger Babson's merchant father was not enthusiastic about colleges. He thought they were playgrounds for rich men's sons. If his son insisted on going to college, the father said, he should have no financial aid unless he went to Massachusetts Institute of Technology. The father believed that was the one school that made the students work. Elbow grease, he thought, was the best part of education.

So Roger left the happy days of Gloucester high school and went to M.I.T. The slender boy had no interest in engineering, so simply took the first course the school listed. That was civil engineering—not the course, one would imagine, to train a man to become a leading investment authority.

He disliked all his engineering classes. The work was difficult for him. He only managed to graduate by the skin of his teeth and the kindness of one of his professors.

Yet Roger Babson says he learned one thing of great importance to him in that dreary course. He learned to make himself do things he didn't want to do.

This lesson—You can make yourself do it!—was the key to his success as the leader in a new business field.

This lesson took him through a setback with tuberculosis at

the age of twenty-five. Though shy one lung, his brain still functioned 100 per cent, and he forced his brain to be active. He bundled up against the New England winters, rested physically in the raw open air while working hard mentally. Writing with mittens on his hands, he began to compile investment statistics that he sold to banks for $12.50 a month. Such were the outdoor beginnings, by a sick man, of the Babson Statistical Organization.

Roger Babson got things done because he had once learned how to make himself do things in the engineering course he detested.

He Made Himself Speak in Public

George Carr Shaw was an easygoing man whom everyone liked. He was pleasant to be with, whether drunk or sober, and he was drunk most of the time. Children laughed at an amusing squint in one of his eyes, a squint that had been made worse by a bungling operation. George Shaw did not mind the squint; he clung to his whiskey bottle and let kind providence look after his family.

That was George Bernard Shaw's father. At fifteen the son had to find a job and landed in a Dublin real-estate office at $4.50 a month. Perhaps that was all the live-spirited boy was worth, for he demoralized work by organizing quartets with the other junior clerks as soon as the boss was out of sight.

At twenty George Bernard Shaw went to London, sporting a downy beard but with no job in view. He floundered for months and would have starved but for his mother, who gave music lessons to earn money.

One foggy evening, in search of something to do that cost nothing, he attended the meeting of a debating society. He became so aroused that he tried to take part in the debate. But he made a complete fool of himself and was heartily ashamed of his tongue-tied incoherence.

This public failure aroused the tall youth. He had been following the easygoing example of his worthless father. Now he swore he would make himself speak in public. He immediately joined debating societies and attended every meeting he could find that was open for public discussion.

He forced himself to think of something to say on every question. He forced himself to stand up, moisten his dry lips, ignore his thumping heart, and speak.

At first he was a general nuisance. But he gradually succeeded in making himself speak well and intelligently. Soon he was actually being asked to speak at meetings in advance. For a dozen years he was in demand as a lecturer.

He applied his newly-discovered talent for making himself do things to writing. He wanted to write, but again had his father's easygoing example to overcome—this time in his personal habits. So he made himself write five pages every day, whether he felt like it or not. In four years he earned a total of $30 from his writing. Discouraging—but he kept on.

He wrote five long novels which sixty publishers rejected.

Discouraging enough to make him quit writing? No, no more discouraging than his failures when he had first tried to speak in public. George Bernard Shaw continued to make himself do things, to turn out his daily quota. He became one of the best-known, best-paid, most-quoted writers in the world.

His squint-eyed father did not make himself do things and was a total failure. The twinkling-eyed son, who had almost no formal schooling, is today one of the world's leading intellectuals because he FORCED HIMSELF to get things done.

The Daily Quota

Let no day pass without getting something accomplished, something done.

Audubon, after failing in business and floundering generally, set up a quota for himself—he would paint a bird a day.

Edna Ferber held herself to her daily writing stint whether in a hall bedroom or in the luxurious compartment of a transcontinental train. Often she had to work in environments that were unfavorable to creative work, but she made herself create. Forcing herself to write when she didn't feel like it sometimes brought her a quarter of a million dollars a year.

Somerset Maugham reports, "Wherever I've gone and whatever I've done I have kept in mind that each day I must write from 1,000 to 1,500 words."

On his fireplace Emile Zola had a Latin inscription that reminded him to make himself work regardless of his personal inclinations. *Nulla dies sine linea.* "Not a day without a line."

Thus have people who were already Achievers kept on achieving—they have looked upon their work as daily work no matter what its character. As Huxley said, "Duty is to do the thing we ought to do, at the time we ought to do it, whether we feel like doing it or not."

Forcing Inspiration

Giacomo Rossini was born on February 29 of the leap year 1792. He had musical fame of a sort, but was inclined to prefer gay companions and the salad dressing he invented, which brought him a Cardinal's blessing. His reputation as a composer was slipping. Then the director of a Naples theater wanted the gay Rossini to write an opera for him. He locked

Rossini up, vowing not to release him until the opera was written. In three days, working under duress, Rossini had composed the entire opera "Othello."

In the same way papa Gautier locked his idling, twenty-four-year-old son, Théophile, in his room and kept him under lock and key while he wrote "Mademoiselle de Maupin."

Mascagni, too, discovered the real inspiration that comes from perspiration. He was twenty-six, a wandering musician, and penniless, as usual, when he learned about a prize competition for a one-act opera. He learned about it only a week before the contest closed. He wrote feverishly for seven days and nights, and the stocky youth's "Cavalleria Rusticana" won him the contest, forty curtain calls on the opening night, and wealth overnight. Until his death, at the age of eighty-one, Mascagni continued to compose, but none of his later compositions reached the height of inspiration of this first one, produced under pressure.

"One day work is hard and another day it is easy," Sir Arthur Sullivan said, "but if I had waited for inspiration I should have done nothing. The happy thoughts which seem to come to one only occur after hard work and steady persistence." This from the curly-headed composer of "The Lost Chord," "Onward Christian Soldiers," the Gilbert and Sullivan light operas, oratorios, cantatas, anthems, and dozens of carols.

Tchaikowsky's wife nearly gave him a nervous breakdown, and she herself was taken to an asylum. Hear what he has to say about making oneself do things.

One cannot afford to sit waiting for inspiration; she is a guest that does not visit the lazy, but comes only to those who call her. Very often one must first conquer laziness and lack of inclination. It is the duty of an artist never to submit, because laziness is a strong human trait, and nothing is more harmful to an artist than to let laziness get the better of him.

This from one of the most prolific of Russian composers, the man who was brought to the United States to conduct some of his own compositions at the dedication of Carnegie Hall.

Men who have inspiration work for it.

LEARNING TO LIKE ANYTHING

Do you remember the first olive you tasted? You probably disliked it and had to use will power to swallow the bitter, slimy thing. There are many other foods we can learn to like by forcing ourselves to eat them despite our first feelings of revulsion.

An American exporter, interned in a prison camp when the Japanese overran Manila, told me his life was saved because he forced himself to eat disgusting food.

He was losing weight daily on the limited rations provided by his captors. For months he struggled to force himself to eat something else, while his weight dropped by more than a hundred pounds. It was six months before he could make himself chop up banana stalks and stew them with alley cats to supplement his prison-camp diet.

"In a few days," he said, "an old tomcat tasted better than spring chicken to me. I would undoubtedly be dead now if I had not, in desperation, made myself eat the first one."

Contemplation had been worse for him than realization. It is thus with many of us. The more we think about a hard job, the harder it becomes with contemplation. If we roll up our sleeves and wade into it, we are soon too busy to bother about the difficulties.

The popular saying that the first thirty years are the hardest is wrong. It is the first thirty seconds.

If we don't face a task squarely during the first thirty seconds, we begin to worry about it, and it takes more and more will power to push us into action. It took the prisoner six months. It took George Bernard Shaw's father all his life, and then he had not yet started.

People can force themselves TO DO almost anything, TO LIKE almost anything. Neurotics humor themselves, increasing their dislikes rather than forcing themselves to overcome them.

Thin, little Nina Wilcox Putnam was huddled beside the radiator in her parents' New Rochelle home, wondering, as children often do on stormy days, why God allowed so many ugly things in the world—snakes, decaying meat, and the hideous brown color her mother made her wear, for instance. In her nine-year-old fashion she concluded that, since God made such things, they must be beautiful, and she was at fault for not seeing their beauty.

Her large eyes searched eagerly for something on which to practice this theory. They lighted on an overripe garbage can! She held her nose and lifted the cover to look in. She forced herself to keep looking at the random harvest until the remains of lettuce and tomatoes seemed a beautiful pattern in greens and reds to her, the broken eggshells hashed up with coffee grounds became an oriental mosaic. She finally made herself see so much beauty in that messy can that she uncovered her nostrils to inhale its incense.

"From that day to this," she said years later, "I have always been able to see beauty first in anything. When I was nine I discovered this source of strength within myself upon which I have had to call many times since."

Let others coddle you now and then if they want to, but **never coddle yourself if you expect to get things done.**

LAZINESS AND INFERIORITY

There are already many versions of the story about the hill-billy too lazy to turn his chair around to watch the circus parade and the tramp too lazy to stoop down to pick up the coin tossed to him. Other versions might be told about you or me. While we love to think "there is not a lazy bone in our bodies," the fact remains that we—like the rest of mankind—are naturally lazy.

Often people work in order to be lazy. The Midwestern farmer toils long hours to make enough money so he can retire and go to California in middle life. Some work their way through medical school so they can make a living later with less work. It is the same with most pursuits. A great many individuals pursue laziness and not a constructive goal.

Surveys show that about 9 per cent of normal women and 14 per cent of normal men have a job intentionally to overcome their natural laziness. The remaining percentages may be enjoying their laziness and not fighting it.

An inferiority complex can make laziness worse. The person who feels he will not get ahead in the world sometimes withdraws into his shell and shows a pathetic mixture of timidity and apathy.

Sometimes, however, an inferiority complex urges a person on to make something of himself, to work everlastingly. A feeling of inferiority has been an asset to many of the world's leaders, because the best-known antidote for such a feeling is hard work.

Laziness may be made worse by physical causes. The shiftless hillbilly's laziness could be increased by hookworm. An executive may lose his enthusiasm for work as he develops a mild case of anemia. An unbalanced diet, unhygienic habits of living may weaken one's body and cause the inborn laziness, which afflicts mankind, to become exaggerated. One's thyroid gland may be slowing down, causing fatigue after only slight exertion.

Get a complete physical examination regularly to make certain no medical condition is making your inborn laziness worse. Then, when assured by the medical examiner that you are able to work like a horse, lunge into the harness and make yourself work.

It is natural to have to force yourself to overcome the handicap of natural laziness. Keep forcing until work has become **a habit that is stronger than your human inclination to loaf.**

KEEP EFFORT ALIVE

At times it takes an emergency to show people how much they have been coddling themselves.

Two emergencies, years apart, opened Sarah Bernhardt's eyes to her own capacities. The first occurred when she was but two years old. The anemic, quick-tempered child had been practically deserted by her butterfly mother. A peasant family in Brittany was raising her.

They found she was least bother when strapped in her high chair beside a table where she could handle pieces of colored paper. One day the peasant woman neglected to buckle the strap. Little Sarah tumbled headlong from the high chair into the wide fireplace full of burning logs.

The screaming child was quickly rescued and plunged, red hair and all, into a churn of milk. It was three months before she recovered from the burns, and she bore the scars on her body all her life. She was given the nickname of "Flower-of-the-milk."

From that painful day she had an intense fear of fire.

Twenty years later Sarah Bernhardt was an actress who had all Paris raving over her dramatic performances. She was living in an apartment filled with bowlegged Louis XV furniture, near the Opéra. Her hobbling old grandmother was living with her, caring for her infant son, Maurice, while the divine Sarah rehearsed and starred in her plays.

YOU GET MUCH MORE DONE

WHEN YOU MAKE YOURSELF

DO IT

One night as Sarah was returning home she found her street crowded with excited spectators. Her apartment building was on fire.

This young woman, who fainted at the sight of fire apparatus, who could not tolerate an open fire, ran breathlessly to a fireman. No, they had not taken a baby from the apartment. She shrieked and dashed up a stairway, pushing aside the firemen who tried franticly to stop her.

Groping desperately through the smoke, she found Maurice, still sleeping. She threw a blanket around him, cuddled him in her arms, and carried him to the street. Then she fainted.

In this emergency she had disregarded her horror of fire and made herself dash recklessly through the very flames.

Wartime, a business depression, and other emergencies may show a person how much more he can do than he ever imagined if he only forces himself to do it.

There is no rule for getting things done that works as well as doing.

THE SOCIAL BUTTERFLY

William James, the jovial, scholarly granddaddy of American psychology, used to say will power could be developed by keeping the faculty of effort alive. In other words, KEEP DOING THINGS, keep making yourself do them.

Edith Wharton could do things, but there were so many interesting detours in Paris, London, Newport, New York, and Lenox that she was not doing them. This society redhead could write and had all the time in the world for it. But she would not make herself sit down and put the words on paper. It was much easier to attend teas and balls.

It was Edward Burlingame, editor of *Scribner's Magazine*, who at last challenged her to force herself to work. He needed a novel for the magazine, to be published a few chapters in each issue. He wanted the first chapters right away because another author had failed him at the last moment.

For months Mrs. Wharton, between teas and benefit parties, had been toying with the idea of a novel about frivolous New York society and how its frivolity destroyed a young woman, Lily Bart. She had the story all ready to tell but had not started the telling. She thought she might start it in a couple of years, perhaps.

Then editor Burlingame came along and insisted on some chapters at once. These were printed before she had the rest of the book under way. Now the dainty hands had the bear by the tail and she had to write for dear life to keep ahead of the printer. Travel, gardening, pink teas had to be pushed one side. She at last had to make herself do things.

"Of all the friendly turns that Mr. Burlingame ever did for me," she commented, years later, "his exacting this effort was undoubtedly the most helpful."

That is how she wrote "The House of Mirth," scribbling reluctantly to aid a friend who was in difficulties. The greater aid was to herself; she learned the usefulness of forcing herself, of EXERCISING THE FACULTY OF EFFORT.

Thirty-two full-length books followed, finished books by a professional who had learned to make herself do it. Edith

Wharton was no longer a society dilettante who could spin stories when she felt like it. She won a Pulitzer prize and the gold medal of the National Institute of Arts and Sciences.

FORCING ONESELF TO WORK AGAINST ILLNESS

When one has a burning goal it is easy to force oneself to get things done, even in the limitations imposed by a hospital.

Take Clara Barton, for instance. She was born auspiciously on Christmas Day. Bright as a silver dollar, she could read by the time she was three. But her stature never kept up with her brain; five feet three inches was as tall as she grew. She was not only short, but also frail and thin as a lily.

At the close of the War Between the States, this tiny woman spent four intense years identifying some 20,000 missing soldiers, both Union and Confederate. The government gave her a tent at Annapolis, a clerk, postage, and the high-sounding title of "General Correspondent for the Friends of Paroled Prisoners." She had to draw upon her savings and give lectures to raise enough funds to run her one-woman bureau of displaced and missing persons.

Then her eyes gave out, she lost her voice, and rheumatic fever racked her body. She was fifty-five when she was taken to Dr. Jackson's private hospital at Dansville, New York. Ten years she stayed there or in a near-by home under sanitarium care. And those were the best ten years of her busy life.

Her body was sadly in need of rest, but her pert little head found plenty of work to do. In the drab sanitarium room, Clara Barton planned an organization to do what she had been doing singlehanded, an organization that would bring medical relief and comfort to displaced and missing persons. She wrote letters by the hundreds from her sickbed, letters to important persons and high officials both at home and abroad. Many did not bother to answer her; many gave discouraging answers.

When she learned that an attempt had been made years before to form an American Red Cross but had failed, she became the more determined. No one would have suspected that this aggressive invalid had once been abnormally timid. Big names and important officials became her targets. From that Danville sanitarium, the pain-racked little woman finally pushed the American Red Cross into being, an accomplishment that had defeated husky men.

How did she achieve this, despite illness and rebuff? How did she keep up with the details of the correspondence that littered her bedside table and overflowed onto the floor? Miss Barton said, "I try hard to get one out of the way so as to go on with the next." She did it, step by step, by constantly forcing herself to work. Since she had a goal that sprang from the depths of her being, it was easy for her to force herself.

A Monument to Washington and . . .

As the Potomac boats passed Mount Vernon they reduced their speed and their bells tolled a mournful salute to the memory of Washington. Pamela Cunningham was deeply impressed by this dirge and as deeply distressed to see how fast beautiful Mount Vernon was losing its beauty and becoming another dilapidated, melancholy Southern mansion. What should be a national shrine was well on its way to becoming a local eyesore.

Pamela Cunningham was a helpless spinal invalid. She had to be carried from bed to her favorite window chair in her South Carolina home. There she could sit for but a few hours each day. Her body was slowly disintegrating. But not so her spirit! She was going to save Mount Vernon! She wrote letters from her invalid's room, thousands of letters, to editors, clubwomen, prominent people, getting a fund-raising movement under way to purchase Mount Vernon for the public as a national shrine.

She raised some sixty-nine thousand dollars before she was carried in her chair to Mount Vernon to talk with the owner. He asked for a larger sum and tried to impose restrictions on the sale. So back to her invalid's chair to raise more money, to press a special act through the Virginia Legislature, and to persuade Congress to appropriate extra funds. All this Pamela Cunningham did; yet she was such a complete invalid that she went into convulsions sometimes when she even exerted herself to write her signature.

Restored Mount Vernon is a monument to Washington and to someone else. **It makes one wonder why many able-bodied men do not accomplish more than they do.**

FLORENCE BARCLAY

Florence Barclay was a minister's daughter and a small-town minister's wife. This dark-haired woman had spirit, imagination, and health. Her energetic life used all her resources to the full.

At forty-three, shortly after the birth of her eighth child, she was laid low by heart disease. For nine months she was bedridden, then convalescent for a much longer period. The first few weeks of her illness she was kept flat on her back. As soon as she could be propped up in bed for a few hours at a time, she asked for paper and pencil and began to write the story of Jane, a story of which her active imagination had been dreaming for some time. Now, at last, she had an opportunity to get the story on paper.

During her illness she finished writing the story of Jane, but when she read it over she almost decided to burn it. Four years passed before she had the courage to submit it to a publisher. Very few people bought the book when it first came out. Yet, by some miracle, demand for it gradually grew and grew. It became one of the world's most popular volumes, appeared in eight languages, and sold more than a million copies.

That is the history of "The Rosary," a book born in a sickroom because a woman had a burning message she wanted to tell and forced herself to tell it.

Borodin—Barrie

"I hope you are ill," acquaintances would greet Alexander Borodin.

A strange, twisted greeting, but flattering! For Borodin, professor of medical chemistry at the St. Petersburg Medicosurgical Institute, was a promising musician and composer. But he only wrote music when he was confined to his room by recurrent illness.

When he was in good health, his teaching and laboratory research kept him so busy he had no time to compose. When struck down and bedridden, he composed without interruption. "On the Steppes of Central Asia," symphonies, string quartets were written from his sickbed. The opera "Prince Igor," started during his last illness, was completed by Rimsky-Korsakov and Glazounov; it took two famous composers to finish what the dying man had begun. Borodin made himself work, not in spite of his illness, but to forget his illness.

Sir James Barrie worked, too, as a means of escape rather than for money. Once, during an attack of malaria, for instance, he locked himself in his room. His eyes were too affected for him to read, so he got a supply of narrow sheets of paper and a pen and made himself write during the weary hours. When he recovered he tucked the writing into a drawer of his desk and forgot it. Years later, when Granville Barker wanted a one-act play in a hurry, Barrie suddenly remembered this "malaria play" and took it from the drawer. That is the story of "The Twelve Pound Look," written when he forced himself to work in order to forget his malarial aches and chills.

ANIMAL AND PLANT EVOLUTION

Alfred Russel Wallace was self-educated. He bought a secondhand book on botany when he was eighteen, and it aroused his interest in natural science. He worked as a surveyor and clockmaker, but was always thinking ahead and looking for opportunities to reach his goal of becoming a naturalist.

When the chance to accompany a naturalist on an exploration of Brazil was finally offered him, the retiring young Wallace seized it eagerly. He would collect foreign butterflies, strange birds, and flowers and sell them to collectors in London. He had a four-year collection on board ship as they started for home. The ship caught fire, it and his precious collection were burned in mid-ocean, and he had to help row the nine hundred miles to Bermuda, the nearest land.

Bad luck—but it could not last forever. So Wallace started out again, now to collect wildlife in the jungles around Singapore, Malacca, and Borneo. More than 30,000 specimens were his harvest the first two years. At the same time his eager, self-tutored mind, absorbent as a sponge, tried continually to fathom some of the mysteries of nature. He was not only a collector, but a born student as well.

One February he was on the small tropical island of Ternate, foraging with his net and collection boxes. The weather verged on hot, 88 degrees, but Wallace was chilly. He wrapped himself in blankets and still shivered. Then suddenly he was in a fever of sweating. The alternation kept up; one hour his teeth chattered in a chill, the next his body was salty with perspiration. A severe attack of intermittent jungle fever knocked him out.

But no tropical disease could completely floor this self-made naturalist who wanted to get things done. Lying in blankets in the dripping hut, serenaded by insects, he kept thinking of the thousands of unusual specimens of plant and animal life he had observed, comparing their similarities and differences.

One particular cold fit lasted about two hours, and during it he thought out a theory of evolution. That evening, in a fever, he wrote down his ideas. Throughout the following two days he continued to work on the theory, despite attacks of chills and sweats, then mailed it to Darwin, thousands of miles away.

When Darwin read Wallace's communication he was flabbergasted; this young man, during his racking jungle sickness, had hit on the identical theory of animal and plant evolution that the older Darwin, after a lifetime of endeavor, had just discovered.

And Darwin, too, had made his discovery by forcing himself to work against chronic headaches and weakness.

KATE DOUGLAS WIGGIN

Kate Douglas Wiggin was from way down East. The death of her stepfather left the family impoverished, so she became a kindergarten teacher. She held a teaching job until she was forty-three, then a painful illness forced her to seek relief in a sanitarium at Pinehurst, North Carolina.

Time hung heavily on her hands there, and she began to think about Rebecca, a girl in a starched yellow calico dress, primly carrying a pink parasol. Miss Wiggin determined to write the girl's story. Against the advice of doctor and nurse, she propped herself up in bed, a thick pad of yellow paper across her knees, and began to write with a pencil.

She filled one pad at Pinehurst, another at a sanitarium in northern New York with the delightful story of "Rebecca of

Sunnybrook Farm." "The nicest child in American literature!"
the critics raved. And the public? They, too, raved about Rebecca. This tale, written by a sick woman who forced herself to
work to forget her sickness, quickly became one of the most
popular books of all times.

THE MURPHY BUTTON

Of course six-foot John Murphy was an Irishman. He was
just thirty-five and doing well in his practice as a Chicago surgeon, when he began to lose weight, cough rackingly, and have
night sweats. His complexion became that of a bereaved man.
Other physicians confirmed his fears, so the young surgeon went
to Colorado, then to New Mexico, to take the cure for tuberculosis.

The restless Irishman was ill at ease as he sat on the sanitarium porch, twiddling his thumbs and listening to the idle
chatter of the other rockers. He put his head to work running
errands, thinking about some of the problems that baffled the
surgical profession. There was still great hazard, for example,
in abdominal operations. In those days a patient with a severed
intestine to be sewed up was almost doomed.

While others rocked and gossiped in the sun, the young
surgeon with the wax-colored hair worked on this problem.
And, on a sanitarium veranda, John B. Murphy invented the
famous "Murphy button," which cleared the field for abdominal
surgery and spread his reputation like a racing prairie fire.

AN INGREDIENT OF GENIUS

"I am a lucky man," white-bearded Pierre Renoir told his
friends. "Now I can do nothing but paint."

He was in a wheel chair, this shy little man, humming off

key, his fingers and joints twisted by rheumatism. Strapped to one hand was an artist's brush, with which he made painful strokes on the canvas in front of him. Yet, to look at his easel, no one would have guessed how much he suffered; he painted only beauty. He was already famous and could have rested on his past glories, but he forced his stony hands to create still more loveliness. Later collectors and museums were to pay small fortunes for the fruits of his determination.

He got things done because he wanted to do things; he could not tolerate doing nothing. But Renoir did not need the heavy time of illness to make him want to do something. He was a genius, and a large ingredient in genius is a wish to get things done that is stronger than one's natural inclination to laziness.

"Whatever happens," Pierre Curie said, "even if one has to go on like a body without a soul, one must work just the same." He also was a genius.

That Hard Job

That hard job we hesitate to start may be a blessing in disguise provided we exert the will power to tackle it instead of passing the buck.

Aristide Maillol was designing and weaving tapestries in a little French fishing village. He became blind for six months when he was forty. Though he slowly recovered his vision, he could not return to his fine work with tapestries.

So, in middle life, he started afresh as a sculptor, working on large statues in the Greek tradition. In the pink stucco house in which he was born, using neighboring peasant and fisherwomen as models, he carved out a new and bigger reputation for himself.

Plaster, stone, and terra cotta took on massive beauty under his strong blows. He liked best to work in stone—hard, resistant stone.

"The harder the stone, the pleasanter the work," he said, "because you can strike with all your might."

When a man really tries he gets things done.

A *small* try, *small* results. A BIG try, BIG results.

You will get much more done if you will only crack the whip at yourself.

All the geniuses I have encountered have been the hardest workers and most indefatigable students I have ever known.

—ARCHIBALD HENDERSON

Do, and don't talk.

—*Motto of* EDWARD WILSON

There is no development without effort, and effort means work.

—CALVIN COOLIDGE

11

How to decide trifles quickly

THERE WAS a stack of printer's proof waiting for me when I arrived in Seattle, so I planned to correct it right away in a restaurant while I ate.

"You pick out a dollar meal for me," I told the waitress, thinking she could save me the time of reading the menu and making my selections.

"Don't you want to pick your own soup?" she asked timidly.

"You go right ahead and select everything," I answered and began reading the two-foot-long proof sheets.

I finished the soup, continued reading proof while waiting for the next course, and finished several pages, too, before the hesitant waitress approached again, "Which meat course would you like?"

"I don't care. You go right ahead and choose my entire meal, just as if I were eating in your home."

But no meat arrived. I looked around for my waitress and saw her in conference with two other waitresses near the kitchen door. She was pointing toward me as she studied the menu, corralling their assistance in selecting my meal.

The blond member of the pair glanced sympathetically in my direction, looked at my whiskers and the long sheets of paper I was scanning. I saw her lips say, "Guess he's some foreigner and can't read English."

But her slouchy, gum-chewing companion had another answer. "Nope," her lips said, "he's just some nut!"

The indecisive waitress blew up completely under the strain of making up her mind what to bring me to eat. I had hoped to save time, but her difficulty in deciding trifles wasted the time of at least four people.

Peter Henderson had better success at teaching others to make minor decisions for him. He trained a waiter near his seed store on John Street to bring him a noonday meal without an itemized order. Moreover, he paid the waiter a weekly tip to watch for his arrival at the restaurant and bring him lunch without delay. Most of us need some sort of training to get into the habit of making decisions more quickly.

Wasting time deciding trifles is one of the big reasons why people do not get more things done. The time itself may not be long, but the habit of indecision is likely to grow on one.

Indecisive people wonder so long what to do or how to do it that they get little accomplished.

They try so hard to decide what is the right thing to do that they do nothing until it is too late.

By trying to be perfect they become second-rate.

Perhaps they do not mean to put things off—they may be sincerely trying to decide what to do—but the net result is procrastination.

P.I.T.T.O.T.

The letters P.I.T.T.O.T. hung in a large frame in Robert Gair's office.

This tall, curly-headed Scot had been following the advice of those mysterious initials ever since his luckless father had fled to America to evade the Edinburgh sheriff.

Robert himself did not sail quite so hastily as his dad. Fourteen years old, he had to seek an opportunity to work his way across the ocean as a ship's carpenter first. He found one on an old sailing ship that was blown back across the Great Banks four times and took ten weeks to reach New York harbor.

As soon as he got his feet under him in the New World, he set up a small wholesale paper business, originated the idea of printing a merchant's name and advertisement on his paper bags. He made the first folding paper box, using a $30, secondhand printing press, and revolutionized packaging methods.

He had his feet on the ground, and no grass sprouted under them. P.I.T.T.O.T. kept him doing things so fast the grass didn't have a chance.

To Bob Gair and the initiated that slogan meant "Procrastination is the thief of time."

Indecision—wasting time and brain power over trifles—is the chief cause of procrastination.

Gair, founder of the modern folding-paper-box industry, did not waste either time or brain power. A printer's blunder, one April morning, gave him the idea for making folding paper boxes. By nightfall the same day he was producing them.

He did not let opportunity slip by while trying to make up his mind. He decided *right on the spot* and *went to work* on his decision.

Four Kinds of Decisiveness

The ways in which people make up their minds separate them into four classes.

1. The die-hard conservatives, who take a long time to think over trifles and end by deciding to do nothing at all.

2. The conservatives, who waste their energy on trifles but usually do something in the long run.

3. The progressives, who reach decisions quickly, go into action quickly, and may change their minds quickly.

4. The radicals, who reach decisions quickly but, instead of going into action, spend their energies in trying to justify these

decisions and who are inclined to hold to their decisions so long that in time they almost qualify as members of the first class.

The people who get things done rarely belong to either of the extreme classes. The Achievers come from the second or third classes.

THE CAPITOL OF THE WORLD

Indecisiveness and delay seem to be an integral part of diplomatic protocol. For more than a year the United Nations had been considering first one location, then another, as a permanent site. Then came a swift-moving December day when a businessman switched the course of history by making a big decision quickly.

In twelve hours this businessman and philanthropist accomplished more than the astute diplomats had in twelve months.

It was at breakfast that John D. Rockefeller, Jr., first learned that the final vote on a permanent site would take place the next morning and that, although the President wanted the site in the United States, indications apparently proved it would not be.

Rockefeller quickly called together two of his sons, an architect, and an assistant. He talked to absent sons over the long-distance telephone as his plans progressed. Almost at once he reached a decision and sent his aides into action.

By dinnertime he had control of eight and a half million dollars' worth of city blocks in New York to give the United Nations for a headquarters. He was also prepared, as an alternative, to present them with more than 1,000 country-estate acres if the Assembly preferred a rural location.

Numerous local booster groups had been scrambling to win the vote for their cities, but this one decisive man swept all their plans off the board.

It even takes decisiveness to give things away.

Quick Decisions Are Usually Sound Decisions

George Horace Lorimer started work at a Chicago meat-packing house, left for a subordinate job with the then struggling *Saturday Evening Post*. He was a young man who reached decisions quickly. No hesitation or shilly-shallying about him.

When Mr. Curtis, the owner of the *Post*, went to Europe, he left Lorimer in temporary charge. The first issue Lorimer produced contained some changes; the next contained more; each issue contained still more changes. When news of the alterations reached Mr. Curtis in Europe, he hurried a cablegram message to Lorimer making him full editor.

Lorimer's prompt decisions and his resulting ability to get things done put new life into a moribund magazine.

Henry Ford, like most men who have founded great institutions, had the priceless habit of making decisions quickly. This is one reason why he has been able to build up, singlehanded, a business more successful than many that are guided by conference discussions. A group of men, such as a board of directors, takes a long time to reach decisions, and the decisions it makes are often the results of compromise.

Quick decisions, strangely enough, are more likely to be right than those we let simmer for days. One's biases and hidden prejudices are given fuller sway the longer one debates. You have probably noticed that people who take a long time to decide not only get little done but also do foolish or impractical things. Their prejudices tend to dominate their decisions.

Decide quickly, and you will probably make a better decision.

Impulsiveness has its good points.

Indecision is inaction.

WORRY ABOUT MISTAKES

Conscientious people have difficulty getting things done because they try to be so perfect they quibble with themselves over trifles. Fear of making mistakes keeps them from accomplishment.

The executive who gets things done cannot have this attitude. He must have confidence in his prompt decisions. As Albert Hubbard wrote, "An executive is a man who makes a lot of decisions—and some of them are right."

James ("Buck") Duke had his first business lessons at nine. He and his father drove their peddler's cart, with its pair of blind mules, all over North Carolina. At that point Buck was a tobacco-chewing, pigeon-toed lad who might have stepped right off the stage of "Tobacco Road." Only a few years later, he dominated the tobacco industry with his American Tobacco Company.

Buck Duke did not debate with himself over trifles. Nor did he lose sleep over any of the mistakes he made. One day, for instance, he met an old friend who had remained a small pumpkin in the industry.

"My partner and I have troubles enough with just two stores," the friend said, "and here you are thinking of opening two thousand. It's a mistake, Duke."

"A mistake!" Duke boomed. "I've made mistakes all my life. And if there's one thing that's helped me, it's the fact that when I make a mistake, I never stop to talk about it—I just go ahead and make some more."

So Duke unhesitatingly went ahead with his chain of retail tobacco stores, and they eventually did a ten-million-dollar business for him each week. He left a hundred million to found

Duke University, only a portion of the wealth he built up by his quick decisions, some of which were right.

Lord Leverhulme's favorite saying was, "The man who does not make mistakes does not usually make anything."

And Cardinal Mercier, heroic Belgian religious leader of the First World War, said, "Don't look back in the hope of gaining complaisant self-respect from the road you have traveled. MARCH ON! PROCEED!"

Making up one's mind may waste so much time that the golden moment for action passes without being used. It is also genuinely fatiguing, particularly so for the self-quibbler.

A few hours of shopping wear a person out because of the decisions he has to make when buying.

Indecisiveness is sometimes the sign of a neurotic nature. Sometimes it can even precipitate a mental breakdown. Such was the case with George III, King of England at the time of the War for American Independence. Five times during his lifetime George III went through periods of insanity.

When sane, he tried his best to be a good king. From childhood his mother had said to him, "George! Be a king!" whenever he did something she did not think proper. And as a man he wanted to "be a king." He worried over possible mistakes, wishing to be a perfect ruler. He thought a king should be infallible.

When he was brought face to face with dilemmas that were difficult to decide, therefore, he blamed himself scornfully for not being able to make up his mind. He would find fault with himself, become melancholic, then pass into a maniacal mood. Many times, he had to be laced into a strait jacket to prevent him from injuring himself and others. His indecision became the cause of five mental breakdowns. Had he been more decisive, or had he had less sense of duty, he probably would not have been subject to attacks of insanity.

INDECISION ABOUT MARRIAGE

Studies show that women have a harder time trying to make up their minds than men but do not change their minds any more often. Women may seem to be more changeable because of the greater length of time it takes them to reach a decision. They are not more changeable, simply spend more hours wavering this way and that before acting.

This womanly tendency to hesitate over trifles is one reason why there are not more women executives.

Queen Elizabeth had a weakness for postponing decisions. She left important offices unfilled because she couldn't make up her mind whom to appoint to them. She couldn't decide whether to move from Hampton Court to Windsor, and for weeks the entire court was half-packed, awaiting her royal decision. Her chronic indecisiveness divided her court into factions and caused endless bickering.

She never wasted time trying to make up her mind about her temper, however. Her anger would flare out like sudden lightning, as befitted that of the daughter of Henry VIII.

She had a weakness for men but couldn't decide which one to marry. She loved generously and was loved amply in return, but she did not make up her mind to marry until it was too late. Her indecisiveness made her reign turbulent.

By way of contrast, look at England's short, plumpish Queen Victoria. The long period of her rule is now called the Victorian Age. She could make up her mind, in affairs of the heart as well as the state.

> # DECIDE MORE THINGS MORE
> # QUICKLY, AND YOU WILL GET
> # MORE DONE

"How does a girl ask a man to marry her?" she asked old Melbourne, her adviser. He laughed, that elegant old cynic who had been prominent in two divorce cases.

The next morning young Victoria went hunting with her cousin, Albert of Saxe-Coburg. At noon, on their return, the mite of a Queen said, "Albert, it would make me happy if you would consent to my wish," and she began to settle upon a date for their marriage.

Victoria was no uncertain coquette. She popped the question herself, then impatiently moved the marriage date ahead, while Albert played the somewhat bewildered silent partner.

Picking out a husband was as easy for Victoria as picking out a new hat. She had the initiative to select one herself rather than trust to intriguing politicians. Like her reign, her marriage was long and happy.

PARENTS DO TOO MUCH DECIDING

Top-notch mental specialists make a strong case for the claim that there are more people nowadays who can't make up their minds than formerly. The experts blame this condition on our small families in which the parents do most of the deciding for the children. When there were many children in each family, each child had a better chance to get practice in deciding.

The way to develop will power for making speedy decisions is, of course, to practice making decisions. When parents or teachers prevent such practice, obviously the will power to make decisions is not being increased.

There are bosses and employers, too, who keep their workers in an indecisive state by telling them, "*I* am the one who is paid to do the thinking in this place."

It was John Ruskin's mother who made a milksop of him. She did not even let him go to college alone; she went, too, to see that he dressed properly, did not fall in with bad companions, and ate the things that were good for him.

Ruskin's mother had him so tightly tied to her apron strings that, after she had picked Euphemia Gray as the girl he should marry, the mother actually proposed to Euphemia for her twenty-nine-year-old son. But the son was too firmly tied to the apron strings to make a satisfactory husband, and in six years Euphemia divorced him in a case that had all England rocking with laughter.

Ruskin was a pathetic man, broken by parental attention. Even he knew that his mother's overprotection of him, her making decisions for him, was the cause of his weakness. "The ceaseless authority exercised over me," he wrote, "left me unable to do any more than drift."

Women of aggressive types, married to men who attend mostly to business and show them little affection, are likely to destroy the decisiveness of their sons by protecting them too much and deciding for them.

Some young men have the spunk to wean themselves, despite their mothers' efforts to keep them closely tied to the apron strings. Strongheaded Bismarck, for example, resisted his mother's attempts to keep him on such a leash.

Dr. Clarence O. Cheney, of the Hudson River State Hospital, gives this advice.

Some mothers, particularly those unhappily married, bestow their whole affection on their boy. They shield him from hard knocks, and have him remain their baby. He is excused if he fails in school or in work, and the blame put elsewhere.

The boy to succeed in life has to learn to stand on his own feet, deriving satisfaction from overcoming obstacles himself, and establishing himself in his own family.

The unwise mother who gets her satisfaction in life by making her boy dependent on her, lessens his chances of development.

Our advice to parents is: *Help and guide your boy to grow away from you.* If increasing signs of independence sadden you, keep in mind the thought that it is only by their independence that your children can be successful men.

LESSONS IN DECISIVENESS

Joseph Henry, the stage-struck Albany boy who became the first director of the Smithsonian Institution, had a well-remembered lesson from a cobbler in deciding things for himself. Those were the days before shoe factories were known, when shoes were slowly made by a cobbler in one's own home town.

The boy's grandmother offered to have the cobbler make him a pair of shoes. There was a choice of only two styles, the round-toe or the square-toe. The boy could not decide which style he wanted. Meanwhile the cobbler was making the shoes. Each day Joseph visited the cobbler's shop, trying to reach a decision about the toes. He waited until it was too late. The cobbler finished the shoes, and one had a square toe, the other a round toe.

Those mismated shoes, a monument to indecision, lasted a long time.

Checker players often spend a long time figuring out their next moves. But mental specialists use checkers to develop speedier habits of decision by putting a time limit on each think period. After only one minute of pondering, they make themselves move.

In a like manner, if one sets a TIME LIMIT on important decisions, it helps prod the sleeping will power.

Tex Rickard, ex-sheriff who became boxing promoter, advised a torpid card player in Nome, Alaska, "Never stare the spots off your cards; play!"

TOSSING A COIN

Many of our daily decisions are so minor they can be made by tossing a coin—which turn to make when walking, for instance, or which necktie to put on in the morning. Make a turn, any turn. Put on a tie, any tie. **Do more things more quickly to wake up your decisive qualities.**

I toss a coin, with a clear conscience, to make many decisions that others stew over. Take haggling about prices. I consider it a waste of time. The time spent haggling is seldom worth the few pennies saved on the deal.

Recently, for example, an editor was interested in an article I had written and offered me a price I considered way too low. "Why waste time arguing or why have bad feelings about it," I said to him. "I'll be a sport, if you will. Let the waiter toss a coin for us. If it comes up heads, you can have the article for a nominal price of one dollar. If it comes up tails, you pay me twice what you offered."

It came up heads.

"Now I have seen everything in editing," the editor said, in amazement. But I didn't lose, after all, for I gained his good will and desire to buy later articles at good prices, and I did not waste time or nerves haggling.

Line fences are another cause of unnecessary quibbling. There was a question of an eighteen-inch strip, 900 feet long, on our line fence. Many big court battles have been fought over less land. I suggested tossing a coin. Again I lost, for although I gained the strip of land, it meant just that much more grass to cut every year.

Tossed Coin to See Where Brains Went

Edward S. Morse was a New England boy who was kicked out of three schools for his mischief. He never went to college, yet became one of America's leading naturalists and received honorary degrees from four colleges. He had to pick up his education the hard way but was not handicapped by indecision.

One example of this is the way he disposed of his brains. Cornell University asked him to bequeath his brains to them when he died. So did the Wistar Institute, in Philadelphia. The peppery scientist did not waste time. He tossed a coin and wrote to Wistar to send a jar and instructions about preserving his brains. He kept the jar in a small box beside his desk, using it as a footstool.

His Life Saved by a Tossed Coin

Looking back on decisions made by tossing coins would almost make a superstitious person believe coins possessed both intelligence and foresight into the future. Decisions made by tossed coins often seem, in retrospect, to have been the wisest that could have been made at the time. This is because for most decisions what we decide is less important than getting something under way. Doing rather than wondering what to do is what counts. And, as one looks back, almost any decision can seem to have been the right decision. The human inclination to try to justify one's actions makes one believe in the rightness of tossed-coin decisions just as firmly as in the rightness of those that have split brain cells.

Yet there are cases, such as the one to be related, where a tossed coin does seem to have had some uncanny foresight into the future. Dr. Morse, who tossed the coin to dispose of his brains, was from Salem, Massachusetts. Another scientist from the same historical seaport is Dr. Frederick B. Knight, educational psychologist and administrator at Purdue University.

Dr. Knight was in New England, on a combination trip for business and pleasure, when he was invited by the dean of the University of Connecticut to join a group at the opening performance of the circus in Hartford. Other friends invited him to go fishing the same afternoon. Never a man to waste time deciding or be tactless with his friends, Dr. Knight flipped a coin to see whether he would go fishing or to the circus.

The coin took him fishing. While he was out, the circus tent broke into a sheet of flame, and every member of the party he might have been with was burned to death. The lucky coin had saved him from the same tragic fate.

THE BANKER TOSSED A COIN

James B. Forgan took the decisive step of his life by tossing a coin; and he was a banker at the time. This Scotch-born redhead was in his early twenties, clerk in a New York City branch bank. One day the bank received a telegram asking that a clerk be sent to the branch in remote Halifax. No one wanted to go there, but young Forgan and another clerk were eligible for the job.

Forgan thought he preferred to remain in New York, but to decide which clerk should go to Halifax he suggested tossing a coin. He lost, went to Halifax like a good loser. The varied banking experience he received there proved to be invaluable as he rose in banking circles to become president of the First National Bank of Chicago.

A toss of a coin determined a major decision for Forgan.

For most daily decisions over perplexing little things, a tossed coin can be recommended without reservations.

A Coin Located an Industrial Center

Three farm brothers, William, Daniel, and John Grant, set out early in life to make their way in the world together. They left their native Scotland to start a business in the lush Lancashire valley. Just where to locate it was their first problem. The three stood on a hilltop, uncertain whether to locate it in the valley to the east or in the equally pleasing valley to the west. But they did not quibble. They quickly tossed a coin, and, in the valley at Ramsbottom, they began the combined cotton mill and printworks which they were to build up into one of the largest organizations of its kind in the world.

Having the best location was no more important to them than having the valuable quality of reaching decisions quickly.

The Use of Rules and Policies

For speeding important decisions, a policy, a set of principles, or a goal is essential.

The young Mayo boys, for example, had a goal; they were going to be top-flight physicians and surgeons. When they were invited to a pink tea they did not hesitate over their answer. They simply asked themselves, "Will this make us better medical men?"

A college graduate in engineering, who inherited a good job in his family-owned factory, was getting nowhere because he could not make decisions. He bit his fingernails, wanted to do things, but could not clear the work from his desk.

His white-haired uncle noticed his indecisiveness and was seriously concerned, since the business might someday fall on the nephew's shoulders. The uncle gave the young engineer a list of principles to guide him in making decisions on the dozens of problems that came to his desk daily.

> Will it make the work easier?
> Will it lower costs?
> Will it make the work safer?
> Will it make the workers more satisfied?

The nephew had been trying to reach decisions on a catch-as-catch-can basis. Each problem had seemed different to him. But with this list of questions as a guide, he was astonished to discover how much effort he had been wasting on things of no consequence and how quickly he could now pick out what was important.

That is a characteristic of most indecision. We gnaw our nails over minor things and overlook the weighty questions.

The decisive person has principles which guide him to the heart of a problem. He can decide quickly, consistently, because **principles dispel confusion and open a clear track to the essential.**

John Wanamaker decided quickly on the basis of definite principles, so found it easy to live up to his motto, "Do the next thing."

The little things in life do not count nearly so much as the indecisive pretend.

You can decide most things more quickly.

Next to being right, the best of all things is to be clearly and definitely wrong, because you will come out somewhere. If you go buzzing about between right and wrong, vibrating and fluctuating, you come out nowhere; but if you are absolutely and thoroughly wrong, you must have the good fortune of knocking against a fact that sets you all straight again.

—THOMAS H. HUXLEY

No steps backwards, but a good many zig-zag.

—BISMARCK

My only regrets are the failures to act on impulse. It is the things one could have done and didn't which are lost opportunities.

—GEORGE BIDDLE

Start—Stick—Finish!

—CHARLES KIRCHNER

12

Getting a vigorous start

ENERGETIC STARTERS need not worry about getting things done, getting in ruts, or lacking opportunities.

Initial inertia is a law of all life, even of inanimate objects. I was reminded of this law the hard way recently by my automobile. The gasoline gauge read empty, but I did not want to refill until I reached a filling station near home where I could get a penny a gallon discount—Scotch, you know.

The engine sputtered and died as I turned into the station, fifteen feet from the gasoline pump. The motor was as lifeless as a banana peel.

"Nice level pavement here," I thought aloud, "so it will be easy to push the car to the pump."

But all 180 pounds of me couldn't make the car move. It seemed to spring in where I pushed, but the wheels were as stationary as the legs of a stubborn mule. Bill, the attendant, came up, leaned his big shoulder against the back of the car, gave a long grunt in which I joined, and we had the car under way in a jiffy. Then he left me to guide and push the gasless wonder in unaided.

With my full strength I couldn't start the dead car, but once it was moving slightly I kept it moving with one hand.

It always takes more effort to get going than to keep going. That is why automobiles have to be started in the powerful low gear. Engineers call this "overcoming the initial inertia."

The first railroad locomotive made in this country had a

"starting pole" to overcome its initial inertia and old musket barrels, which served as pipes, to carry the steam from boiler to cylinders. It was built by Peter Cooper for the Baltimore & Ohio Railroad.

The locomotive would not start when the engineer opened the throttle. He had to push against the ground with the starting pole to get it moving. When there were passengers, he used to ask them to give a push on the sides of the cars. There was no danger of the passengers being left behind for, at top speed, the train could not go quite so fast as a man could run.

People, too, need starting poles to get going, to overcome their initial inertia to get things done.

It requires an extra push at the start to get going.

Human self-starters give that extra starting push.

A Bungstarter

The opening sentence is the hardest part of a letter. A starting pole is needed to overcome indecision and hesitation.

Hiram Maxim used a starting pole for his correspondence. He had difficulty recalling names, but did not allow that to waste time or cause indecision when he was dictating a letter. He would lean back in his chair and begin.

"Dear Mr. Bungstarter . . ."

His stenographer had to look up the correct name afterwards. Maxim was an expert on explosives, and he used explosive starts in his own work. No hemming and hawing. No head scratching over a name. HE BEGAN.

Several professional writers always start an article or story with "Now is the time for all good men to come to the aid of their party." They write something, anything, to get under way, to overcome the starting lag.

Sixty thousand salesmen report that the hardest part of selling is starting a sales talk. Once they get uncorked, the rest is easy.

The beginning is the chief point of resistance in any task. That is when extra horsepower, one's full will power, needs to be turned on.

Starting the Day Vigorously

"They might as well open the office half an hour late," an office wit observed, "for no one gets anything done the first thirty minutes."

A half-wit used the same logic when he figured railroads should leave the last car off trains, since that was the one usually damaged in accidents.

The first half-hour of the working day is usually as unproductive as a man bailing water out of a boat with a sieve. People get up steam slowly unless they put on extra effort to get started.

A few do not get going full force until afternoon. They idle along in the morning letting nature take its course when they should use starting poles, extra steam, and get under way.

Each new day, like each new task, requires an initial push to get it going. The vigorous pushers accomplish things. The slow pushers have more things left over to do tomorrow—or next week.

Perhaps sleep lingers in your head, and you are slow waking up. Then force yourself to a sudden start; that is the best way to clear out the cobwebs. Inactivity encourages drowsiness; activity makes for wakefulness.

Do your coasting afternoons. Put forth all your horsepower mornings, right from the first upward slope. Dress vigorously, put some enthusiasm into your breakfast, dig into the work with all your might.

Weak starts make deep ruts. Energetic starts pull people out of ruts.

Forceful Starters

Well started is half-finished.

Henry Baldwin Hyde came from the Catskills, worked seven years in the office of a life-insurance company. The tall, bushy-browed man was cashier at twenty-five, with ideas for expanding the business. One blustery March Saturday he talked these ideas over with the company president. The president promptly fired him.

On Monday young Hyde rented a second floor back room at 98 Broadway and started his own company. It was only an idea. There was no capital. There were twenty strong established companies with which to compete. Financial conditions that year were topsy-turvy.

But young Hyde made a vigorous start. He did not wait for more favorable times. He jumped right from being fired into the work of building a new company along the ideas he had developed in the cashier's cage. His Equitable Life Assurance Society did not get off to a flying start—no new business ever does—but Hyde got it off to a good start, and without delay.

"A step each day" was Hyde's favorite motto. Promptitude was his middle name. He worked like lightning, put on extra effort at the outset, and licked initial inertia. He did not stall at the start.

The Electron Microscope

Jim Hillier was newly married and teaching a full schedule of physics classes at the University of Toronto for $1,100 a

---

PUT ON EXTRA PUSH AT THE
START OF EACH TASK AND
EACH DAY

---

year. He had been interested in telescopes ever since his eleventh birthday, when his father had given him a small one. At that time the eleven-year-old had taken the telescope apart and in a few days discovered how to make a microscope from its lenses.

But now he was twenty-two. It was 1937, and he was earning less than $100 a month and doing little with telescopes.

A professor who had just returned from a visit to European laboratories told Hillier about a new kind of microscope the German physicists were trying to develop. This new German supermicroscope, as it was called, magnified things enormously, but the images were blurred and quickly faded. Perhaps the principle on which it worked was all right, but the mechanism itself was not yet practical. The Toronto professor thought he and Hillier together could use the principle and make it work properly.

"When do we start!" Hillier exploded eagerly, and he immediately began to think about making the idea practical. Already doing a full load of teaching, he took to working at night, often until five in the morning.

The pair used some thirty thousand volts of current. Once Hillier was knocked across the room when he accidentally came in contact with a charged part. They borrowed equipment, made parts, worked feverishly as the momentum of their vigorous start carried them along.

Then one day Hillier climbed the short ladder in the darkened room to take the first look through the new electron microscope that was taller than a man.

"Sharp as a razor's edge!" he shouted to the men who were working the switches and generators. "And it stays in focus—not a bit of blurring!" He had licked the problem; the electron microscope was now practical. It magnified objects to a power thousands of times greater than any ever known before.

His success took him to the RCA laboratories at Princeton, where he found how to cut the cost of the electron microscope in half and to reduce it to a mere sixteen inches in height.

And with equal vigor he plunged into another problem, the solution of which added to his triumphs—he created the micro-analyzer.

His vigorous starting helped science to see small.

WHITNEY AND THE BLACK CAT

Eli Whitney had been working for some time to develop a practicable cotton gin. He was visiting the plantation of one Catherine Greene, a comely Georgia widow with several attractive daughters. All of them, the widow included, were in love with the young Yale graduate. Whitney scarcely noticed his admirers. He was deeply puzzled about his cotton gin.

For weeks he had been up against a blank wall. The gin would not work, and Eli sat in his work shed, beside a chicken yard, in deep thought.

One day his dreaming eyes happened to fall on a large knothole near the bottom of the chicken fence. Suddenly a huge, black paw was thrust through the knothole. Eli straightened up, wondering what the black tomcat was up to.

He had an answer in a few minutes, when an unsuspecting hen walked past the knothole. The black paw shot through the opening, claws extended, and pinioned the hen to the ground. The hen struggled, squawked itself free, and ran out of sight, still squawking in panic.

The cat's paw held a clawful of feathers which it pulled back through the knothole.

Whitney jumped to his feet, his face alight. "That's it!" he exclaimed, as he rushed inside to grab a piece of charcoal and a drawing board. "If a cat's paw can pull feathers through a knothole," he mumbled to himself, "a wire hook will pull cotton through a slot and leave the cotton seeds behind."

He started sketching the mechanism INSTANTLY, started work on the actual construction **instantly**.

Daughter Cornelia Greene came into the shed, poutingly looking for attention. Whitney ignored her, neglected her objections as he tore apart a cage she had made for a mockingbird. He wanted the wire to use for the "cat's paw action." He worked continuously, carried by the momentum of his vigorous start. For two successive nights he went without sleep to follow through his idea. And his cotton gin worked.

Whitney was an energetic starter in all his inventive work. A few years later he returned to his New Haven factory by boat, and friends met him at the dock with bad news; his factory had burned. Whitney was flushed and hot with malarial fever.

For a moment he stood like a bronze monument. Then he pushed Harry Todd firmly away from the gangplank.

"In the last ten minutes the fever has left me," Whitney said, as he walked firmly off the boat to Wooster Street where his factory was a heap of smoldering ashes.

He was already at work planning the reconstruction of the burned building, and by nightfall the small wing that had been saved was rearranged to manufacture gauges and treadle drills to replace those lost in the fire.

Whitney was a self-starter. Malaria and flames together could not delay this man who was to become the father of mass production. We will learn more about his methods of getting things done in a later chapter.

DIAMONDS IN HIS BACK YARD

David Ross was an Indiana farm boy who wanted to go to near-by Purdue University. His father objected, but his aunts, who made most of his clothes with their own needles, talked his father into allowing him to take an engineering course.

Upon graduation David Ross did not leave Lafayette for an engineering job, as did most of his fellow graduates. Two things kept him there. For one thing, his father was steadily losing money on the swampland farm and needed David's help. For a second, while in college the young man had heard Russell Conwell's famous talk, "Acres of Diamonds," a lecture depicting the folly of those who looked for opportunities in distant places only.

David Ross was famous for getting things done. He soon had the old farm drained and running on a paying basis. His head hatched ideas easily and, more important, he went to work on these ideas right away. HE HAD THE ENTHUSIASM TO MAKE EVERY START A VIGOROUS START.

He got an idea for improving the steering mechanisms of automobiles and trucks, promptly started developing it in an old horse barn. That was the start of the Ross Gear & Tool Company, a dominant firm in the enormous growth of the automotive industry. He invented his steering gear before he knew how to drive an automobile.

After he had learned to drive, he noticed one night how the

eyes of a cat beside the highway reflected the beam of his head-light. As soon as he reached home he sketched a little device of metal and glass, the size of an overcoat button, that could be placed along dangerous road banks to warn motorists of danger. That was the birth of "cat's eye" reflectors, which have saved thousands of lives on the highways. This man, whose shaggy eyebrows were like dark caterpillars, did not hesitate over his ideas; he started each one vigorously.

When he saw a tunnel being dug into the Purdue power plant, he stopped in his tracks. "Look at that!" he snorted. "They dig a tunnel. In a few days another gang comes along to brick it up. Then another gang puts the dirt back over it. Too much waste!"

By the end OF THE SAME DAY he had developed a plan for parabolic shapes of cast concrete that would fit together and support themselves at the top. They could be put in place, section by section, as a tunnel was dug, so tunnels could be finished in jig time.

Where others made timid starts and timid tries, David Ross jumped into every job with both feet and got it done. He was granted eighty-eight patents, most of them important and money-making. He started things vigorously, found acres of diamonds right in his rural community, and gave more than two and a half million dollars to Purdue University.

Start of Memorial Day

James Redpath also put on extra starting power. While Superintendent of Schools at Charleston, South Carolina, he inaugurated the nation-wide observance of Memorial Day.

One evening Redpath talked with Charles Dickens. The famous English novelist told him about the many annoying experiences he had undergone while on a lecture tour he arranged himself.

At breakfast the following morning, short Redpath commented, "Celebrities should not have to make their own lecture arrangements and dates. There should be a bureau to do the job on an efficient basis, and I will start one."

He went into immediate action. In a friend's office on Bloomfield Street, Boston, he started the first lecture bureau. He made up his business from odds and ends; there was no regular routine at first. Each task was something new to be started. Redpath was a man who could put all the extra effort needed into each new start.

He built up the great lyceums that spread entertainment and culture, then the chautauquas that were held under canvas during the summer months. He was an Achiever.

Redpath did not wait for inspiration. He used the VITAL MINUTE, the first minute.

Such energetic starts prevent procrastination.

Stage Fright

An energetic start whips stage fright, too. Florenz Ziegfeld, the great theatrical producer, knew this. He applied it on opening nights to bring out top performances by his stars who were afflicted with first-night jitters.

Ziegfeld would stand in the wings beside a star nervously awaiting her cue. When the cue came, Ziegfeld would give the star an unexpected kick on the posterior, pushing her onto the stage. Surprise would displace nervous tension, and the star would do her best.

The first seconds of any public appearance are the hardest. Give yourself a swift kick and get under way.

Discover what you can really do by putting on extra power at the start.

You can't begin by coasting.

Things started energetically almost finish themselves. James B. Duke saw Rockefeller consolidating small oil companies to form a business giant. He scratched his red head, allowed he could do the same thing with tobacco.

"Then," Buck Duke said, "I *started* out to do it." It was as easy as that.

Another tobacco man, long before Duke, also accomplished much in his lifetime. This was Sir Walter Raleigh.

"How do you ever get so many things done?" Raleigh was asked.

"When there is anything to do, I start it."

Don't look at a thing; START IT.

Don't imagine it is *too difficult*; START IT.

Don't *put it off* a day; START IT.

Don't look for *someone else to do it*; START IT.

Don't pretend you must *think it over*; START IT.

Don't start halfheartedly; put everything you can muster into your start.

Morale is that something in the human will which releases the extra effort needed to get started. Your timidity may say, "It can't be done," but with a forceful start you can do it.

You have probably done things all your life without using this extra force at the start. Think how much more you could achieve by making an enthusiastic start each morning at each task.

Start it hard!

It is the man whose enthusiasm lasts for thirty years who becomes a leader.

—EDWARD BURGESS BUTLER

Labor ipse voluptas. (Work is its own joy.)

—*Latin motto of*
CAIUS COLLEGE

13

The best hours for getting more done

CHUCKLING HARRY LAUDER wrote many popular songs, but none was more true to life than his "Oh! It's nice to get up in the mawrning! But it's nicer to lie in your-r-r bed!"

Getting under way mornings is a real task for many. Yet there is gold in the morning hours, and it is worth the extra effort to establish the morning-work habit. The old adage **"Get up early three mornings and gain one day of time"** is more than true.

Human efficiency rises and falls. Bodily processes have both high and low points during the course of the day. Mental powers wax and wane as the hours progress. This "diurnal course of efficiency," as it is called, can be used to get more things done.

The daily rise and fall of mental efficiency follows a course something like this for most persons.

Morning
8 o'clock	105%
10 o'clock	102%

Afternoon
1 o'clock	101%
4 o'clock	96%

Evening
8 o'clock	98%
10 o'clock	97%

Surgeons have long taken advantage of this diurnal variation. Most operations are performed during the morning hours, many at what seem to us outrageously early hours. The early hours are favored because surgeons find their HEADS ARE CLEARER and their HANDS STEADIER at the start of the day. And, possibly, the patients' vitality is higher in the morning.

An astonishing number of self-made men and women have been morning workers. Whether they were so from deliberate practice, or whether it was just natural with them, it has unquestionably assisted their climb in the world. It has helped them get more things done quicker and better.

THE LIBERATOR OF CHINA

There is an old Chinese proverb that if you lose an hour in the morning, you have to hunt for it the rest of the day.

Generalissimo Chiang Kai-shek started as a common soldier. This tall, slender man, with his short legs, has done more than any other person to liberate modern China. He has made himself a world personality.

Soldiers, of course, are used to rising early and working in the morning. But gray-eyed Chiang did not remain an ordinary soldier. He used to get up before the bugler. Throughout his great career he has generally risen at dawn, worked from then until breakfast. In the hours when his rivals are doing nothing, he does his most important work.

WANAMAKER

Ruddy-faced John Wanamaker was one of the first men at his store mornings. He took the seven-o'clock train to New York; his buyers left an hour later. He carried work on the train each day.

As Postmaster General, he almost stirred official Washington from its morning lethargy by opening his office ahead of everyone else in the capital.

At seventy, still erect and with only a few gray hairs, he inspected the floors of his great stores in New York and Philadelphia at 7 A.M. and had suggestions for the sleepy-eyed managers when they arrived a couple of hours later.

THE SOAP KING

William Lever was one of the ten children of a small wholesale grocer. Starting in an inadequate rented factory building, he built up Lever Brothers' Company. Its plants soon covered every civilized country and plantations of thousands of acres dotted uncivilized lands.

He remained a morning worker, even after he became one of the world's richest men and was honored with the title of Viscount Leverhulme. He got up at 4:30 every morning, whether at one of his town houses or his half-dozen palatial country estates.

He took brief setting-up exercises immediately on rising, followed by a cold bath to "get the sleep out of his system." Then he worked until breakfast at 7:30.

When his secretaries appeared, each found a day's work laid out for her. Lever used to make notes in red pencil or green ink on the margins of letters or write slips of instructions on colored paper while the secretaries were getting forty more winks.

LUCKMAN

At thirty-seven, Charles Luckman, who sold newspapers as a boy in Kansas City, became the three-hundred-thousand-dollar-a-year president of Lever Brothers Company in the United States. Like his company's founder, Chuck Luckman is on the job early. Every day he is up at 5:30, works until break-fast. He puts in ten more hours of work in his office after that.

WEBSTER

Daniel Webster also came from a family of ten children. This short, swarthy son of a New Hampshire farmer made himself a national leader. His farm habit of getting work under way early in the day helped take him up the road to fame.

Four o'clock was his favorite hour for starting the day's work. By breakfast time he had finished what would have been an eight-hours' job for many men, and he had the rest of the day thrown in for good measure.

"I never let the sun get the start of me if I can help it," he told his friends.

EDISON

Thomas A. Edison, the electrical wizard, had only a few months of formal schooling. His family had neither the influ-ence nor the cash to help him along. Almost on his own he made himself one of the world's greatest inventors. Everyone has heard the stories of how he used to get along on short amounts of sleep during the intense periods when an invention was being rushed to completion.

Few know, however, that it was the deaf wizard's habit to be up and at work by 6:30 each morning. He did a couple hours' work every day before other budding inventors had gotten up.

He did not get along on small amounts of sleep. He averaged seven-and-a-half to eight-and-a-half hours' sleep out of the twenty-four. But during the intense periods he would take less of this at night and have numerous catnaps during the day.

Early rising does not necessarily mean that one gets less sleep.

Going to bed early at night makes up the difference before it is lost.

The modern use of electricity has turned night into day for many people. They stay up later, enjoying the glamour and entertainment afforded by electric lights. Unquestionably they would be more efficient if they got up early instead of staying up so late.

The Meat Barons

Philip D. Armour, a short, broad-shouldered boy from a family of eight children, was expelled from Cazenovia Seminary because he played truant one fine spring day. He went buggy riding with a girl instead of going to classes.

At nineteen he joined the Gold Rush but found no gold. He made gold later, however, by working with an established meat-packing firm. In a few years he owned the firm himself.

Shortly before seven every morning Armour was in his office. He got up at five. While his competitors enjoyed an extra hour of sleep, P. D. Armour built one of the country's great fortunes, revolutionized the meat-packing business.

Thomas E. Wilson was in his twenties, a clerk for the Burlington Railroad. A Chicago meat-packing firm was having difficulty keeping track of its refrigerator cars, so asked the railroad to detail a man to help straighten them out. The first man the railroad sent objected to the early hours and poor working conditions at the stockyards.

Young Wilson offered to try the job. Early rising was nothing new to him; it was his habit to eat breakfast at 5:30. He showed the packing firm how to keep track of their special cars, then stayed on with them to help in other ways.

When the firm name was changed to Wilson & Company and the onetime railroad clerk was made president. he was still eating a 5:30 breakfast.

McCormick

Cyrus McCormick, a tall, square-shouldered youth with a high, intellectual forehead, followed his father's example and invented a reaper for small grains. His father had invented one, but the son's differed from it in an important respect; the reaper Cyrus invented actually harvested the grain.

The idea of a reaper was in the air those days, and at about the same time a dozen other inventors brought forth reapers that worked. McCormick had patent protection for his only during the first eight years of its life. And during that eight years he sold 778 reapers at an average profit of just $20 each. You can figure out how fast he was becoming a rich man.

Unlike his inventive competitors, McCormick used to wake up at five o'clock. He liked to consider his business problems in the solitude of the early morning hours. He prepared for this early rising by taking a long nap after his evening meal, before he went to bed.

Without benefit of patent protection he either outdistanced or absorbed all his competitors.

Two University Builders

You will enjoy becoming better acquainted with two infant prodigies who turned out all right.

First meet Timothy Dwight, New Englander, who could read the Bible when he was four years old, who read Latin two years later. His father tried to keep him from reading so much, hence, boylike, young Timothy read all the more eagerly on the sly. At eight he was ready to enter college, but his parents sensibly kept him at home until he was thirteen.

When thirteen-year-old Timothy entered Yale he began to

have the time of his life. He could do better work than the older students without bothering to study. So he played cards for most of his first two college years. When he reached the mature age of fifteen, he went to the other extreme and remained there the rest of his days. He abruptly quit gambling, buried his nose in books, and began getting up at 3:30 in summer, 4:30 in winter. He taught at Yale at nineteen and was later its president for nearly a quarter of a century.

As president, the only thing he could never control was the undergraduate propensity to do damage to the outhouses on Halloween. He had the "necessities" built of solid brick, even roofed with brick. At last he would surely foil the mischief-makers! The following Halloween the students blew up the buildings with blasting powder!

We have already made the acquaintance of the other infant prodigy, pudgy William Rainey Harper, the Ohio storekeeper's son, who started the University of Chicago and scheduled each hour of his day. Harper also made himself an early riser, was often dictating to his secretaries at five o'clock in the morning.

When his son was seventeen, President Harper used strategy to get the son into habits of early rising. He made a written bargain. The boy was to be paid for getting his father out of bed early. President Harper understood human nature too well to nag the youth about late hours; getting up early enough to disturb the father's rest was something different for the boy, especially when he got paid for it.

Incidentally, the careers of both these prodigies were cut short by cancer, though this had nothing to do with their early rising.

SEARS, ROEBUCK & COMPANY

A railroad-station agent in a small town in Minnesota hit a bonanza when he accidentally started a mail-order business by disposing of a C.O.D. shipment of watches that the local jeweler refused to accept. But Richard Sears, the station agent, lacked the imagination to see the future of the mail-order business he developed from this modest beginning.

Sears was a relatively young man when he sold out his interest in the firm. The stout, optimistic son of an immigrant peddler, Julius Rosenwald, bought a quarter of the interest for $37,500, most of which he had to borrow.

Rosenwald was an energetic chap, all industry and on the job early in the morning. When he wanted to select a lawyer for the firm, he went to a lawyers' office building at dawn to see who came to work first. He hired that man, eventually took him into the firm.

An early bird, Rosenwald built up Sears, Roebuck & Company, gave away more than sixty million dollars. He used to phone his department heads before nine to make sure they were on the job in their offices.

The Sage of Monticello

A redheaded farm boy from the Virginia hills went to William and Mary College, bringing with him his violin and his "work kit." He was nicknamed "Long Tom." Keep an eye on this tall boy and his work kit. In those days Virginia gentlemen liked to sleep late mornings and stay out and enjoy themselves late evenings.

But when young Thomas Jefferson spent week ends on plantations he got up early, opened his work kit, and invested his extra time. Before anyone else was awake, Jefferson used to get a lot of work done.

"I have made it a rule," Jefferson said later in life, "never to let the sun rise before me."

RULERS

Charles II, King of England, of whom it was alleged "he never said a foolish thing, nor ever did a wise one," was another early riser. But, history reports, he got up early merely to have more time to play, because the lack of electricity kept him from playing at night.

Christina of Sweden usually studied for five hours every morning before the other members of her court were up and around.

Frederick the Great also worked before his court was awake. He started the day at five o'clock. Later he had himself awakened at four to get in another hour of work.

SOUNDWRITING

Isaac Pitman's father did not approve of Isaac's going to college, perhaps because his eleven children overtaxed the family resources. So Isaac went to work in an office when he was fifteen and picked up an education for himself by getting up at four o'clock to study. This four-o'clock rising hour became his habit for life.

He was twenty-seven when he developed the new system of Pitman shorthand, based upon the sounds of words. The system was adapted to fourteen languages.

Pitman shorthand was the direct result of reading Isaac Pitman did in his teens, before breakfast. For his self-education he secured a copy of Walker's Pronouncing Dictionary, which he read through in order to learn how to pronounce every word with which he was not already familiar. His familiarity with the sounds of language served as the basis for his improved system of soundwriting.

Geniuses Who Met the Sun

Some people think geniuses can take things easy. Inquiry into the private lives of famous creative workers shows, on the contrary, that very few have allowed themselves to sit back. *Would-be geniuses* may take up irresponsible habits of Bohemian life, but *actual geniuses* PUSH their talents in the morning hours, the early-morning hours.

Antoine Lavoisier, the father of modern chemistry, was a wealthy Frenchman who did not permit his wealth to stifle his ability to get things done. He was up and at work by six o'clock. Evenings he worked from seven until ten, a combination that reminds us of the two shifts of the French author, Balzac. Lavoisier's wife, with whom we shall become better acquainted in a later chapter, worked with him.

Alexander von Humboldt did poorly at school but came to his senses later, settling down to the scientific work in America and Europe that earned him permanent fame. He made it his practice to be up at four o'clock.

John Wesley, founder of Methodism, was also a four-o'clock riser.

John Hunter, the Glasgow boy who became surgeon to the king and discovered how to resuscitate apparently-drowned persons, was a five-o'clock riser. He is buried in Westminster Abbey.

George Bancroft, the historian who became Secretary of the Navy, also rose at five. He started the Naval Academy at Annapolis, and in the large dormitory named in his honor early rising is still the custom.

F. Marion Crawford, the man who wrote in spite of his wealth and turned out nearly a five-foot shelf of novels, was at his desk between six and seven every morning.

Buffon, the great naturalist, was at work before six and worked standing up. We will learn more about people who worked standing up in a later chapter.

Goethe as a young man tried a devil-may-care existence. For half a dozen years work was only an interruption to his idleness. Then he settled down and began each day in earnest. "I learned to work mornings," he said, "when I could skim the cream off the day and use the rest for cheesemaking." Later, when a committee was talking over plans for a Goethe memorial, they suggested using a lamp as a symbol of his industry. "No, gentlemen," he advised, "for I have never worked at night. I work mornings, where the gold lies."

John Milton as a young man also tried to turn night into day. His first wife stood for this for a month, then returned to her family. It was not until middle life that Milton became a morning worker. It was after the change that he wrote his chief masterpiece, "Paradise Lost." He started work at four in summer, at five in winter. He was busy until noon, then again from two until six. He ate supper at eight.

Charles Dickens, the boy who blacked shoes while his father was in debtors' prison, liked to work early in the morning. "There is something incomparably solemn in the still solitude of the morning," he commented. But his wife was a sluggish sort of woman, perhaps a victim of inadequate thyroid glands. She preferred to sleep late. This was one of the unfortunate differences that made their married life unhappy.

Beethoven was short, swarthy, awkward. His grandmother died in an insane asylum, and his father was a worthless drunkard. Beethoven overcame these handicaps—and the handicap of early deafness—by getting up at daybreak, winter and summer alike, to work on the musical compositions that have made his name permanently famous.

STARTING AN HOUR EARLIER

IN THE MORNING MAY MAKE

YOU AN ACHIEVER INSTEAD

OF AN ALMOST

Rubens was the richest, busiest, most famous artist of his day. By four o'clock each morning, summer or winter, he was ready for work.

Naturally lazy and given to procrastination, Mozart nevertheless got up at six o'clock and worked.

Immanuel Kant, the philosopher, was up and starting work at five.

Gustav Mahler, composer and conductor, was also at work before breakfast; he started at six and rose even earlier.

Brahms started work before Mahler, at five o'clock, and went through the day without stopping.

Sir Walter Scott, a victim of infantile paralysis, got up at six, built his own fire, shaved, dressed, then sat down to write. By the time the family gathered for breakfast he had, in his own words, "broke the back of the day's work."

Fannie Hurst, nearing sixty, world-famous and wealthy from her short stories and novels, still rises at six, walks in Central Park, and, at seven, settles down to work in a room with stained glass windows and paneling out of a medieval French church. Her fame was not an accident.

Arnold Bennett deserted a law career to become a novelist

and playwright. He worked before breakfast, often starting at two o'clock.

Rousseau, whose romance, "Emile," revolutionized education, was an early-morning worker.

John Calvin's writings brought about the Reformation of religion. He started work at six.

Bertel Thorvaldsen, the timid son of a man who carved crude figureheads for the ships of Copenhagen, became the leader of the Classical Revival in sculpture. He was at work shortly after five mornings.

Rosa Bonheur first learned drawing from her father. At seventeen she was making copies of famous paintings, which she sold to help support the family. At thirty-one, after a year and a half of work, she finished her gigantic painting "The Horse Fair." She used to get up at 6 A.M. and be at work in her studio before seven. She worked through the day until dusk stopped her, then took a twilight walk to think over new subjects for her brush.

Slender Leonardo da Vinci became a painter against his father's wishes. A morning worker, for months he climbed the scaffold in the monastery of Santa Maria della Grazie each day at early dawn to toil at his painting, "The Last Supper." He worked until the evening shades forced him to leave the scaffold.

Joshua Reynolds' schoolmaster father could not teach his son to spell, but the boy got other things done by being a morning worker. Before he was thirty, he was receiving commissions for nearly 200 paintings a year. He used to work at his easel before seven. As a morning worker, he finished an amazing number of paintings.

Corot, in contrast, did not find a market for his talent until he was fifty. But, for years before he made his first sale, this man of more than six feet used to go out in the countryside singing softly to himself, waiting for the first vague outlines of dawn, at three o'clock. He tried to catch the creation of each new day on his canvas. He remained in the field until the sun sank in the west, to record the changing scene. "I paint and I paint and I paint," he wrote a friend. He painted that way for nearly thirty years until—Bam!—belated fame discovered him.

Being an early bird is one of the signs of genius.

Forcing an Early Start

Early rising is apparently something that can be LEARNED.

John Curran, for instance, found it perfectly natural to sleep overlate in the morning. As a young man, he devised a machine for getting himself up at 4:30. He described it as follows: "Exactly over my head I have suspended two tin pans, one above the other. When I go to bed, which is always at ten, I pour a bottle of water into the upper pan, in the bottom of which is a hole of such size as to let the water pass through so as to overflow the lower pan at 4:30." When the overflowing water soaked his head, he got up. John Curran made himself a famous Irish orator and judge.

John Jay, the American statesman, had himself waked at sunrise by cutting a hole in the window shutter. The hole was placed so the first rays of the sun fell on his face.

Kosciuszko, Polish patriot and one of George Washington's generals, was trained in the Royal Military School in Warsaw. There he paid a watchman to awaken him at three each morning. The watchman pulled a cord that hung out of Kosciuszko's window. The other end of the cord was tied around the young cadet's wrist.

Frederic Sauvage inherited a shipyard and became one of the world's outstanding inventors of ship improvements. He also invented a machine to get himself up early mornings. His machine was similar to that devised by Judge Curran, except that Sauvage did not get his face wet. He had two pans arranged on a seesaw. When the water slowly dripped from one pan, the seesaw tilted the other way and set half a dozen bells ringing.

Morrell Mackenzie, an insurance-office worker, was taking evening courses in medicine. He wanted to get up at five o'clock to do his studying. He tied strings to his thumbs to awaken him. He became a renowned throat specialist and, as Sir Morrell, was paid sixty thousand dollars for services to the German Emperor.

Aristotle, who lisped and spent a long, wild youth, finally settled down to brass tacks after he made a contrivance that got him up at daybreak.

Georges Buffon was a young French count who did not have to work. As a young man he didn't work. Family friends claimed he was unusually lazy. Their good-natured teasing about his lying abed made him determine to do something about it. He tried to get up earlier but couldn't. Then he offered his servant, Joseph, a cash reward for each morning he got the foppish count out of bed before six o'clock. Joseph took the ways and means of getting Buffon up into his own hands, dashed buckets of cold water on him. Joseph finally made Buffon an habitual early riser. When Buffon later became the leading French naturalist, director of the Royal Museum, and a member of the French Academy, he said he owed Joseph three or four of the forty-four volumes on natural history he had written. Once Buffon had got the habit of starting early in the morning, he was able to work through without a break until two in the afternoon, then again from five until nine in the evening.

Like Buffon, William Prescott was without financial worries. He was also decidedly on the lazy side, especially when it came to getting up mornings. When he was in his twenties, blind in one eye and losing the sight of the other, he decided to do something about his natural indolence. He gave a servant a cash bonus for getting him up early. When the servant called him, young Prescott used to count to twenty and then arise. On the few occasions when he went back to sleep, the servant would enter the room and take away his bedcovers. The servant, Nathan Webster, was with Prescott more than thirty years and was generously remembered in his will. Prescott himself became an early bird and a before-breakfast worker. He was up before the sunrise he could not see, this blind rich boy in Massachusetts who made himself one of America's greatest historians.

John Muir, the nature supersalesman who became the father of the United States national park system, was an inveterate inventor in his younger days. His inventions, however, were not for profit; he just liked to make useful things for himself. When he was working in a sawmill, for instance, he constructed an early-rising machine that was as complicated as the sawmill but very successful. Its levers and cogwheels turned on a lamp, lit a fire in chilly weather, and tilted a bed up on end so the sleeper was pitched on the floor.

This machine, which made enough noise to awaken the sleeper without throwing him out of bed at all, attracted much local attention. Muir was asked to exhibit it at the Wisconsin state fair. It became the talk of the fair, and the twenty-two-year-old inventor was kept busy the whole day tossing spectators out of the bed.

When he went to college, Muir took his early-rising machine along but had to discontinue its use because other students in the dormitory set up loud complaints against the unearthly noise it made every morning. But he continued to get up early; he hired the night watchman to pull a string that was tied to his big toe.

Another early riser, who in effect worked two shifts a day, was Balzac. He first supported himself as a printer, so his writing had to be done at night. This started him in the habit of forcing himself to work. After he was able to give up typesetting and devote full time to writing, he made himself do *two* eight-hour stints daily. His first stint was from two to ten mornings, after which he took a two-hour pause. Then he started work anew at noon, continuing until eight in the evening.

Balzac was so short he wore high heels to make himself look taller, but his early rising and double shift gave him a stature of lasting fame as France's greatest novelist. Playful by nature, he used to say he had been born a day late so worked two shifts to catch up. His neck was thick, but not his head.

Jean-Baptiste Colbert came from a family of storekeepers, worked his way up to become Controller General to Louis XIV. He untangled France's perplexing financial condition, developed her industry, created her Navy, established his country as a productive international power.

One day his son asked him if it were better to work in the evening or the morning.

"Son," he said, narrowing his deep-set eyes under their bushy eyebrows, "it is necessary to work in the morning *and* in the evening.

A small daily task, if it be really daily, will beat the labors of a spasmodic Hercules. The tortoise always catches the hare while the latter is losing time in preening himself for a quick spurt.
—ANTHONY TROLLOPE

When a man begins to turn over it's time to turn out.
—DUKE OF WELLINGTON

I have always believed in long hours. It is the only way to get things done.
—ELIHU THOMSON

14

Working for quality

HERE IS another story about Eli Whitney. After graduating from college he went to Savannah, Georgia, to study law. There he heard people talking about the need for a speedy way to remove the seeds from cotton pods. As it was, one worker had to spend an entire day tediously picking the seeds from a single pound of cotton. Consequently, cotton was too expensive for most folks to buy.

"You are a good tinkerer, despite all your book learning," Governor Greene's widow said to Whitney. "Couldn't you devise some way to get rid of the seeds?"

Whitney closed his law book and gazed across the room. He was thinking of some of the machines he had made on his father's farm back in Massachusetts.

"Perhaps I could make something," he finally answered. "May I use your shed as a workshop?"

After many false starts, he produced a contraption that removed the seeds from cotton a hundred times faster than the most skilled human fingers. When he applied for patents on his cotton gin, however, several states refused him, and, in other states, piratical manufacturers took away his business. He brought lawsuits to protect his patents; these suits consumed his business, leaving him nearly penniless. Yet his invention more than doubled the wealth of the cotton territories.

He gave up his cotton-gin business and, after a period of

apprehension, converted his small factory in New Haven to making rifles. He started work on a government order for 10,000 new model rifles, to be sold at ridiculously low prices.

"How can he ever do it at that price?" knowing friends asked. In those days every rifle was painstakingly made by hand, and gunsmiths commanded top wages.

Washington officials began to hear strange rumors about Whitney's factory; he was making guns without any armorers. They rushed an inspector to New Haven to see what it was all about. The inspector had trouble getting into the factory, and when he did get in Whitney evaded his questions; the unfortunate experience with the cotton gin had made him secretive, even with government agents.

A week before the first rifles were due to be delivered, more inspectors called. Whitney did not have a single rifle ready to show them.

"Come back in seven days, gentlemen," Whitney told them. "Those rifles—and many more—will be ready for you."

The door shut in the puzzled inspectors' faces. Was this man out of his mind? Making rifles without gunsmiths or armorers, and not a gun finished yet! The inspectors shrugged their shoulders. It would be his funeral, not theirs.

A week later, back they came. This time there was no secrecy about Whitney. Haggard but smiling, he took them into a long room. At one end were empty crates, waiting for guns. Inexperienced young men and women were working at long benches down the sides of the room. There were small bins beside each worker. The inspectors watched in amazement as each worker put a couple pieces of a gun together, then passed it to the next worker, who added a few more pieces.

"Man alive!" the visitors exclaimed, "do you expect those parts to fit into any gun? The government will never accept such rifles. Every gunsmith knows that each part has to be individually filed and fitted to each gun!"

Whitney rubbed his hands together, motioned the inspectors to follow him to the end of the other long bench. There was a pile of completed rifles. Whitney took three of them, removed all their parts, and scrambled the pieces together. Then he had an Irish boy put them back together in five minutes flat.

"I still don't believe it," said Inspector Orr in amazement.

"There is some trick. Let me see if I can do it with some other guns," said Inspector Gansevoort.

But the astonished inspectors quickly proved to themselves that they, too, could put the rifles together without filing and fitting the parts. Whitney was not playing tricks on them.

"Wonderful! How on earth is this possible?"

"There are two essentials," Whitney replied blandly. "*Accuracy*. QUALITY."

For the first time in history identical parts had been made, a feat that other manufacturers considered impossible. Whitney had developed special machines to finish the parts cheaply—and with amazing accuracy. One part was just like another to the thousandth of an inch. That accuracy spelled economy, since it eliminated the need for slow hand-filing. Whitney's rifle parts snapped together like the sections of a watch-case cover. Now an army could interchange pieces of weapons at random on the field of battle. They would need only to carry extra parts instead of complete extra rifles.

Quality made it possible for Whitney to make more rifles—and better rifles—at less cost. His pioneering work on quality manufacture marked the birth of modern mass production. It is quality in details that makes mass production possible.

Many people presume that mass production means fast work. What it depends on is accurate work.

Quality Begets Speed

And, with the individual, **emphasis on quality helps get more things done.**

Take learning to use the typewriter, for example. Experiments with beginning typists show that those who aim for speed right from the start do not acquire the most speed in the long run. The ones who get more speed ultimately are those who at the outset direct their attention to accuracy. This is not as paradoxical as it may seem.

Those who emphasize accuracy from the start do not have to make so many erasures and corrections. They *get it right* without backtracking to cover up blunders. They do not form incorrect habits which they will have to break later.

People who are not quality workers have to do many things a second and third time. Of course, they get less done.

The thing to speed up is quality.

Right and Speedy

The old saying "Slow but sure" does not imply that "Fast but inaccurate" is also true. Dozens of experiments and business records show beyond a doubt that the inaccurate worker is the slow worker. The slow learner is the one who has more things wrong—to learn over. Keep the emphasis on being sure, not on being slow.

Get it right, and you'll learn faster.

Keep the quality up, and you'll get more things done and done well.

Keep tabs on your quality rather than on your amount.

Just as the adage "Slow but sure" may be wrongly interpreted, so may the other old adage "A good workman never complains about his tools."

The good workman sees that he has good tools. He emphasizes quality. He keeps his tools sharp and true so they will work properly and get things done accurately. He doesn't complain about them, for he keeps them in perfect condition.

One of Solomon's Proverbs runs, "He that despiseth little things shall perish little by little."

THE FIRST TELEPHONE ENGINEER

Wiry John J. Carty, a Boston Irishman, was fired from his first job, that of messenger boy of all work to a firm that sold electrical novelties. His next was switching telephone calls. Lacking a college education, he trained himself in electrical engineering during his spare moments and for half a century remained with the telephone company.

As chief engineer he was responsible for engineering improvements which extended the range of a long-distance conversation from a line between Boston and Providence to a coast-to-coast hookup. He carried the telephone across the ocean.

And, always, it was quality he emphasized.

"Let's do it right, boys!" he told his assistant engineers. "And then we shan't have any bad dreams."

He also used to indoctrinate his enormous engineering staff with the idea that "the highest form of success is that internal satisfaction which every man can get from doing his absolute best."

ILLUSTRIOUS EXAMPLES

William S. Burroughs, onetime bank clerk who invented the first workable adding machine, did not make his sketches on paper. He etched them accurately in fine lines on metal plates, full-scale. He just naturally emphasized quality.

When he was superintendent of railway mail clerks, Theodore Vail speeded up output by periodically giving special

DO WELL,

AND YOU WILL DO MORE

examinations to test the clerks' accuracy. In sorting mail, he had them emphasize quality.

Georges Buffon, the great naturalist about whom we learned in the preceding chapter, was racked with pain from cancer in middle life. He rewrote his books on natural science eleven times before sending them to the printer, although he had already spent half a century on the subject.

Sir Isaac Newton rewrote some of his books fifteen times before they were set in type. The things he did counted because he emphasized quality.

David Belasco was born in a California cellar, educated in a monastery, and started his career as a bareback rider jumping through flaming hoops. He became the preeminent impresario of the theater because he emphasized quality while other producers were still letting their audiences live on cheap make-believe. When Belasco wanted an actress to give a more realistic scream, he jabbed her unexpectedly with a pin. When his actors were supposed to be eating a meal in the second act, they ate a real meal, piping hot, that the audience could smell. When he did not think his newly painted scenery accurately depicted a house, he chopped it up with an ax.

Belasco rehearsed his plays twice as long and three times as hard as other producers. He took an unknown, unattractive, redheaded, moody, big-nosed Kentucky woman, who had just left her husband, an elderly manufacturer of liver pills, and by emphasis on quality made Mrs. Leslie Carter the rage of the stage for fifteen years. (King Edward VII went to see six performances of one of her plays, cried copiously each time.)

J. C. Penney, one of twelve children of an *un*paid (not merely *under*paid) minister in Missouri, went to the Rockies to cure his tuberculosis. In a twenty-five-foot-wide building on a side street of a small Wyoming coal-mining town, he started a store. He lived in a sloping-roofed attic above the store with his bride. He built that store into a chain of more than 1,500 stores, all of them on main streets. "It is neglect of little things," he said, "not hard luck nor lack of talent, that trips up most men."

Watch quality, and you will not neglect the little things.

Johann Schiller watched quality, though at thirty-two he contracted tuberculosis, from which he never fully recovered. Tall, thin, with hollow cheeks, he worked until four mornings, kept awake by drinking coffee. Before his death at forty-five, this fertile poet said, "Only those who have the patience to do simple things perfectly will acquire the skill to do difficult things easily."

SATISFACTION IN QUALITY

Dwight Morrow was a short, headachy boy who wore his brother-in-law's castoff clothes at college. He entered college with eight conditions against him—not an auspicious start for a man who was to become a Morgan partner, an ambassador, and who was to reject offers of university presidencies. But this Irish lad was a quality worker. "More real satisfaction is to be gotten from the way we do our work than from the work we do," he said.

"I know what pleasure is," remarked Robert Louis Stevenson, "for I have done good work." That is the comment of a craftsman, not a conceited man. Craftsmen get things done because they emphasize quality. Stevenson had been trained in engineering, where accuracy was paramount. As a writer he still kept the engineering ideal. His life was cut short by tuberculosis, but, in the twenty years allotted him for work, his emphasis on quality gave him a permanent place among the front ranks of craftsmen.

Ignatius Loyola did not start grammar school until he was thirty-three, but at forty-three he was busily organizing the Jesuit Order. Later he was placed in the catalogue of saints by Pope Gregory XV. Saint Ignatius wasted half his life before he found himself, but after that self-discovery he emphasized quality and avoided shallowness. "He who does well one work at a time, does more than all," he stated.

Trifling with Perfection

Benjamin West died before the telegraph was invented, yet he helped invent it. A tenth child, he was born prematurely to his Quaker mother in Pennsylvania. Although he did not see a picture until he was six, he became America's first internationally famous painter. He was taught to mix colors by the Indians, and he made his first brushes with hairs plucked from an unwilling cat.

A young Yale graduate went to London to study painting under West, who was then at the Royal Academy. The student made a drawing of the statue of the dying Hercules and showed it to West.

"That is a good start. Go on and finish it," West told him.

"But I thought it was finished," the student answered in surprise.

"Those finger joints are not clear," West said. "And it needs more work here—and here."

A week later the student reported again. The finger joints were now as real as life. "That's an improvement; now go on and finish it."

The youth wanted to break the drawing over his instructor's head. Dejectedly, he toiled for three more days.

"Now you have learned your lesson, and I will not harass you longer," West told him at the end of that time, with a beneficent smile. "It is not the half-finished drawing but one thoroughly finished that makes the craftsman."

That was the way Benjamin West got Samuel F. B. Morse to emphasize quality in his painting.

The lesson later helped Morse develop the telegraph as a side activity to his painting. His first telegraph model worked as soon as he tried it. He had made it by painstaking quality, not fast, furious trial and error.

It was a favorite maxim of Michelangelo that "Trifles make perfection, and perfection is no trifle."

And O. S. Marden's motto, which he picked as a schoolboy and kept in front of him throughout life, was, "Let every occasion be a great occasion, for you cannot tell when Fate may be taking your measure for a larger place."

There is no compromise between quality and speed. Quality brings speed.

Don't half do a job; you may be neglecting the half that is important.

Accuracy is a duty and not a virtue.

—A. E. HOUSMAN

I cannot recall ever starting a job without thinking out how to do it better than it had been done before.

—JOHN EDSON SWEET

15

Doing two things at once

IT IS APPARENTLY a mathematical impossibility to be in two places at the same time, but it is of practical importance to do two things or even more at the same time.

Take Walter, for instance. He started with nothing and at forty was worth a million. Along came the financial depression and wiped him out. Walter was wiped out only, though, not licked. There is a big difference.

He took the reverse on the chin and immediately began to stage a comeback that amazed his acquaintances.

"How on earth does he do it? What is his secret?" they asked each other.

I learned the answer not by asking Walter but by accidentally observing him one spring morning. I was waiting for an appointment in a New York office. I sat idly admiring the pretty receptionist and wondering whether she was a natural blonde.

Walter breezed in. He walked right past me and never noticed I was waiting. But he, too, had to wait a few minutes for his appointment.

"The wait is all right," he told the girl, "if I can just use one of your telephones for some outside calls until Mr. Smith is ready to see me."

No idle daydreaming for him! He didn't seem to notice whether the receptionist was blond or bald. He drew a chair up to her desk and made his business calls, some of them to competitors of the firm whose reception room he was using as his temporary office. And there I was, letting the grass grow around me.

Walter got more accomplished by doing two things at once. **He put his spare time to work.**

Carl Winkler, apprentice machinist who founded the U. S. Machine Corporation, knows how to do two things at once. I was in his office one day autographing a couple of boxes of books he had bought to give his employees. He was talking over long distance, buying several thousand dollars' worth of machinery for his factory. I saw that, while he was busy with his telephone call, he was also busy using his free hand and his eyes to scan and sign a thick pile of letters.

Sir Walter Scott's motto was "Never be doing nothing."

Voltaire's was "Always at work."

Carl Winkler would add **"And do several things at the same time."**

THE SPARE-TIME NAVIGATOR

We have learned in an earlier chapter how the Bowditch boy read an encyclopedia in his spare time. He left school when he was ten to work with his father making wooden barrels. He kept an open book on the bench in front of him and taught himself algebra while he was using his hands at the cooper's trade. Evenings an old sailor talked to him of the simple and inaccurate way in which ships were navigated.

When he began selling ship's supplies, he read the encyclopedia in spare moments on the job and at night.

At twenty-two young Bowditch went to sea; he could find more time on a ship than in the store. When his ship, the *Henry*, was attacked by privateers, he was assigned the job of passing ammunition to the deck. But during the lulls in the fighting he worked problems in his new method of navigation on the powder kegs.

All his life Nathaniel Bowditch was doing two things at the same time. He was not quite thirty years old when he finished his "New American Practical Navigator," the spare-time accomplishment of a busy man. Five years afterwards he declined an appointment to a professorship at Harvard and later turned down similar flattering offers from the University of Virginia and the Military Academy at West Point.

By doing two things at once and investing his spare time, he made himself an insurance actuary and one of the world's leading mathematicians and astronomers.

THE ORIGIN OF SIDEBURNS

Ambrose Burnside was one of a family of nine children who lived in a small Indiana village. He learned the tailor's trade, worked in a busy shop where there was little spare time. But the tall, good-looking Burnside boy soon discovered how to make spare time by doing two things at once.

One day Congressman Caleb Smith came into the tailor shop, saw the boy busy at work with a book propped up against an iron. Heavy tailor shears held the book open, leaving both his hands free to work.

This impressed the congressman, who offered the young tailor an appointment as a cadet at West Point. Ambrose Burnside's ability to do two things at the same time carried him to the rank of major general. He invented a new breech-loading rifle, became treasurer of the Illinois Central Railroad, was three times Governor of Rhode Island, and declined a fourth term.

He found he could also make spare time by shaving only his

chin. The result was the style of whiskers called "sideburns," after Burnside, who was a popular national hero.

EVENING MAGIC

You can't buy time at a store, but you can make more time for yourself without infringing on any patents.

The evening hours, when the bread-and-butter routine of the day is over, offer you the opportunity to do something different, something for your future.

A tallish young Boston lawyer worked evenings for a dozen years preparing a study of the common law; it boosted him on his way to become Justice Oliver Wendell Holmes of the Supreme Court.

A plant engineer worked twelve hours a day for forty-five dollars a month at a Detroit electric company. Nights he worked in an old shed behind his house, while his wife sat on a box watching him. After more than three years of this evening toil, Henry Ford had his first automobile ready to run. At three o'clock one rainy May morning he hung a kerosene lantern on the dashboard, got the one-cylinder engine running, and took his first automobile ride. He went right across his wife's flower bed and smashed the clothesline pole.

John W. Hyatt went to work as a printer at sixteen. He kept his brain busy at other things while he was setting type. He spent his evenings putting together the ideas he hatched during the day. He invented a family knife sharpener, a method of making solid emery wheels, a machine for making billiard balls. With these evening spare-time activities, he laid the foundation for his later invention of celluloid and spiral roller bearings.

PUT YOUR SPARE MOMENTS

AND YOUR SPARE HAND

TO WORK

George Eastman left school to help support his mother when he was fourteen. He became bookkeeper in a bank at Rochester, New York. He invested his spare time in his mother's kitchen, developing the first successful dry plate for photographers. The hundred-million-dollar Eastman Kodak Company was started in that kitchen.

Albert Payson Terhune was six feet two inches tall and built proportionately. He liked boxing, took boxing lessons, and seriously considered becoming a prize fighter. But, at thirty-two, he was working in a newspaper office nine hours a day and getting nowhere. He decided he was a lazy failure and must make a big change in his life if he was to get anywhere. He recalled his training as a boxer, figured he must force an opening, just as he had been trained to do in the fight ring. So he started working for himself five hours a night, five nights a week. That was his beginning as a famous author who was to receive as much as $2,500 for a simple dog story.

Henrik's father lost his business and moved with the eight-year-old son to a dilapidated farmhouse on the edge of town. At fifteen the son was taken from school, told to get rid of his silly artistic notions, and sent to work with a druggist in a melancholy little town on the southeastern coast of Norway. He was hemmed in by the hills around that village for six years. Hemmed in? Well, not exactly. His workday in the smelly shop was long, but, after the store closed evenings, he lost little time in climbing to the garret room above the shop. There he was secretly writing. In two years he had finished—at twenty— a three-act tragedy. He went to Christiana to get a producer for it. No producer wanted it. So he published it as a small book. The book sold thirty copies.

But, when Henrik Ibsen was in middle life, a famed playwright and director of the National Theatre, this attic-written tragedy, "Catilina," was at last produced and raised from its years of obscurity. Those youthful, productive evenings in the attic kept Henrik Ibsen from spending his life unhappily as a poor prescription compounder on an isolated seacoast.

Morning Magic

Perhaps you have no spare time in which to work for yourself evenings. Such was the case with Dr. Samuel G. Howe, who revolutionized the care and treatment of the blind, deaf, feebleminded, and insane. Dr. Howe made spare time for himself by getting up several hours before breakfast. He got more things done because he started work at four every morning. He followed the admonition "Arise, therefore, and be doing."

Betty Smith had what many would call a full-time job. She was keeping house and helping her two daughters through the university. Yet she made enough spare time mornings, between six and seven, to write a story she had long wanted to tell. The house was quiet then, and she could work without being distracted. In two years her book, "A Tree Grows in Brooklyn," was finished. Its great sale made publishing history; its earnings made it possible for Betty Smith to forget financial worries.

Emile Berliner, spending his days in a Washington dry-goods store, made spare time by getting up before sunrise to work for himself; he invented the microphone into which we speak when using the telephone.

Old sailors have a saying, "In rough weather you should use one hand for the ship, one for yourself." The sailor who does not steady himself with one hand may be washed off the deck or tossed from the rigging. People who make extra time for themselves and use that time to advantage sail through life more smoothly.

Odd Moments Add up Rapidly

One has many opportunities for investing odd moments right on the job. One of Einstein's first positions took him as patent examiner to Berne, Switzerland. It was a dull, routine job, with many idle moments he could have spent visiting the other examiners. But the short young man with the dark, rumpled hair invested those moments developing the first of his papers on relativity. The atomic bomb which brought the Second World War to an end was a practical application of the theories he originated.

Twenty-one-year-old Joseph Lockyer also had a routine job —in the London War Office. During slack moments he read scientific books, particularly books on astronomy. Soon he was no longer an office clerk but an astronomer. He became director of the Solar Physics Laboratory and Sir Joseph. He was the first to discover helium in the sun.

Thomas Huxley used his spare time on the job to change the course of his life, too. A young physician just out of medical school, he became a naval doctor. He was assigned to *H.M.S. Rattlesnake*—awesome name!—which was starting a prolonged cruise to explore the seas around Australia. John MacGillivray, son of a distinguished Scotch naturalist, was the scientific chief of the expedition.

Slender Huxley, with his fiercely serious face, had little to do as ship's doctor. He might have made the cruise into a mere pleasure trip. But, serious as his expression, he took advantage of his situation to do two things at once.

He offered to help the professional naturalist, but the gruff Scotchman told him to stick to his pills. Huxley kept his thoughts to himself and also his spare time. He devised a towing net in which he caught rare specimens of marine life. He studied the strange creatures minutely, accurately, and began to understand the principles that governed their strangeness.

The official naturalist of the voyage simply pickled his odd specimens and sent them home as curiosities. Huxley studied his, intent on discovering the reasons for their weird shapes. For four years he continued studying in his spare time on shipboard. He sent several reports on his findings back to naturalists in England and, upon his return, was astonished to find the scientists talking about his discoveries.

No longer an obscure young physician, at twenty-seven he was awarded the medal of the Royal Society. The scientists ignored MacGillivray, who had spent his odd moments at card games with the ship officers.

Huxley dropped his medical work, became a full-time naturalist and one of the most prominent of his day. To the end of his life, he always invested his spare time.

And, in Dayton, Ohio, the two bachelor Wright brothers took advantage of a seasonal slack in their bicycle-repair shop to build the world's first successful airplane.

Odd moments add up rapidly to give large amounts of time. "Many a mickle makes a muckle," says the old Scotch proverb.

Taking an hour off is easy; the difficulty is putting it back.

Thieves of Time

Constantly improving factory and office methods, better transportation and more home appliances are giving the world more and more spare time with each passing year. The work week gets shorter; farm and home work is now finished sooner than formerly.

Extra time is literally being showered down on us, but we have to collect the droplets and use them before they run away.

There are many people who are unable to meet the emergencies this spare time brings to their lives. They can withstand anything except leisure, spending it on what the French call "The Street of Lost Time."

There is one personal problem in connection with leisure: how to keep others from using our spare time. Remember John Ruskin, who asked his friends to consider him dead for a few months when he wanted to work? That was about the only spunk he showed in the fitful yet creative life that his mother nearly ruined.

Thieves of another man's time ought to be whipped. Avoid them like the plague, even if they are entertaining companions.

Napoleon used to tell such people, "Ask me for anything but time."

And, in Arthur Brisbane's office, a large sign warned stallers, "Five minutes is a long time."

Edwin Forrest bluntly exclaimed to an actor who was late for rehearsal, "Sir! You are late. You have taken from these ladies and gentlemen that which Almighty God Himself could not restore to them—their time!"

"Idleness," said Jeremy Taylor, "is the burial of a living man."

Put Both Hands to Work

Are you right-handed? Twenty-four people out of twenty-five are.

The twenty-fifth person is left-handed. Women are seldom left-handed.

Yet everyone, whether right- or left-handed, uses his other hand regularly for minor tasks. **The best helping hand you can find is your other hand.**

In eating, for instance (which is not a minor task for all), both hands are used, though one hand may do most of the work. Dressing requires the cooperation of both hands, especially when tying a necktie. Violinists and typists use both hands; in fact, the typewriter keyboard gives the left hand about half again as much work as the right hand. The skilled housekeeper dusts with both hands and uses both together in the kitchen.

Much of our modern improvement in factory productivity is due to application of the principle that only half a man is at work when only one hand is used on a job. Assembly and machine operations are now arranged so both hands are kept busy.

While we are all a little ambidextrous in many things, there are a few persons—perhaps one out of every 500—who can use either hand or both hands with equal facility.

Leonardo da Vinci is the most famous example of a person who had the natural ability to use both hands simultaneously, or to do work as finely with his left hand as with his right. Baden-Powell, founder of the Boy Scouts, Edwin Lanseer, artist, Edward S. Morse, naturalist, and Dwight Morrow, financier-statesman, were all ambidextrous. So was frog-jawed Irving S. Cobb, the humorist.

They Learned to Use Both Hands

There are other famous examples of people who have exerted effort to LEARN TO USE EITHER HAND with equal skill in order to get more things done. They were not going to let one hand remain idle.

Maybe right-handedness is born in one, maybe not. Scientists do not know for certain. But they do know that people who want to get things done can usually make themselves use either hand until they have such facility with both that it is difficult to decide whether they were originally right- or left-handed.

It is a different story, though, when parents try to make a left-handed child conventionally right-handed, punishing it for using the left hand. I was "born" left-handed, and my early schoolteachers tried to made me right-handed without success. Later in life I lost part of a left finger in a laboratory accident and, while that hand was useless, began to make myself partially ambidextrous. I did not discontinue the use of my left hand, however. I merely used my right more and used both hands in coordination whenever possible.

In Plato's plan for his ideal new Republic he stated that all persons should be taught to use both hands. An unpopular provision, though one that would doubtless have enabled the citizens to accomplish more!

When Sir James Barrie's right hand gave out, he practiced writing with his left to keep up his work. By the time he had recovered the use of his right hand, he had so much skill with his left that from then on he used both simultaneously. He would work at a play sitting between two tables placed at right angles to each other. With his right hand he would write dialogue on one table, while, with his left, he would write stage directions on the other.

Consider another Scotchman, Patrick Nasmyth, who played truant from school to sketch in the fields around Edinburgh. Boyhood accidents made him prematurely deaf and deprived him of the natural use of his right hand. He forced himself to learn to use his left hand and became a famous painter of countryside life and scenes.

His brother, James Nasmyth, was "naturally" left-handed. His parents tried to prevent him from using his left hand. But the son, wiser than his elders, insisted not only on retaining the skill of his left hand but also on learning to use his right. He made himself ambidextrous, became a leading engineer, and invented the steam hammer.

Robert Ripley, of "Believe It or Not" fame, persisted in drawing despite his father's objections. "Artists starve to death," his carpenter father exclaimed. "Learn to drive a nail and pay the rent." The son was just getting his famous informative cartoon series established when his right arm was shattered in an accident. The doctor told him it would be at least a month before he could draw again with his right hand. So, painstakingly, he began to draw with his left, and the eighty million readers of his daily cartoon did not know the difference.

It was a case of love combined with blood poisoning in the right arm that made the naturalist Edward S. Morse become skilled in the use of both hands. He was twenty-three at the time, devoting himself to science, despite the protests of his father. When the poisoning rendered his right hand temporarily useless, he wrote daily love letters of two-dozen pages with his previously unused left hand. By the time the poisoning was gone, he could write well and easily with either hand and did so for the rest of his life. His famous drawings of sea shells and Japanese pottery were made with either hand; often he used both hands simultaneously. In Chap. 11 we learned how he tossed a coin to decide where his brain should go after his death; it was partly on account of his acquired ambidexterity that two research institutions wanted to study it. And, let it be added, those long love letters, written laboriously with the left hand, helped him win his girl!

John James Audubon failed as a New Orleans merchant. He started a sawmill in Tennessee; that failed, too. Then, an event apparently worse than failure, he seriously injured his right hand in the sawmill. He forced himself to use his left hand, drew portraits of his friends in black chalk. His later, world-famous paintings of birds were drawn with both hands.

Nikola Tesla, six feet two inches and built like a bean pole, gave the world alternating electrical current though his mother could neither read nor write and his professor at the Gratz Polytechnic Institute had "proved" alternating current impossible. Tesla was "naturally" left-handed. At the age of ten he found this a handicap in a freehand-drawing course which he disliked. But he made himself learn right then to use his right hand and retained the almost equal use of both hands throughout life.

As a boy, Raymond Ditmars went without lunch at school so he could save up his lunch money to buy a snake. Then he decided he was going to military academy and become a general. To provide for the possibility of his right hand being shot off, he began to use his left hand and was soon ambidextrous. He never went to military academy. Instead he became a naturalist specializing in reptiles, and when only twenty-one started the Reptile House at the New York Zoological Park. That skill he had acquired in using both hands equally was literally a life-saver when he was catching poisonous snakes in the Florida swamps.

TWO-FISTED MEDICAL MEN

Physicians and, particularly, surgeons must be able to work quickly and surely with both hands. Ability to use both hands may save them minutes that mean the difference between a life saved and a life lost.

Dr. Charles E. Brown-Sequard, father of the modern study of glands and hormones, was "naturally" left-handed. He made himself learn to use his right hand too in laboratory and surgery. H. MacNaughton Jones, famed English surgeon, also forced himself to learn to operate with either or both hands.

Dr. Chevalier Jackson, inventor of the bronchoscope, is well known for his dexterous use of both hands, developed intentionally since boyhood. He advocates that children be taught to use both hands with equal facility.

It is a common sight in the internes' quarters of any large hospital to see an eager, young, right-handed physician shaving a glass bottle with his left hand, in order to develop razor-sensitive skill in both, or practicing surgical knots using first the right hand, then the left.

Speaking of shaving the bottle reminds us that Frank Gilbreth, originator of the idea of work-simplifying motion in factories, practiced what he preached; he learned to shave himself using two old-fashioned straightedge razors simultaneously. Simon Bolivar, the undersized millionaire who lost his money and became the liberator of South America, not only held his razor readily in either hand but also his sword and gun.

And, speaking of two-fisted surgeons, we should give some recognition to the great skill possessed by our old frontier gunmen. There was redheaded James Butler Hickok, for instance. He stood six feet two in his boots, which he never removed. How he got the frontier name of "Wild Bill" is not known; there were others much wilder. None was a better marksman, though. He started shooting at eight, trained himself to use either hand, and as a result lived longer. Once, when ambushed by four cowpunchers in southern Nebraska, a shot passed through Wild Bill's right arm. He instantly switched his gun to the left hand and brought down three of his attackers. The only way a man with such ambidexterity could be bested was from behind; he was finally shot in the back of the head while enjoying a card game.

More saintly warriors than Wild Bill Hickok have profited by being able to fight with both hands. In the twelfth chapter of *Chronicles*, we read about the army King David raised to do battle with King Saul. "They were armed with bows, and could use both the right hand and the left in hurling stones and shooting arrows out of a bow." King David's ambidextrous warriors were, of course, the victors.

Franklin's Petition

Franklin wanted educators to train children to make more use of the left hand. Here is the clever but still unheeded petition he addressed to the teachers and parents of the world.

I address myself to all the friends of youth, in order to remove the prejudices of which I am the victim. There are twin sisters of us; and the two eyes of man do not more resemble, nor are capable of being upon better terms with each other than my sister and myself, were it not for the partiality of our parents, who made the most injurious distinction between us. I was suffered to grow up without the least instruction, while nothing was spared in her education. More than once I have been beaten for being awkward. It is true, my sister associated with me upon some occasions; but she always made a point of taking the lead, calling upon me only from necessity.

It is the practice of our family, that the whole business of providing for its subsistence falls upon my sister and myself. If any indisposition should attack my sister, what would be the fate of our poor family? Alas! we must perish from distress; for it would not be in my power even to scrawl a supplicant petition for relief, having been obliged to employ the hand of another in transcribing the request which I have now the honor to prefer to you.

Condescend, sir, to make my parents sensible of the injustice of an exclusive tenderness, and of the necessity of distributing their care and affection among all their children equally.

I am, with profound respect, Sirs,

Your obedient servant,

THE LEFT HAND

MORE WRITING—QUICKER

You probably save some time in making notes by writing "&" in place of spelling out "a-n-d." That common symbol "&" is part of the shorthand system invented by Marcus Tiro. It was back around the year 60 B.C. that the Roman public asked for a record of the rapid-fire speeches of the great Cicero. Tiro devised a laborsaving and timesaving system of shorthand to take down these orations. His system was so useful that for several centuries it was taught in the schools of Rome.

In the intervening twenty centuries shorthand of one system or another has helped many businessmen and scientists get more things done. It saves time for them and helps them make more complete notes with less effort.

Dwarfish Steinmetz, the electrical wizard only four feet tall, taught himself a Swedish system of shorthand while still a student in the University of Breslau. This system was not speedy enough to please him, so he improved on it. A few years later he devised an entirely new system that he used the rest of his life. Although his unique system was a handicap if others wanted to read his notes, he used the system not for secrecy but to get more things done.

Hugh Callendar, the physicist who invented the platinum-wire thermometer, also invented a new system of shorthand to speed up his work. He measured the time necessary to write various symbols and saved only the speediest for his system. He became a Fellow of the Royal Society.

Another physicist, and a colleague of Dr. Callendar's, was Sir Joseph Thomson. He was attracted to Dr. Callendar's system as a way to get more things done. And, although Sir Joseph was in middle age at the time, he learned the system like any schoolboy. He was later awarded a Nobel prize for his discoveries in physics.

Timothy Dwight, early president of Yale University, also invented his own system. His scheme was largely an abbreviated language akin to the codes used by air lines or to the abbreviations used by physicians and nurses.

Clarence Birdseye, office boy, found a shorthand book on the sidewalks of New York. He studied it, bought a more advanced book, and for half a century used shorthand in his scientific work. He is the man who developed the first quick-frozen foods.

Dr. Morris Fishbein, major-domo of the American Medical Association for more than a quarter century, studied shorthand during his senior year in high school in Indianapolis. He thought it would help him in his medical studies. He continued to use it throughout life, often giving notes to his secretaries in shorthand.

One summer while tending the bar in his father's crossroads hotel, Frank Gannett taught himself shorthand during the dull moments between customers. That fall he entered Cornell University with total cash resources of $80. He graduated with a handle-bar mustache and $1,000 in cash. With this $1,000 start he built a series of daily newspapers worth some eighteen million dollars. His shorthand pothooks and curlicues were used almost every hour of the day in his business climb.

Financial reverses in Holland forced the Bok family to America when Edward was still a small lad. As an office boy, he decided shorthand would help him, so he enrolled in a course at the Y.M.C.A. But he wanted to learn faster, so he enrolled at the same time for the same course in a business school. He used shorthand the rest of his life, from the time he organized one of the first newspaper syndicates at the age of twenty-three through his editorship of the *Ladies' Home Journal* and his foundation of the American Peace Award.

John Muir's father was a silent man who deserted his wife and six small children. While working for a garment firm, left-handed, redheaded John took a night course in shorthand. Of the dozen who started in the class, he was the only one to complete the course. He practiced by taking down sermons and conversations he overheard. Using his shorthand to help get more things done, he climbed through the railroad ranks, became a member of the New York Stock Exchange, and originated odd-lot trading and the baby bonds of the First World War.

Another youngster practiced his shorthand in church. This was Raymond Ditmars, who was destined to make himself a world authority on reptiles. He took his shorthand notebook with him to St. Andrew's Church in New York City and sat in the first row directly in front of the minister. During the prayer he reverently refrained from taking notes but noticed that the minister opened one eye to see if he were recording the prayer.

William Lever, who built the world-wide Lever business from his father's small grocery firm, learned shorthand early in his business life. Later, as head of a business that spread over two-dozen countries, he was up before dawn using shorthand to complete two or three hours of work before his seven-thirty breakfast.

Thomas W. Wilson, a young Georgia lawyer, taught himself shorthand so he could take more complete notes in court. His famous book, "The History of the American People," was written first in shorthand. When he moved into the White House, as President Woodrow Wilson, most of his speeches and state papers were composed in the same shorthand. And his shorthand signature appears on his seal on the peace documents of the First World War. Here is the story: When he married Edith Bolling, the state of California sent a nugget of gold to be made into wedding rings. For his signet ring made from this gold Wilson designed a monogram out of the shorthand characters that spelled his name. This Arabic-appearing design was stamped into the seals of the documents when Wilson pressed the monogram into the hot wax.

James Byrnes was a small boy in South Carolina when his father died. Jimmie's earliest memories are of delivering dresses for his mother, who supported the family by doing sewing. She encouraged him to learn shorthand. That was his start as a lawyer, for soon he was a court stenographer. Up he went, still using shorthand, to United States Senator, Supreme Court Justice, then Secretary of State. The only records of many of the conversations of Churchill, Roosevelt, and Stalin are in James Byrnes's stenographic notes of their momentous conferences.

George Bernard Shaw learned shorthand early in life, also. He always carried a notebook and pencil and wrote in shorthand while he took walks. When he was eighty, he said, "My longhand notes show senile decay, but my shorthand does not. I can write shorthand while walking along the road, or while riding on a train. I work in the open air whenever possible. In this way I combine exercise with composition."

John Wesley, smallish son of a family of nineteen children, also did two things at the same time—and also used shorthand to speed up his accomplishments. He wrote his sermons and plans for Methodism in shorthand while riding on horseback from one city to another. He founded the modern Methodist

Church, though he parted his hair in the middle like a bartender.

Emil Ludwig, an eye specialist's son, taught himself shorthand and used it even while shaving. He became one of the world's best-known biographers.

Another writer, Charles Dickens, spent his entire savings as a young man to buy a secondhand course on shorthand. For a while he made his living as a shorthand reporter, but he later used his shorthand to facilitate his work as an author.

More convincing to me than such stories is my own experience in the usefulness of shorthand in getting more things done. I must confess that I use a "hunt-and-pick" variety. It started during my college days when I wanted to save time in writing laboratory notes and to have more complete notes. First I tried to invent a system of my own, but I was a poor inventor. Then I found a standard shorthand manual from which I learned the more common symbols. Ever since my writing has been a combination of longhand and shorthand and a great timesaver and work expediter.

Shorthand does not exactly put the other hand to work. But it does get more work out of one hand in the same time and is often as good as doing two or even three things at the same time.

Put your other hand to work. The result will be one further illustration that you can do more than you realize if you will only force yourself to try more.

Your work will become easier, too, when you use the other hand more.

Put the other half of your body to work.

Put the other half of your P. T. to work.

It's those who keep everlastingly at it, who actively invest their P. T., that get things done.

It is by their use of P. T. that professionals can be distinguished from amateurs, the Achievers separated from the Almosts. Elizabeth Davis is a skilled pianist who specializes in accompaniments for vocal artists. She has worked with top-flight opera stars and would-be society sopranos.

"The professional singers," she says, "were eager to take advantage of every precious moment."

P. T. means "Precious Time."

Time is my estate.

—GOETHE

No person will have occasion to complain of the want of time who never loses any.

—THOMAS JEFFERSON

You will never "find" time for anything. If you want time, you must make it.

—CHARLES BUXTON

A wise man will make more opportunities than he finds.

—BACON

16

The best place to work

THE MOST embarrassing self-survey I ever made, and I've made lots of them, was one New Year's Day when I counted the BLANK SPACES I had left in my life the day before. Most of the blank spaces were not my fault; but it was my neglect that I had not realized they were good places to get things done.

The traffic snarl that held me up a few moments was not my fault. But when Noel Coward was caught in a taxicab by a traffic jam he wrote his popular song, "I'll See You Again."

Nor did Arthur Brisbane let a traffic delay make a blank space in his life. He dictated his famous editorials into a dictating machine he carried in his automobile or read an encyclopedia that was part of the automobile's equipment. So now I always carry a book in my automobile, and one blank space in my life has been eliminated.

I had not looked upon time spent in the bath tub as a blank space until I learned that William Osler, the great physician, read while he soaked himself. Stocky Enrico Caruso, at the height of his fame, rehearsed while taking a bath; an accompanist played a piano just outside the door. And didn't Archimedes discover how to determine the purity of the gold in King Hiero's crown while he was deep in water and active thought at the same time? So now I review facts I have recently read and want to remember or the names and faces of people I have recently met while lathering and showering. (Frederick the Great kept bath time from making a blank space in his life by going for years and years without washing himself.)

Shaving I had previously decided was a waste of time, so grew a set of whiskers. But perhaps I was hasty in doing this. Emil Ludwig, the biographer, works while he shaves. He keeps a note pad near his shaving mirror and jots down his shaving ideas.

Theodore Roosevelt conducted conferences as he was shaved by the White House barber.

The time spent dressing is apparently unavoidable, but I also learned it need not be a blank space. Bewhiskered George Bernard Shaw reads standing up while dressing and undressing. And fat, rheumatic Catherine de Medici, oblivious to all modesty, gave audiences on state business while she was dressing.

Redheaded, diminutive Sarah Bernhardt was another woman dynamo of energy who got things done. Always in a hurry, she always used her time well. Modesty did not prevent her from making stage plans with managers and authors while she was in her bath tub; as a concession to modesty, however, she sprinkled powdered starch in the water to make it opaque, which gave rise to the legend that she bathed in milk.

Dressing, like shaving, may keep both your hands busy, but you can always use your head to think.

Eating also seems to be unavoidable, but mealtime need not be a blank space. In monasteries the monks meditate or take turns reading aloud. Big-nosed Charlemagne had books read to him at meals though he was no monk—merely an obscure king from an unknown birthplace who founded the Holy Roman Empire.

Johann Strauss, the waltz king, wrote his "Acceleration Waltzes" on the back of a menu card while eating in a Vienna restaurant. He did not allow blank spaces in his life, and his wife finally left him because he wrote music at the dinner table instead of encouraging her idle gossip.

Traffic jams, bathrooms, meal tables are all good places to work with one's head.

And may I add here, without the knowledge of Eleanor C. Laird, that people can work in bed—when they have the determination. When the proofs for this book were arriving from the publisher, she was confined flat in bed for several months, after a spinal fusion operation. But she insisted on reading the proofs which had to be held upside down while she studied through them for misprints. "If Clara Barton and Pamela Cunningham and all those others could work while they were incapacitated, I can at least try," she said. And she took further advantage of her condition by learning Chinese from Fei-Bik Yap and Yin-Suan King. (I hope she forgives me for telling this tale out of school, but it is evidence of how the stories told in this book do things to people.)

Kitchen Workers

This college president baked bread. Mary Lyon, who, single-handed, started Mount Holyoke College, personally baked the college bread during the first lean years of the institution. She made more than bread while sitting beside the hot ovens. She kept a portable writing table near her and buried her long nose in the college correspondence, answering letters in her own handwriting, while the bread browned.

Harriet Beecher Stowe had an absent-minded college professor for a husband and a large family to care for. There were boarders, too, but she did not have kitchen help. A neighbor came into her Maine kitchen one day and found her kneading bread dough, holding a pencil between her teeth. She was writing a book in the blank spaces of her kitchen work, a book which freed her from kitchen work, "Uncle Tom's Cabin."

Working While You Walk

Short John Wesley parted his hair in the middle. He founded the Methodist Church, walked twenty-five miles a day from one congregation to another. He read as he traveled, possibly to forget his nagging wife. While he walked he made notes—in shorthand to save more time. He kept the blank spaces out of his life in this and similar ways for half a century or longer.

Rufus Choate was on his own at nine after his father's death. He made himself a leader in the legal profession, this tall, gaunt man who loved to read and walk. He combined his loves by reading as he walked.

"The best story teller that ever lived," they said of Thomas Macaulay. He was a blond, fat bachelor who persistently cut himself while shaving. Perhaps clumsiness with the razor caused the nicks, or it may have been his habit of doing two things at once. He read while he walked, and he walked a great deal. He had a dual career as statesman and writer.

Cornelia Chase Brant was thirty-six, married, and had three children when she decided to study medicine. This slender, dark-eyed wife kept up her housework and carried on her medical studies at the same time by using the otherwise blank spaces in her life. She cut her thick anatomy book into sections small enough to carry in her handbag and studied on the subway or while waiting for her turn at the grocer's. Eventually she graduated with the best grades in her class, became dean of the New York Medical College and Hospital for Women.

Other boys rode or walked to the small Ohio school, but seven-year-old Clarence DeMar went at a dogtrot to and from school. Later, when he went to the University of Vermont, he worked his way through doing odd jobs. He went from job to job at a dog trot—and not just to save time or keep warm either. At twenty-one he became a printer in Boston, ran to and from work, a total of seven to fourteen miles each day. Strangers occasionally stopped him, offered him dimes for carfare. But for twenty years his trotting to and from work kept DeMar the greatest marathon runner of recent years. Seven times he won the Patriot's Day marathons and, at the age of fifty, was still a first-class competitor. The hours going to and from work were not blank spaces for him.

IMPROVISED LABORATORIES

William Beaumont was not discouraged because he lacked a well-equipped place to work. He was a Connecticut Yankee and country physician who became an Army surgeon because he needed a regular income.

One day a drunk French-Canadian half-breed was brought to him. A gaping gunshot wound through the man's abdominal wall exposed the interior of his stomach. Beaumont recognized this as a rare opportunity to study the stomach in action and discover what happens in digestion.

With primitive equipment and with only his small army salary to draw on, he kept the half-breed near him for years. As Beaumont moved from one army post to another, he took the half-breed along, paying his "human test tube" a small wage for the privilege of watching his digestion through the open wound in his belly wall.

From his observations, Beaumont wrote the famous "Experiments and Observations on the Gastric Juice and the Physiology of Digestion," which is considered the greatest single contribution to human knowledge on the subject of the stomach's functioning.

Medical societies are now named in honor of Beaumont, a backwoods physician who did epoch-making work in spare moments, in kitchens and sheds, on an illiterate man who usually had to be sobered up from an alcoholic debauch before the observations could be made. *Any place* was a GOOD WORKPLACE to William Beaumont.

THE NEWLYWEDS IN A SHED

David Bruce, an Australian boy just graduated from Edinburgh Medical School, was mouse-poor and deeply in love. So he, too, became an Army physician to have a regular salary of $1,000 a year on which to get married. The medical service's gruff director disregarded Bruce's request for a specific station. Instead, he promptly shipped the young fellow and his bride off to the garrison at Malta.

The strong island of Malta was a dreaded post. A mysterious disease flourished there. It gave even the strongest men headaches, pains in the lower back, fever that came and went, sweating, and growing weakness. Treatment for this so-called Malta fever was as unknown as its cause.

Bruce found an abandoned shack near the post and, in odd moments when he was not consoling sufferers of the fever, started experiments to discover what it was. The Army not only gave him no assistance but also objected to his work. Obstinate young Bruce went ahead anyway, regardless of official scruples.

He got his wife to help him. From their $1,000 salary they bought monkeys at $1.75 each, into which they injected sick soldiers' blood. The sickened monkeys bit Mrs. Bruce, but fortunately she did not get the Malta disease. That made them revise their theories about the transmission of the sickness. They tested other theories in their shed. Then the infuriated Army ordered Bruce away, and the newlywed scientists were torn from their little laboratory.

But the quest they had started in that shed at Malta did not

KEEP BLANK SPACES OUT OF
YOUR LIFE BY WORKING
ANY PLACE, ANY TIME

end. When Bruce was thirty-two years old, they discovered a new bacteria in the form of short, oval rods, as immobile as Gibraltar itself. They found these in milk and in the blood of Malta-fever sufferers. They made crucial tests and saw that the mysterious fever came from milk. Then they found diseases that resembled Malta fever in other localities, in each case accompanied by the short, oval bacteria in the milk.

These bacteria have been named *Brucella*, in honor of the Bruces. The search that was started in an unfriendly shed, with scant equipment, showed the cause not only of Malta fever but of undulant fever, mountain fever, and a dozen other related fevers as well, which medicos now lump together under the name of brucellosis, the fevers solved by Sir David Bruce, who discovered first that *any place* is A GOOD PLACE TO WORK if one really wants to work.

THE RADIUM SHED

Think of another famous couple who made their fame in another deserted shed, Pierre and Marie Curie, the discoverers of radium. Marie did her preliminary experiments in an unused storeroom in the basement of the School of Physics. It was a dark, damp room. The moisture was hard on instruments as well as humans.

There she worked on the unknown rays given off by uranium, with the temperature often as low as 44 degrees and no way to keep warm.

Then the Curies started their big, joint work, using refuse pitchblende from the St. Joachimstahl mines in Bohemia. The basement room was not large enough for this new labor. But they did not wait until a comfortable place could be built to house their great discovery. Instead, they moved at once into an abandoned shed behind the school.

It was a wooden shack with a leaky roof. The floor was the ground itself. The old potbellied stove did not heat the shed in winter; the wind and cold swept in too fiercely through the large cracks. The dirty skylights intensified the heat that beat down on it in summer. The Curies had to build covers for their instruments to protect them from the rain that leaked through the roof at all seasons.

It was a discouraging place in which they worked, day in, day out, for four intense years to trace down the world's first radium from a ton of discarded pitchblende. It was a good workplace, however, since they had work they wanted intensely to do. **It is the work not the place that makes a workplace.**

THE DISCOVERIES ON THE SIDE PORCH

Emmy Koch was complaining. Her round-headed husband, Robert, was neglecting his medical practice in the small village of Woolstein in eastern Germany. Little wonder he had few patients! He was more interested in his new microscope. "Wasting his time," Emmy called it, as she shooed him and his microscope slides out of the kitchen. He looked at things with the worst smells! Why had she ever given him that microscope on his twenty-ninth birthday? she wondered.

Shoved out of the kitchen, Robert Koch rigged up a place to work with his microscope and foul-smelling specimens on the side porch.

When he went to call on a patient, he often never reached the sickbed. For on the way his nearsighted eyes would see a dead sheep or cow beside the road. That year they were falling like flies. Small sores or carbuncles would appear on an animal, and in a couple days it would collapse and die. Sometimes this puzzling disease, anthrax, would infect humans.

Robert Koch could not pass an anthrax-killed animal on the roadside. He would load it on his vehicle and turn back to his side-porch laboratory, forgetting the ailing human he had set out to examine.

He admittedly neglected his medical practice, but he was not wasting time on that makeshift side porch. By the age of thirty-three he had discovered and proved the cause of anthrax beyond doubt. Then he got a better laboratory. He was not yet forty when he discovered the tubercle bacillus and proved it to be the cause of tuberculosis.

He had to wait until he was past sixty before the Nobel prize caught up with him, this man who did as important work in his porch laboratory as he did later at the University of Berlin. There, as director of the Institute of Hygiene, he was given every facility he desired. But, back on the Woolstein porch, he already had the most vital equipment for getting things done, the intense desire to do them.

THE QUIET MONK

Robert Koch was the father of bacteriology. Now meet Gregor Mendel, the father of genetics, or the science of heredity.

Plump Gregor was raised on a poverty-stricken farm in Austria. His father could devote only part of his time to the farm, because he was forced to work three days each week on public works for which he received no pay. Gregor helped him plant seeds and harvest ripened crops, even when they were scarcely worth the harvesting. Every grain and seed was precious in that family.

Quiet Gregor felt called to the priesthood but failed when he was installed in a parish. He was too tenderhearted to stand the calls he had to make on the poor, the sick, and the dying. So, at twenty-eight, he was transferred to a monastery as a teacher. As he failed to pass the examination for a teacher's license, he served as an extra teacher only.

At thirty-four he again took a teacher's examination and once more did not pass it. So he had to remain an extra teacher at the Brunn monastery, smoking the twenty cigars a day he hoped would keep his weight down.

Discouraged? Perhaps. But he had a small plot, thirty by seven feet, for a garden, and that he enjoyed. Denied the right to be a regular teacher, he now began to study seeds, which had interested him since he was a boy.

For eight years he experimented with crosses of ordinary garden peas in the shadows of the plain, gray monastery walls. For eight years he kept detailed notes of the color and size of the peas grown from each crossing. He smoked his cigars and dreamed about what would happen to the seeds next year and the next.

Then came a winter night that Gregor thought important but that the world overlooked for thirty-five years. On that night he nervously read a report of scarcely a dozen pages in which he told about his experiments on the heredity of garden peas. Members of the Brunn Natural History Society gave him silent attention, then perfunctory applause. The local physicians and professional men who constituted the society thought it fitting to encourage the humble monk, though privately they believed he was puttering his time away on peas; peas were to be eaten, not studied. They did not discuss his little report and promptly forgot all about it.

But, fortunately for science, the report was published along with some other papers the society thought were really important—it didn't want to slight the monastery, you know. About 120 copies of the resulting book were printed, and it was sent to a few large libraries to be indexed and forgotten.

Gregor Mendel went back to his monastery duties, worked faithfully, and in due course died, thinking he had never made a stir in the world.

Sixteen years after his death, thirty-five years after he read his little report on *Experiments in Plant-Hybridization*, it was rediscovered by scientists who were investigating heredity. In the long-buried pages they found the key that unlocked the mysteries of genetics. For nearly a century now, Mendel's opinions on dominant and recessive traits in inheritance have stood unchallenged. They are the basis for all scientific work in heredity, these findings of a plump monk who toiled with nothing but a tiny parcel of earth and a handful of pea seeds but who did not let meager facilities nor failure in examinations discourage him. **His work was where he was.** He did not wait for a better place to work. Only an extra teacher, but he did an extraordinary job!

"Shiftless" Morse

The Reverend Jebediah Morse had eleven children. Only three lived through infancy, all boys. The favorite son was called Finley. He graduated from Yale, undecided whether to be a scientist or a painter. He went through life without deciding and is consequently known as both. But it was his invention in

The Best Place to Work   243

an unused, fifth-floor room that won him election to the Hall of Fame.

He first tried to make a living by painting small portraits and large historical scenes. The small ones he sold cheaply. The big ones were a drug on the market. His income was precarious, so his wife stayed with his parents while she waited for him to get established. But she died at twenty-five and had been buried a week before her husband could reach home.

Sandwiched in between paintings Finley invented a fire pump and a marble-cutting machine. But these did not make a living for him. Then he got his idea for a telegraph. He was forty-one, a widower, and broke. Ability and an idea were all he had.

Where could he find a place to work on the model of his telegraph-instrument idea? His more prosperous brothers lent him a room on the fifth floor of their building at Nassau and Beekman Streets. He slept on a cot in this room and hid the cot during the day so his visitors would not discover his poverty.

He cooked his meals in this room, too, bringing back small amounts of food at a time so his friends would not see him carrying it into the building.

He used an old picture frame, gear wheels from a broken clock, pieces of carpet binding, and other odds and ends to make the first model telegraph set.

The janitor said Samuel Finley Breeze Morse was rather shiftless and wasted his time over some funny machine.

The "shiftless" man was, in truth, a determined man, doing his best to work with what facilities he could get. He worked regardless of location or equipment, and did not allow his days to become blank spaces while waiting for better working facilities to turn up.

OFFICES IN HATS

Any place can make a good workplace for the person who wants to work or who has to work or who is too lazy to look for a different workplace. That is why a few people find their hats make good offices.

"My father taught me to work, but he never taught me to love it," Abraham Lincoln told one of his employers. And that employer corroborated Lincoln's opinion of himself, "He was awfully lazy."

Lincoln's favorite position was flat on his stomach on the floor.

His favorite office was his tall, stovepipe hat which he filled with memoranda. When he thought of a sentence for a speech or some defense for a law client, he would doff his hat, reach inside for a pencil stub and a scrap of paper, and make a note right on the spot. He did not waste time hunting for complete equipment nor take a chance on forgetting the idea before he returned to his other office.

When he did return to his other office, his work was done and stored in his file cabinet, his hat, size $7\frac{1}{8}$. So he would pursue his favorite other-office occupation: tilt far back in his chair, hoist his feet on his unused desk, and dream or swap yarns with visitors. This may not be the Lincoln you have imagined, but it is the true one.

He had his hat organized for work and could work any place because that was the laziest way, after all.

There was nothing lazy about George M. Cohan. He was a peppery hustler who refused to have an office. His office, literally, was his derby hat. He wrote plays and songs in his hat— on trains, subways, street corners, and in theater lobbies. As he acquired age he swapped the hard derby for a slouchy felt. But it was still his office, organized for work any time, any place.

When the United States entered the First World War, Cohan read the news in his morning paper at his home on Long Island. He began to hear a bugle call in his head as he trembled at the

announcement of war. The bugle became clearer; its call began
to vary. He got in his car to ride to New York City, started to
write words to go with the haunting bugle call. By the time he
had reached his destination, his hat-office carried the complete
words and music for "Over There," *the* war song. For that song
he was awarded a special Congressional Medal.

Brusque Oliver Newberry, pioneer Great Lakes shipbuilder
who became the largest shipowner on the Lakes, also carried his
office in his hat. His hat was so crowded with papers that he had
to tilt his head forward whenever he removed it. Usually,
though, he kept his hat on to protect the papers, regardless of
the weather or the presence of ladies.

Robert Dick, plagued with rheumatism, was the best biscuit-
maker in the little Scotch city of Thurso. In his spare time he
also was a student of natural science and took daily walks to
build up his natural-science collection after his morning baking
was done. His office was a threadworn, out-of-date hat. When
he discovered a new beetle, an ancient fossil fish, or a rare speci-
men of grass, it was carefully stored away on top of his head.
The small boys and puzzled citizens of Thurso thought he was
touched, and sometimes they jeered at the ancient hat as they
passed him on the streets. But their tune changed when the big
man of the day came to their isolated city to get acquainted with
the discoveries of the baker-scientist who carried his laboratory
in his hat and who became one of the leading Scotch naturalists.

Now meet another producer who always has his office with
him. He is Henry Cohen, grand old citizen of Galveston. But
his office is not in his hat but on his starched cuff. As a young
man of eighteen, in London, he began using his cuff as his office.
Through South Africa, the West Indies, and for half a century
in Galveston he has written on it memos for the day's activities,
pausing in the middle of the street to study the entries or to cross
off those he has completed. His flying short legs and careening

bicycle have taken him to many places where charity or assistance was needed; and his office-on-the-cuff has seen to it that he missed none of them.

Hat, attic, shed, or side porch—one can do good work anywhere. More depends on a person's desire to get things done than on the place in which he has to do them.

What many need is not a better workplace but a stronger desire to work. Those who really have the desire to work do not let mere circumstances fill their lives with blank spaces.

Producing Even in Prison

Charles Goodyear, in prison for debt, won the jailer's friendship and so was able to send out for small amounts of chemicals, which he used to continue his experiments on vulcanizing rubber, until his creditors relented and he was released.

Thomas Paine came to the United States, a bankrupt mechanic, with an unusual penchant for putting his finger on the weaknesses of officials. Quite naturally this made his life stormy, for the athletic man preached the gospel of freedom; there was no reason at all why people should kneel to nobles and landowners, he maintained.

One might have thought his important work in the War for American Independence would have satisfied Paine, but he just couldn't keep out of the French Revolution. He landed in Luxembourg prison where he could hear the swishing of the guillotine and the carts rumbling away with the headless dead. Would he be next? He didn't let the thought bother him, for he was busily using the otherwise idle time to write the second part of "The Age of Reason."

François Villon richly deserved his term in prison. He was lean and lousy. He had stabbed a priest, who forgave him with his last breath. In addition, he was a born mechanic who could pick any lock in Paris and had picked many of them, even to rob the poorboxes in churches. He had traveled to small towns and sold paste jewels as priceless stolen diamonds.

He was given a death sentence, but it was commuted to a term in prison.

He did not mind the damp straw of his cell; he was used to the seamy side of life. He spent his time behind bars composing many of the 173 sections of his long poem, "The Great Testament," with its ballad of dead ladies, its laments of the old hag, the fat Margot, and its touching prayer of the old mother.

He always imagined he was on the verge of reforming, but his only reform was his constructive use of the blank spaces in his life when jail prevented him from making merry.

John Bunyan, a wild, tinsmith's son, did reform. Then he went to the other extreme. Like Thomas Paine, he was too aggressive and too outspoken in his criticisms of worldly authority. Bunyan ended in prison for preaching without a license.

He wrote nine books there, was released, but was soon back on the straw bunks again. He took up where he had left off and wrote his immortal "Pilgrim's Progress" during his second term.

Marco Polo journeyed to China, found Kublai Khan's court, and ate noodles and spaghetti, which he brought back to become the national dish of his fellow Italians. He also brought back stories, jewels, and a restless, exploring nature that even twenty years in China had not quieted. His restlessness earned him a prison sentence from the Genoese. While in prison he dictated to Rusticiano, a fellow inmate, "The Travels of Marco Polo."

Adolph Hitler was thirty-four. He had an intense fire in his eyes and bad breath. His Munich revolt was unsuccessful, and

he was given a five-year prison sentence. During the nine
months he actually served, he used his time to dictate to his
fellow prisoner, Rudolf Hess, the book in which he organized
the ideas that were to plunge the civilized world into the Second World War. "Mein Kampf," perhaps even the plans for
Hitler's tragic rule, were produced during the blank time he
spent in prison.

François Arouet was half dead at birth and the midwife said
he could not possibly live longer than four days. But he was
obstinate from the start and stuck it out for eighty and four
years.
    He was built like a human skeleton, his face scarred by small-
pox pits, his eyes beady. Perhaps the homeliest man in France,
he was surely the most sarcastic and fearless. He especially enjoyed venting his sarcasm on higher-ups.
    When he lampooned the Regent, he ended behind the stout
walls of the Bastille, sharing his cell with visiting rats and ver-
min. He tried to tame several rats during the eleven months he
was there but spent more of his blank spaces writing "La Hen-
riade," an epic on the life of Henry of Navarre. He published
it under the name of Voltaire, the name by which he was hence-
forth known. Let us recall from an earlier chapter his motto,
"Always be working."

Keep Work Ahead to Avoid Empty Spaces

People can get things done anywhere, any time. Any place
can be a workplace. Of course, an office, shop, or laboratory is
handy, but the person who works only in one spot usually
doesn't get much done.
    And the person who works only during his regular office
hours may find himself outdistanced by those who have learned

the trick of working at odd moments in odd locations and doing two things at once.

Back in my high-school years I worked for a farmer on the edge of an Iowa village for my room and board. The old homesteader had for years been buying up more land and taking on more work as he went along. He seemed to think from the way I ate I should work like a horse, too.

The first rainy Saturday morning that fall I rejoiced secretly; the weather meant I would not have to follow the gray team at fall plowing or wrestle to hold the plow in the tough old pasture he was turning over. The farmer thought too much of the team to work them in such weather.

After his second cup of coffee, he wiped his shaggy, black moustache on the back of his hand. "Well, it's raining, so we can't work today," he said seriously, "so now we can just husk the corn in the west barn."

He always had work stored ahead to take care of the blank spaces.

I thought this plain man a slave driver at the time, but I have since been thankful for the lesson he taught me: **Always have productive work on hand for odd moments.**

He helped me learn that, when we imagine it is no time or place to work, we are really trying to get out of work.

No man distinguishes himself in any art who is not ready to beat heat, cold, hunger and thirst. He who imagines that he can become great by taking his ease in pleasant surroundings is much mistaken.

—GIORGIO VASSARI

Keep on going and the chances are that you will stumble on something. I have never heard of anyone stumbling on something sitting down.

—CHARLES F. KETTERING

17

Get someone else to do it

YOU ARE GOING to like the idea in this chapter. You recall the story of how Tom Sawyer whitewashed the fence? He pretended he was having so much fun that his playfellows actually paid to whitewash it for him. That story is more than an entertaining Mark Twain yarn. Tom Sawyer's successful way of getting others to do his job works in real life. It works with adults as well as children.

Andrew Carnegie did not live a Tom Sawyer boyhood, but as a lad he practiced the habit of getting others to do his job. Later in life the same habit helped make him a steel millionaire.

There was the affair of Carnegie's pet rabbits, for instance. The undersized boy started with only a few rabbits. But you know how rabbits are. Soon he was busy building new hutches. His other chores were also increasing at geometrical rates. The rabbits became too much work for one boy.

Shrewd young Andy solved the problem easily. He offered to name a rabbit family after any playmate who would take care of it for him. The boys volunteered their services in droves, proud to see their names painted in crude letters on a hutch.

Years later, when Carnegie was building his iron and steel empire, he recalled this boyhood method and applied it to adults. The president of the Pennsylvania Railroad became one of Carnegie's unpaid salesmen, for instance, because Carnegie named a steel-rail plant after him. Of course, after that the railroad bought all its steel rails from this plant.

For years I have had neighborhood boys run errands for me and help me enthusiastically with odd chores. But I must admit that the bait I use has not added to my popularity with their mothers. Many boys are not allowed to have air rifles, but I keep one on the side porch in full view of passing small fry.

When I have an errand I want run, I fire a few pellets at a tin can. Boys come running at the sound. When they have done the errand I pay them off by giving them ten shots at the can. Occasionally, after a really big errand, I reward them by letting them use my twenty-two.

Those boys work harder for ten shots with a B-B gun than they would for ten dollars. They don't feel they are doing dirty jobs for me. They are flattered because I share my prized possession with them. The boys and I both have fun, and I get more things done with their help. (To date no windows have been broken by random shots.)

EDISON VS. TESLA

Some experts claim that Nikola Tesla, inventor of alternating-current transmission, was a more brilliant man than Thomas A. Edison. But Edison accomplished much more and had more inventions patented. Edison's name is well known to this day; Tesla's is known only to engineers and scientists.

The Austrian-born Tesla had a suspicious streak in him, which was intensified after he was cheated on one of his early inventions. Thenceforth he was extremely difficult to work with and insisted on carrying out his experiments in complete secrecy.

Edison, in contrast, encouraged other young engineers to do much of his work for him. Many of them became important inventors in their own right, started amazing new industries. They were proud of their share in the inventions of the Wizard of Menlo Park and later organized themselves into an exclusive mutual-admiration society called the "Edison Pioneers."

Edison not only got more done for himself but also developed other men who helped develop the electrical field. Not a lone worker, no one-man wizard, Edison headed the first research *group* in the world.

Whether Tesla was more brilliant than Edison, I cannot judge. But I am very certain Tesla did not get so much done because he would not let others do things for him.

He Got the Indians to Do It

Samuel Hancock was one of those sturdy prospectors who tore to Sacramento in the Gold Rush. He had good luck. Some days he gleaned as much as $500 in gold. But at the end of each week he would find he had little left. Thieving freebooters stole what he did not spend for costly sugar and flour. His long head soon figured there must be other undiscovered minerals that would be worth more than gold in the long run. Coal, for instance.

So he left Sacramento and its rowdies to search for coal. Frontiersmen told him there were some peculiar black rocks in Oregon. Sam Hancock, searcher, was off to explore the waters that emptied into Puget Sound. He found there too many long rivers for one man to search, so he got others to do his exploring for him.

He showed Indians coal in lumps. It frightened them, because they thought it was solidified gunpowder and would kill them. Hancock proved to them it would not fire a musket. Their confidence won, they agreed to paddle up the rivers for him, looking in the shallows and on the banks for the black stones. And Hancock became the owner of the first coal mines in the West by getting others to do his job.

Samuel Hancock became a coal magnate because he did not try to be a one-man band.

INANIMATE HELP

A Baptist minister's son who attended an upstate college in New York used a nail to help him in his evening studies. He nailed his lounging slippers to the wall and each night would stick his feet in them and work for hours without exerting himself to hold his feet up. Fraternity brothers told Charles Evans Hughes it was laziness that made him use nails to hold his feet up. Hughes responded that it was silly to do something he could get done for him so easily. Hughes became Chief Justice of the United States Supreme Court.

Once I heard of a man who used inanimate objects to light his matches for him. He carried old-style matches that lit anywhere and would hold one against the side of a passing truck to be ignited. Perhaps that is the height of laziness.

In Seattle, Mrs. Guy Bowden observed a janitor using a passing truck to wring out his mop. He thrust his wet mop underneath the truck's wheels and let them wring it dry quicker than he could have done by hand and with practically no effort on his part.

AN ORGANIST'S SECRET

Friedrich Wilhelm Herschel migrated to England to try his fortunes when he was twenty. He wanted to be an astronomer, but had no training in science. He used his natural musical ability plus ingenuity to make his living while he was studying astronomy.

Seven men were trying out for work as organist in a certain church—a job Herschel wanted. They drew lots to determine in which order they should play. Herschel drew third place, following Dr. Wainwright, a famous Manchester organist, who was noted for his rapidity in fingering the keyboard.

What chance would an unknown young amateur have after this professional?

"Fingers alone will not be good enough," Herschel thought, as he ascended to the organ loft.

He took a few moments to adjust himself at the keyboard. Then the pipes burst forth in a crescendo of slow, extraordinarily full chords. Herschel improvised a few bars, swung into "Old Hundred." The committee thought they had never heard the familiar hymn played so richly or movingly before. The young German won the job.

Old Snetzler, the organ builder, asked Herschel how he had produced such fullness from the new organ. The blond winner held up two small pieces of lead.

"I used more than my fingers," he said. "I placed these weights, one on the lowest key of the organ, the other an octave above. By thus accompanying the harmony, I produced the effect of four hands instead of two."

As Herschel developed from an amateur into a professional astronomer, he improved the telescope so it too would do more work for him. He got his old-maid sister, Caroline, to labor at his side, and she became a great astronomer herself. Friedrich Herschel got things and people to help him until, at forty-four, he became the Royal Astronomer and Sir William.

How to Tell a Little Man from a Big Man

Little men want to do it all themselves.

Big men get someone else to help them.

Frank Woolworth was a little man. He failed in his first few attempts to start a five-and-ten-cent store. When he was at last beginning to make a go of one, he had a serious illness. This illness changed him into a big man.

"Up until that illness," he observed, "I thought I must attend to everything myself. But thereafter I indulged in the luxury of a bookkeeper, and at great effort I broke myself of the conceit that I could buy goods, display goods, run stores, and do everything else better than any man associated with me. That marked the beginning of my success and enabled me to expand in a large way."

Shortish Alfred Nobel, a bankrupt dreamer's son, was a tremendous worker himself. But Alfred's blue eyes were ever looking for someone to give him a helping hand at his work.

To his brother, who was trying to build up their chemical and manufacturing business, Alfred wrote, "It is my rule never to do myself what another could do better, or even as well. Otherwise I should long ago have been worn out, and probably ruined as well, for if you try to do everything yourself in a large concern, the result will be that nothing will be done properly."

He had reason for writing in that vein. The brother was trying to do it all himself, and his branch of the business was bogging down as a result.

Look now at another man. Tall, every inch the polished gentleman, he had a way with the ladies and a genius with the brush and palette. This was Peter Paul Rubens, the great Flemish painter we have seen before. Unlike many artists, he did not hesitate to let others of lesser skill help him get things done.

Scarcely thirty years old, he had more orders for paintings than he could produce alone. So he employed outside men to prepare his canvases and paint in the foundation details, while he himself applied only the finishing touches. As his fame grew, he sometimes had as many as fifty artists at once doing the rough work for paintings that he, the master, finished.

PEOPLE WHO GET THINGS
DONE SELDOM TRY TO DO
IT ALL THEMSELVES.

Rubens was applying John H. Patterson's motto, "Never do anything if you can get someone else to do it."

You will get more things done by applying that motto, and at the same time you will develop responsibility and loyalty in those who help you.

TRAINING OTHERS

There are secretive and mistrustful souls who seem constitutionally opposed to enlisting the aid of others. They are apprehensive lone wolves. They fear other people will take credit for their ideas, beat them out of their jobs, or steal their secrets and compete with them. So they try to do it all themselves.

The Chicago plant of the Western Electric Company had a complicated piecework method of computing wages. One old-timer had discovered a short cut for calculating the wages in his head. But he would not divulge his secret to the other pay clerks. He wanted to remain the indispensable man.

Walter Gifford was just out of college and had gone to work at the factory against his father's advice. Gifford thought if an old-timer could figure out the wages in his head then a chap with a college education should be able to, too. For several weeks Gifford spent his evenings trying to discover the short-cut. Finally he hit on it. Gifford proceeded to make himself indispensable not by keeping the method a mystery but by teaching it to all the pay-roll clerks.

When a new manager was needed in the company's Omaha branch, the old-timer who had not trained others was overlooked. Instead, the job was given to Gifford. That was his first step upward. Other promotions came rapidly, and at forty he was president of the American Telephone & Telegraph Company. Gifford got more things done because he TRAINED OTHERS to do them for him.

Victor Cutter graduated from Dartmouth Business School, then went to Costa Rica to learn the banana business from the plantation stage up. Everything he learned there he passed along to others so they could help him get more done and he could work less himself.

Soon when there was a big job to do the boss gave it to Cutter, for he had the habit of getting more things done by more people. Enlisting others to carry out his job brought Cutter the presidency of the United Fruit Company.

Pigeon-toed James B. Duke, already an old acquaintance of ours, kept an approving eye on the man in charge of the Far Eastern export market of his then-young American Tobacco Company.

"How many people have you in China who could take your place if you were killed?" he bluntly asked James A. Thomas, on one of the latter's trips to headquarters.

Thomas pulled out a pad and began to write down names cautiously.

"There is a list," he said, pushing the pad toward Duke. "Any of them could now step into my shoes."

"Whew! Twelve men," the chief said. "Well, J.A., if you've

trained a dozen men to do your work for you, you're worth more money to us."

"The training of men is the chief job of any executive," said Cyrus McCormick.

And the best way to train men is to have them help you at your own work. The opportunity to do more important things usually goes to that individual who has had others help him and thereby trained them to do his work.

GIVE OTHERS CREDIT

Get others to help you and give them more credit than they deserve for their assistance. You may discover they have unusual talent, and the credit you give them will earn you friendship and loyalty.

Henry Thornton was a broad, loose-limbed boy from Logansport, Indiana, who started as a draughtsman for the Pennsylvania Railroad. He worked up to become president of the twenty-one-thousand-mile Canadian National Railways. This towheaded giant accomplished the near-miracle of transforming a national white elephant into a national resource.

He worked the way he had played football—intensely and by getting others to carry the ball. The teamwork of those around him was superb because he gave them more credit than they deserved for every yard gained.

"His story is a tale of loyalties that strayed across the years of his life," his biographer records—loyalties, be it emphasized, that he built up in his railroad work on three continents by getting others to help him and giving them more credit than they deserved.

Rugby School was petering out. It seemed to be losing the

struggle for existence until Thomas Arnold became headmaster. He converted it into the famous school it now is by surrounding himself with men he could trust and then trusting them. He got others to do his work and gave them more credit than they deserved.

START WITH CHILDREN

Do you think a family of five children would be a handicap in getting things done? A large family is a decided help to the parent who knows how to get others to help.

One of the gayest social butterflies I know is a career woman turned housewife. She has five children, no household help. Yet she attends teas, receptions, committee meetings, dances, first nights, or dinners almost daily. She gives brilliant parties in her own home.

And she neglects neither her children nor the housework. She has the children help her. The older children have definite duties for definite hours; they look after the younger ones. Each, even the youngest who is learning to walk, has something to do around the house. All help with the family dinners and at homes, thus making them parties for the children as well as the grown-ups.

The woman could afford to employ household help and a governess. But she insists it is better for parents and children both if all pull together.

The children take their share in the work for granted. Assuming responsibility seems to come naturally to them, for it has been delegated to them by their mother since they can first remember. She does not slight her family or herself. She merely divides the labor, just as she did when she was a successful executive. She is not raising a one-mother family. In her household, the family has six mothers.

Parents who think they are too busy to get outside things done should follow her method of delegating the chores. It is even better for the children than for the parents.

The basis of all education is to LEARN BY DOING.

ASSISTANCE AND MENTAL HYGIENE

Conscientious people are inclined to try to do everything unaided. Yet they are the very ones who mental-hygiene experts say should have others help them.

Take the case of George William Frederick, for instance. We met him earlier, in the chapter on "Making up One's Mind Quickly," under his better-known name, George III, King of England.

He had seven brothers and sisters. And too much mother and too much grandfather. His mother nagged the children even when they were fully grown. And his grandfather, George II, complicated her nagging by his efforts to instill kingly qualities into the character of George William Frederick.

When in his early twenties this bulging-eyed boy became king, he wanted to be a one-man band. The early training of his mother and grandfather had shaped him to the mold. He struggled against his ministers, tried to abolish the party system. Opposition made him nervous, yet by trying to do everything he created more opposition for himself.

At twenty-seven he had a mental breakdown, which was followed at intervals by four other attacks of insanity. Each attack was more severe. Psychiatrists who have studied his case since report that he probably would never have become insane if he had been able to delegate much of his work to others. It was not overwork, but conscientious over-worry about the work he had to do alone that made him in his insanity interrupt church services, hide under a sofa, choke his physician, and, at seventy, imagine he was only seventeen and could talk to people long dead.

Both for the sake of getting things done and your mental health, don't be so conceited as to imagine you must do it all yourself.

Get someone to do it for you whenever possible.

Light is the task where many share the toil.

—HOMER

Almost all the advantages which man possesses arise from his power of acting in combination with his fellows.

—JOHN STUART MILL

18

Work for more than money

SLAVES HAD to work, whether they liked it or not. So do many free men, as far as that goes. Their pocketbooks are in their jobs, their hearts elsewhere.

But most of the world's doers spell money in small letters, WORK in capitals. Getting things done is their main objective, not getting things.

There was that redheaded shoe-factory worker, for instance. He landed a foreman's job by mistake. George F. Johnson started work in a basement shoe factory in Massachusetts at thirteen. One day a letter arrived addressed to "Mr. Johnson"; it described an opening for a foreman in a new factory at Binghamton, New York.

It did not occur to the ruddy twenty-four-year-old that the position might be intended for his father. He started at once for Binghamton, where they were decent enough to give him a trial as foreman. The trial was a success.

But the small factory had many periods of idleness, and finally it reached the stage where the stockholders had trouble borrowing the money to keep it running.

"Let me run the factory for a year, and I'll show you how we can make better shoes for less money," the foreman told the principal holder. And he hastened to add, "You needn't pay me more than I'm getting now as foreman."

So the bench foreman was given charge of the business as a last resort.

In a few months things were going much better in the plant; the stockholders no longer needed to borrow money and were gradually paying off their notes. In two years the factory was turning out eighteen times as many shoes, week after week, as ever before.

Johnson was offered a raise.

"Let's wait and see what happens," he replied. "We've got to make all we can *of* this concern, not try to take all we can *out* of it."

At forty-two George F. again refused a raise; instead he bought a half interest in the business with borrowed cash. That was the start of the Endicott-Johnson Shoe Company, which George F. built into an organization of more than two dozen factories, turning out some one hundred and seventy-five thousand pairs of shoes and boots daily from the green hides to the finished product.

This thirty-odd-million-dollar corporation was built by the redhead, once hired as foreman by mistake, who was more interested in trying out his ideas of industrial democracy and management than in getting a raise. When he came to be a millionaire in spite of himself he continued to live in a house so plain that it might have belonged to one of his workers. He worked for more than money; he worked to introduce his new ideas in industrial relations to the world, ideas that were to create two model cities in a beautiful river valley of southern New York State.

"Not what I have, but what I do is my kingdom," said Carlyle.

THE MASTER OF STEEL AND HIMSELF

When the Bethlehem Iron Works wanted a new plant built, they called in a Pennsylvania Dutchman to build it. John Fritz was a broad-faced farm boy who started blacksmithing at sixteen. He worked in many of the Pennsylvania mills, changing jobs not to get more money but to vary his experience.

Once when he was twenty-seven, for example, he left his job to work for a new blast furnace and rail mill. The new position paid barely half the wages he had been getting, but he was working for more than money. There were things about iron-and steelmaking he still wanted to learn.

He went after experience systematically, and it was worth more than money to him in the long run. He was not yet forty when he won the responsibility of building the first of the great Bethlehem plants. He was only forty-two when the United States government gave him full rein and a blank check to build the country's first armor-plate mill.

John Fritz made himself the great engineer of the iron and steel world by working for more than money. Each year now the John Fritz medal is awarded by American engineering societies for notable scientific or industrial achievement. Its recipients—George Westinghouse, Alexander Graham Bell, Thomas A. Edison among them—are people who have found how to get things done.

THE NICKEL-AND-DIME MILLIONAIRE

A tall, thin, rather frail farm boy also wanted to learn how to do things more than he wanted to make money. Frank Woolworth's first job was in McNeil's small country store in northern New York State. Woolworth, nearing twenty-one, was pleased as Punch to get the job, though it paid him precisely nothing.

His second job, with the American Store in Watertown, was quite an advancement for him. Now, though he was still working for no pay, he was in a city store. It was at this store that he got his idea for a five-and-ten-cent store, which was to earn him one of the world's great fortunes.

Exactly a dozen years after he went to work in the American Store for more than money, Frank Woolworth came back to Watertown on a visit. Already he was successfully operating several of his new five-and-tens. But when he went into the old store he found it depleted of stock, run down, and wavering on the brink of bankruptcy. He rolled up his sleeves, opened his pocketbook, went back to work for nothing so he could put his ex-employer back on his feet.

He Lived on Sparrows

Emil Zola learned the hard way that money can be very important. His parents became impoverished in his youth. His mother sold their last four pieces of furniture to get enough funds to go to Paris, hoping to find something better for them there.

"My stomach and my future always bothered me," Zola said, years later. His stomach did bother him that first winter in Paris, when he was twenty-one. He lived mostly on sparrows, which he trapped and broiled on the end of a curtain rod. He sold many of his clothes and walked around his barren lodgings draped in a sheet like an Arab.

Yet he went to work for nothing. For a month he wrote for the new magazine *Figaro*. "After a month," the suave publisher told him, "we shall see what you are worth."

At the end of that time the publisher gave the nearsighted, threadbare youth one of the largest checks in the magazine's existence. The size of the check was not determined by Zola's need, but by the value the magazine had received from this man who was working for more than money.

Then and later, Zola was working to make himself one of the immortals of French literature.

WEBSTER DECLINED THE JOB

Swarthy Daniel Webster was the ninth but far from the last child of his parents. The family was so large that frugality became a necessity. When he was in high school, Daniel wrote his brother this parody of a popular song.

> I'll never make money my idol,
> For away our dollars will fly.
> With my friend and my pitcher,
> I'm twenty times richer
> Than if I made money my idol.

But he forgot that verse when he began his law practice. He was given the opportunity to become clerk of one of the New Hampshire courts. The salary, plus fees, made the offer look attractive. Daniel was elated. Now he could live in comfort and help support his brothers and sisters. He would earn more than the judge himself! He hastened to tell his father and then Christopher Gore, the distinguished Boston attorney who had trained him for law.

"You have climbed pretty well up the hill," Gore told the excited Webster. "But if you take that job you will stand still. You will merely rust out. Your mission is to make opinions for other men to record, not be the clerk who records the opinions of others."

Webster cooled down, thought it over, and declined the clerkship. He trudged through the snow to break the news to his father.

"Are you crazy?" his father exclaimed. "Just as your mother always said—you will amount to nothing!"

Another man took the juicy job as clerk of the court, lived in comfort, and the world does not remember him.

Webster rented an office for $15 a year over a red store near his home in Boscawen. For two years he did not even earn enough to pay the rent. But he did have time to delve deeper into the law, to study harder. He worked for more than money and became one of America's most famous lawyers and orators.

HE WOULDN'T RUN THE FACTORY

Now look at this shy young man. Perhaps his shyness was due to the frightful birthmark that disfigured almost the entire right side of his face. Perhaps it was due to his extreme near-sightedness, which caused him to pass friends on the street without recognizing them. It was not helped by the fact that, just as he was completing his college course, his parents lost their money, so he had to help support them.

Such was Charles W. Eliot's start in life.

At twenty-one he began teaching chemistry at Harvard. Five years later he was out of a job, ousted by faculty politics. For two years he was without work. Then he received an unexpected and flattering offer from the Merrimac Mills. They wanted him to run their plant and offered him a salary twice that of the Harvard president.

It was a strong temptation for a man not yet thirty with a wife, baby, and aged parents to support. It took him only a week, however, to decide to turn it down. There was something else that, in spite of the lower pay, he wished to make his life-work.

A month later he accepted a job teaching at Massachusetts Institute of Technology for one-third the Merrimac salary.

And, when he was thirty-five, a widower of a few weeks, the school that had fired him as a young instructor begged him to return as its president. Eliot became "King Charles," for forty years president of Harvard. He converted Harvard from a small Puritan college into a great university, turning it over like a flapjack.

If perchance you have his famous five-foot shelf of books, you will want to read his full life story in it.

That "Better Job"

How about these tempting offers that come from rival firms? Alexander Legge, who was working for the McCormicks, once received an offer from a rival manufacturer of farm machinery. He told his old Scotch father that he planned to change employers.

"Bide where ye are," his father advised. "Dinna ye ken that the McCormicks'll fin' it ot if ye are worth more than ye are gettin'?"

Legge remained with McCormick, became president of the organization, and later helped found the gigantic International Harvester Company. It would have been slavery for him to have accepted another job merely to make more money.

"One should never trouble about getting a better job," Calvin Coolidge wrote, "but one should do one's present job in such a manner as to qualify for a better job when it comes along."

"Ambition and pride keep a man at work when money is merely a by-product," said Philip D. Armour, who referred to himself as a butcher rather than a packing-house millionaire. To his sons he wrote shortly before his death, "Don't try to get rich too fast, and never feel rich."

Turn back to Chap. 8 for other examples of people who worked for more than money and turned down attractive offers because they had something more important in view.

The Wages of Genius

Something more valuable than money must keep geniuses at work, for the exceedingly small remuneration that the early work of some famous men and women received can certainly not have encouraged them to continue. Yet they kept on working until they became known in their own rights.

George M. Cohan, for example, sold his first song, which bore the touching title of "Why Did Nellie Leave Her Home," for $25.

"Sweet Genevieve," a perennially popular song, earned the huge sum of $5 for its author, George Cooper, who had married sweet Genevieve. On her untimely death the grieving husband wrote this charming, melancholy air. Cooper lived to be ninety but never remarried. He produced many other song hits, but the greatest of all brought him only a $5 bill.

Richard Henry Dana, who came of a long line of jurists, was a sailor, lawyer, author. He was kicked out of Harvard but later readmitted. At twenty-five he wrote "Two Years Before the Mast," a classic of sea adventure. He received $250 for this book, although it rivaled "Robinson Crusoe" in popularity.

Richard Pease Danks was a Connecticut Yankee and musician who moved to the Midwest. He wrote many anthems and popular songs. His "Silver Threads Among the Gold" brought him just $30.

Eugene Field, who loved children and was called the "Poet Laureate of Childhood," received $5 for his "Little Boy Blue."

Stephen Foster, composer of "Old Folks at Home," and many other long-time favorite songs, was the ninth of ten children. He quit his work as bookkeeper in Cincinnati to pour out his spirit in songs which made him "America's Troubador." At thirty-eight, when his wife was working as a railway telegrapher to help make a living, brown-eyed Foster died in a charity ward at Bellevue Hospital. The total he had received from his many songs was barely $15,000. After his death his heirs received only $4,000 more. In his pocketbook at the time of his death were 85 cents and a corner of an envelope on which he had written "Dear friends and gentle hearts."

Oliver Goldsmith was a pug-nosed Dublin Irishman whose head was almost large enough for two ordinary mortals. He became a physician, but disliked the work almost as much as his few patients disliked his medicine. So he turned to writing, living on borrowed money, and produced "The Vicar of Wakefield," which enriched him by exactly $300.

Dark-haired, shy Nathaniel Hawthorne wrote stories, only to burn most of them in his fireplace. But he sold some of his "Twice-Told Tales," for $3 each. He kept himself alive by working as customs collector while his wife kept him scribbling by a mixture of nagging and encouragement.

Henry Wadsworth Longfellow started to study law but switched to the literature in which his heart lay. For "The Wreck of the Hesperus" he received the large sum of $25. He supported himself by teaching at Harvard until his writing became so prolific and popular that he could live by his pen alone.

Medium-sized, oval-faced John Milton led a stormy life for such a calm philosopher and poet. He was thrice married, each time unhappily. At fifty-two he became blind, though he still worked. For his masterpiece, "Paradise Lost," he received $50, and it became so popular that it went through twenty printings in twenty years.

Walter Hunt, an upstate Quaker who stood six feet four inches tall, married a young widow with one child and moved to New York City. Invention, invention, invention was his inner urge. He invented the double lock stitch for sewing machines and the safety pin. For the safety pin he received only $400, kept right on inventing, and produced the first metallic cartridge and dozens of less important gadgets. C. Austin Miles was a graduate pharmacist who could make a living mixing pills and sundries. But there was music in his soul; at twelve he had substituted for the church organist in his home town of Lakehurst, New Jersey, shocking the congregation when he played the Lohengrin wedding march at a funeral. He wrote some three thousand hymns, most of which were sold for $2.50 each. His most popular, "In the Garden," went for a higher price, $4. More than 3,000,000 copies of this $4 hymn were sold by the publishers.

The Frank Merriwell stories of virile boyhood appeared in editions totaling over a hundred million copies. Their prolific author, six-foot George W. Patten, never received more than $150 a week at the height of his popularity. At seventy-three he had to fight eviction from his home. For his first two stories together he received $3.

John Howard Payne, thirty-one, was in a Paris garret trying to write an opera. Overcome by homesickness for his family cottage on Long Island, he interrupted composition of the opera long enough to write the words of "Home, Sweet Home." These he set to the music of an old Italian air. For his immortal song he received $250; and the publishers made $10,000 from it the first year.

That neurotic genius, Edgar Allan Poe, received $15 from a second-rate magazine for his poem "The Raven." The most he ever made from his writing was $100 for the story "The Gold Bug." No wonder he took to drink and died early!

George Bernard Shaw, determined to become a writer, earned the vast sum of $30 from the efforts of his first four years.

PEOPLE WHO GET THINGS

DONE SEE MORE THAN

MONEY IN THEIR WORK

Charles M. Sheldon was the Kansas minister who wrote "In His Steps," one of the most popular religious novels of all time. He did not copyright the manuscript. More than thirty publishers issued it in book form. Only one publisher paid him anything for it. In later years he wrote three other works.

"The Washington Post March" swept into popularity overnight. Dancing masters used it to introduce that newfangled dance, the two-step. John Philip Sousa, the composer, had sold the march for $35. Many of his famous march compositions were sold for $5, while some went for the "high" figure of $50.

Anthony Trollope worked in a post office but wanted to write, and he did write in every minute of spare time he could garner. His book, "The Warden," earned him $95 in ten years. But he stuck to his ambition and finally wrote volumes that earned him as much as $17,000 each.

Genius must work for something more valuable than mere money.

"Wealth, notoriety, place and power are no measure of success whatever," said H. G. Wells. "The only true measure of success is the ratio between what we might have been and what we might have done, on the one hand, and the thing we have made and the thing we have made of ourselves, on the other."

SCIENTISTS' LOVE OF WORK

Look where you may, but you will not find a happier lot of people than the creative scientists and scholars—or a more underpaid one.

Their work taxes both their ability and patience. They put in long hours; and when they leave their laboratories their work goes with them in their thoughts, often pestering their sleep. They spend a lifetime in preparation for it. After they land a job they like, it pays half or less than many jobs they could get in the commercial world.

Yet of all the varied people I know none are happier than these intellectual workers who do so much for the world and get so little of the world's goods in return.

Perhaps the secret of their happiness and their ability to get things done lies in the fact that they are working for more than money.

Take the story of Vitamin G, for instance. It was given this alphabetical designation to honor its discoverer, Dr. Joseph Goldberger. He called it by another name, but after his death scientists rechristened it with Goldberger's first initial. Vitamin G is a symbol of what one may do when one works for more than money.

Goldberger was raised in the teeming ghetto of New York's infamous lower East Side. Illness and death stalked his foul tenement. His parents, toiling in their little grocery that reeked of pickled fish, hoped their oldest and brightest son, Joseph, would become an engineer.

But this curly-headed eighteen-year-old wanted to be a physician; he wanted to learn how to relieve the suffering that he saw around him everywhere. After long family conclaves

Joseph won, and his parents agreed to make the sacrifices necessary to help him through medical school.

At Bellevue Medical College he ran away with every honor, yet he graduated a disappointed young man, for he had learned that many human ailments were still a mystery to medical science. He had found that medicine was full of blind-alley diseases. While a physician could make good money in private practice, it was hard to live and at the same time carry on research which would aid the mass of mankind. Goldberger wanted to find the cause and cure of those ailments that afflicted his tenement neighbors and others all over the world, ailments that medicine seemed hopeless to relieve.

So he entered the United States Public Health Service—at the munificent salary of $1,600 a year—and devoted thirty years of his life to removing diseases from the blind-alley class. Yellow fever, dengue, typhus, diphtheria, parasitic worms, pellagra were some of the medical mysteries he helped solve. He answered the riddle of pellagra alone. He boldly experimented on himself and twice nearly died from fevers he contracted from his laboratory specimens.

When New York City looked over the country for a director for its new health laboratory, forty-year-old Goldberger was the first man chosen. The city authorities offered him the position, a position that would have put an end to his monthly struggle to pay his bills. But he did not hesitate. He quickly answered no. For he was deep in another mystery; only a month previously he had been asked to tackle "one of the knottiest and most urgent health problems," the plague of pellagra that had puzzled doctors for two centuries.

At half the salary he would have received in New York, Goldberger went into pellagra-infested sections of the Southland to eliminate this new medical blind alley. He discovered the cause and cure of pellagra and the vitamin that proudly bears his initial. He was working for more than money; he was working to do some of those things his youthful observation in the ghetto had told him needed to be done. To him, human suffering was more of an incentive than money.

They Did Not Take Out a Patent

The Curies had just discovered radium. A fortune was within their reach if they patented the discovery. One Sunday morning Pierre showed his wife a letter from a Buffalo firm asking permission to exploit radium in the United States.

"We have two choices," slow-talking Pierre told her. "We can describe the results of our research without reserve, or we can consider ourselves the proprietors of radium and patent our technique."

He pointed out how much it would mean to their children's future, in their own old age, if they patented the technique and reaped a fortune.

Marie thought silently for a few minutes. "It is impossible to patent it," she replied. "It would be contrary to the scientific spirit. Radium will be useful for treating diseases. It would be impossible to take advantage of that."

"Yes," Pierre echoed. "It would be contrary to the scientific spirit."

It took no longer than fifteen minutes one Sunday morning for them to decide to keep on working for more than money. And, months later, when the Nobel award dropped unexpected thousands into their laps, they gave most of these away to needy relatives and charity.

Perhaps they recalled Anaxagoras, the ancient Greek scientist who inherited a fortune from his rich father. He gave it to the poor and the state so he would not have to worry about it and could devote his time to thinking. He made himself a pauper, died a pauper; but his thinking won him a fortune in fame that has lasted for centuries.

Consider also Sir Humphry Davy. When asked why he did not patent a safety lamp he had invented for use against gases in mines, he replied, "More wealth might distract my attention from my favorite pursuits." His favorite pursuits were the study and advancement of science.

The Hardest-headed Scientist

"I cannot afford to waste my time making money," Louis Agassiz replied to an offer from the West. His scientific work in zoology at Harvard was the important thing to him. And, when an offer reached him to take charge of the Jardin des Plantes at Paris, with a seat in the French Senate thrown in, he answered that he was engaged in important zoological research in the United States and nothing could separate him from what he was doing.

A large marble statue of Agassiz stands in the quadrangle at Stanford University. During a California earthquake that destroyed more than two millions of the university property in less than a minute, the statue of the zoologist tumbled off its twenty-foot pedestal. It fell head downward, crashed through a concrete sidewalk so that only the legs remained above ground.

When the upturned statue was excavated authorities were astounded to find that only the nose had been broken. Agassiz' noble dome had crashed through concrete and deep into the earth without a bruise.

"I always knew he was a hardheaded old chap," commented a fellow zoologist.

THE LANGUAGES OF THE MYSTERIOUS EAST

Max-Muller was only four years old when his father died. His mother spent the balance of her life grieving over her loss and kept the children in a continual state of depression by taking them to their father's grave for an hour daily to weep. The family was poor in worldly goods, too; it lacked many of the simple essentials of life.

But language study finally opened a new and cheering world for the boy; languages made him forget the family poverty and bitterness. Soon the childless Prince of Dessau wanted to adopt Max-Muller and put him in the diplomatic service where his command of tongues would make capital. The latter protested; he wanted to learn more about languages not use those he knew for political chicanery.

By the time he was twenty-four this brilliant young man had turned down several other offers. He had decided to continue in genteel poverty rather than desert the thing he wanted most to do. Then he got an offer from Oxford. He accepted it eagerly, for it allowed him the time and facilities he required to learn more about languages. Half the time he taught; the other half he devoted to mastering his beloved Sanskrit manuscripts. Later he gave up the professorship altogether to devote his life to editing the fifty-one volumes of "Sacred Books of the East."

Working for more than money, Max-Muller became the world's leading philologist and orientalist.

THE TWO-WAY ATLANTIC RADIO

Reginald Fessenden, a minister's son, looked at the world through his thick, indispensable glasses and saw visions of things he wanted to do. He was a mathematics teacher but taught himself chemistry, persisting in it until he landed a job as a chemist with Edison. After he had made several discoveries for Edison, he was offered a third interest in the Pratt & Lambert Paint Company. He turned it down to finish work in which he was engrossed. This, when the youth with the wide forehead was only twenty-three years old!

Later he turned down further flattering offers—a partnership with Andrew Carnegie, a powerful position in the Baldwin Locomotive Company, and others. Instead, he took a poorly paid teaching job at Purdue University, then one at the University of Pittsburgh. These jobs were to keep him from starving while giving him an opportunity to do some of the things he wanted to get done.

He was not working for money, but for a chance to invent heterodyne radio circuits, the wireless telephone, the submarine telephone, the first two-way Atlantic radio. In the richly paying varnish firm, Carnegie steel, or the Baldwin Locomotive Company, he would not have found it. They would have kept him from making his real contributions in electricity.

HEALING WITH LIGHT RAYS

"Small ability and total lack of energy," reported the academy principal when he dropped Niels Finsen from the class rolls. But later events proved it was the school rather than the young student from Iceland that was lacking. For it was Dr. Finsen who discovered how to use the ultraviolet rays of the sun to treat previously incurable skin tuberculosis and how to make artificial ultraviolet light by electricity.

When Denmark built a special institute in which he could continue his experiments on the medical uses of light rays, Finsen bluntly refused any salary until his theories had been proved valid beyond a doubt.

Less than ten years afterwards, he received the Nobel prize for medicine. The Finsen Institute, in Copenhagen, is like its namesake, world famous.

The Electron Expert

Like Fessenden's, Robert A. Milliken's fame lay in a field in which he had taken no formal courses. He began teaching physics before he had taken a course in the subject, kept about one lesson ahead of the class. Soon physics absorbed all his interest. He went to Europe to study with top-notch physicists and win a doctor's degree.

Back in America again, he received an enticing offer; he turned it down to take a job worth only half the salary with famed Albert A. Michelson, at the University of Chicago. There he could continue the research he wanted to do. He could work for more than money.

He, too, won a Nobel prize, for separating and measuring the evasive electron.

The Coastguardman on a Horse

Charles W. Peach was an enlisted man in the Coast Guard. He rode on horseback along the Scotch coast to watch for smugglers. He also rode a hobby: collecting odd sea shells, specimens of marine life, and fossils. In the course of duty he chanced across many interesting specimens lying on the seashore. Off duty he studied these specimens or went on trips inland to explore other regions.

As his service in the Coast Guard lengthened, he was given the due promotions. His fame began to spread amongst scientists, and he reported some of his discoveries at scientific meetings.

Soon Coast Guard officials were told they should give enlisted man Peach a still better rank. The authorities moved slowly, finally offered Peach a choice of two posts, one of which would almost have doubled his salary. But it also would have taken him to a location where the opportunities for spare-time natural science were relatively barren. He accepted the poorer-paying post in the location he wanted to explore. It was this coastguardman who became president of the Royal Physical Society of Edinburgh and was honored by the Neill prize for his work in natural science, work made possible by his taking a poorer-paying job.

HE BECAME A TRAMP

We learned earlier about the astonishing bed John Muir invented to tumble sleepers onto the floor early in the morning. He invented other things that were equally profitable and more practical, though he would not patent them. Some gadgets and a machine he worked out for making wagon wheels caused his employers to offer him a partnership in their prosperous factory. He was thirty at the time.

The partnership would have made him a wealthy man. But he rejected the offer and became a tramp. He began a thousand-mile walk to the Gulf of Mexico to study nature and gather specimens. He camped nights in cemeteries to avoid being molested by prowlers. He made the continent his playground, reaping its treasures for his notebooks.

"Just an unknown nobody of the woods," he would say, as he disproved the theories of distinguished scientists. When he settled down in his adopted habitat, the Yosemite Valley, the distinguished scientists came from all over the world to beat a path to his cabin door.

And John Muir beat a path to politicians' doors, eventually

winning his fight to preserve our natural beauty and wildlife by establishing a national-park system.

When E. H. Harriman, the railroad magnate, visited Muir, the Scotchman's blue eyes twinkled, and he said, "I don't think Mr. Harriman is very rich. He has not as much money as I have. I have all I want and Mr. Harriman has not."

THE DINOSAUR EGGS

The Andrews boy, of Beloit, Wisconsin, had trouble passing his courses in mathematics. And throughout life he had to add, subtract, and count by using his fingers; numbers did not interest him in the least. Always, however, he wanted to be a naturalist. As a small lad he kept the house littered with bird and animal skins.

When he graduated from the local college, he had no doubt about where he wanted to work. He traveled across the continent to the American Museum of Natural History. The director received him in a friendly manner, regretted there was not a position of any sort open in the museum.

"You have to have someone clean the floors," said young Andrews. "Couldn't I do that?"

"But a man with a college education doesn't want to clean floors!"

"No," Andrews replied, "not just *any* floors. But the museum floors are different. I'll clean them and love it if you'll let me."

So on Monday morning Roy Chapman Andrews reported for work with a mop and broom. He came nearly an hour early. He worked Sundays and holidays. He cooked most of his own meals or ate cold lunches he prepared himself.

When a minor vacancy appeared in the taxidermy department, Andrews was promoted to it. In a few years an opportunity opened to study whales off the Alaskan coast; Andrews volunteered to go without salary. A few years more, and he was acknowledged to be the world's foremost authority on whales.

Then he went to Asia and the Far East—not for money but for the opportunity to seek out the things he wanted to find. He discovered the world's only dinosaur eggs, returned to the New World with a shipload of new knowledge about the Old, became director of the museum whose woodwork he had once scrubbed.

Many people who GET BIG THINGS DONE are happy because they are working for love rather than money. Their careers remind us of Kipling's lines

> And no one shall work for money, and no one shall work
> for fame;
> But each for the joy of working. . . .

Of such are the scientists and scholars who have led civilization to new heights.

Look around at the great work of the world and see if it has been done by men who have worked for more than money. And review the study of George Washington Carver, told in Chap. 3.

It's good to have money and the things money can buy. But it's good, too, to check up once in a while and make sure you haven't lost the things money can't buy.

—GEORGE HORACE LORIMER

The more I think and reflect, I feel that, whether I be growing richer or not, I am growing wiser, which is far better.

—ROBERT NICOLL

19

Take on more work

THIS CHAPTER is not going to increase the authors' popularity with a lot of people. But, for some, it should prove a turning point in the climb upward.

Is there something wrong with the person who works near the limit of his capacity, who actually takes on more work without having it forced on him? Well, such a person is at least different.

Thousands of factory and office workers were asked, "Do you think a person should turn out as much work as he can on his job?"

About two-thirds of the office workers questioned thought one should do all one could. Slightly less than that number of the skilled factory workers agreed with them. But, of the unskilled manual workers, barely half thought they should do all they could on the job.

In other words, from one-third to one-half of all people are shirkers rather than workers.

Some maintained that if they worked as hard as they could they feared it might injure their health. Others said they held back from doing their level best because they did not want to put poor workers out of their jobs. Many more claimed they did not want to make themselves unpopular by working too hard. And a considerable number pretended they held back from doing their best so the boss wouldn't expect too much of them.

There is one note of cheer in these otherwise doleful figures

—cheer for the ambitious person, not for the employer or the ultimate consumer of the labor's produce. The large number of shirkers lessens the competition for the man or woman who wants to get ahead. The shirkers make the real workers loom extra-large in contrast.

When James B. Duke was creating his mammoth tobacco business, for instance, he overheard a young accountant ask the office manager for more work.

"Well, I'll be danged!" Duke boomed. "Move a desk into my office for that fellow who wants more work."

This is how simply George Allen, a North Carolina boy, became the tobacco tycoon's right-hand man and soon took charge of all his foreign interests. Upon Duke's death, Allen was bequeathed the job of administering the fabulous millions of the Duke estate.

His Extra Calls Grew into a Colossus

At sixteen William Lever left school to work in his father's small wholesale-grocery business. The business barely provided enough to feed the family of ten children. After three years of inside work—cutting and wrapping soap, breaking down lumpy sugar, keeping books—young Lever went on the road to solicit orders for his strict, conservative father.

For five years he made routine calls on the firm's regular customers in the area the elder considered its territory. The son represented his father well. A touch of prosperity came their way, though only a touch.

One afternoon William completed his last call on the farthermost customer early. He looked at his watch. Three-thirty. Good! He could go home and spend the rest of the afternoon with his bride.

But he looked at his watch again, did some mental calculations, and reached a quick decision. He drove to the next town where the firm had never done business before.

He made no sale at the first grocer's, who had never even heard of him. At the second he sold seventy-five pounds of sugar on a trial order. The third and fourth grocers placed full orders. The fifth bought nothing. Then he turned homeward.

He had taken on more work for himself and secured three new customers out of five prospects. But his father hit the ceiling when he heard the news. He did not want their territory extended. He preferred to leave well enough alone.

Young William, however, continued to take on more work until he had enough new customers to warrant establishing a branch warehouse in the new territory. He was placed in charge, of course. Like the tail that wagged the dog, he developed this branch into the gigantic Lever Brothers Company. His habit of taking on more work built the firm up to more than 400 subsidiaries with 600 factories in nearly forty countries—one of the world's largest and most prosperous organizations.

This grocer's boy became Lord Leverhulme, who always took on more work and worked to the limit of his capacity. *Both* man and business *thrived* on his philosophy. BOTH USUALLY DO.

Most of us still work in low gear, even when we imagine we are doing our best. One of the best ways to get into high gear is to take on more work. Then we have to do the job or go under in a mess of unfinished odds and ends.

The person who takes on more work has the bear by the tail; he does not dare let go until he has done something. An easy work schedule brings out one's natural laziness. **A stiff work schedule brings out one's better side.**

A great many men and women need the extra pressure of extra work to start them rolling at their real capacity. It takes a superhuman task to bring out the superhuman in them. Thousands are not aware of what they might do because they have never had to do the superhuman.

There is a certain hazard, of course, in this business of taking on more work; it may just add to one's stock of unfinished things. But, in such an event, the stock would probably have been large, anyway. The extra work is more apt to result in extra things accomplished.

One of the key officers in the atomic-bomb project had an illustrated motto on his office wall. It showed a turtle lumbering along as rapidly as it could. And beneath the picture was this admonition, "Behold the turtle! He makes progress only when he sticks his neck out."

Human beings, too, have to stick their necks out by taking on extra work, regardless of the hazards, to get more things done.

We can do when we have to do.

More about a "Great Little Guy"

George M. Cohan accomplished big things by sticking his neck out and taking on more work. His parents were vaudeville actors, so he did not get a regular schooling. Yet he wrote three hundred songs and half a hundred plays, most of them highly successful.

He moved deliberately from predicament to predicament. He would get the general idea for a new play, for instance, then hire the cast, rent a theater, have the scenery constructed, lay out the advertising. Not until all these costly commitments were made would he get busy writing the play. By that time his neck was out, all his money invested in a play that was not yet written. Unless he made good he would be the laughing-stock of the theatrical world and a ruined man.

So he would lock himself in a hotel room, draw the curtains, put on slippers and dressing gown, and write furiously. He would work for twenty-four hours at a stretch, consuming gallons of black coffee to keep himself awake. He would not dare quit because his neck was out. Sometimes he would finish a last act just as the overture was struck on opening night.

Cohan, "the Song and Dance Man," did not stick his neck out cautiously to see which way the wind was blowing. He stuck it out full length to make himself work; and he won every time.

Breaking the Low-level Habit

Keep work piled ahead of you. This puts on the pressure and forces you to work nearer your top capacity.

Such was the practice of a sandy-haired farm boy, John H. Patterson, who built up the National Cash Register Company from nothing. He followed it with others as well as himself. He gave his salesmen and production departments high quotas that seemed unreasonable, but at which they usually arrived ahead of time.

He often did things the costliest way intentionally to show how much more one could do when one had to. He used a tatterdemalion foundry yard, for example, to demonstrate to a gang of sluggish yard laborers how much they might be doing. Always an untidy place at best, he told the gang one Thursday morning that he wanted the yard covered with nice green sod by Sunday. It was costly work, under forced draft, but it accomplished its purpose of arousing the yard laborers from their lethargy. Patterson jarred them out of their habit of working at low level.

There is merit in taking on extra work; it breaks our long-established custom of doing less than our best. All of us fall

THE SUREST WAY TO GET

SOFT IS TO BE SOFT

WITH YOURSELF

into periods of low-level working. Industrial psychologists call this stereotyping, working at a slow pace that only an emergency can change. It is not deliberate stalling, not intentional laziness. It is just a too-easy working gait that keeps us from top achievement.

Take on extra work to break your easy-going work habits. FIND OUT WHAT YOU CAN REALLY DO before you get caught in an emergency.

The Blind Boy Who Cured His Laziness

He was blind, crippled by rheumatism, naturally lazy, and the son of rich parents. Now there is a combination of factors that could well keep a man from doing anything.

But William Prescott always wore a contagious smile and worked like fury. This tall Bostonian, with his light-brown hair, had plenty of excuses for just sitting back. Yet he systematically took on extra work to force himself to do ever more and more.

He taught himself Spanish in order to study certain historical documents in their original language. He learned to write in large letters with a device that guided his hand by sixteen parallel wires going down a sheet of paper. Sometimes he had to lie flat on the floor while he worked because of rheumatic twinges. Since he could not see to read notes, he had to use brute force to memorize reams of minute historical details.

Obstacles galore, yet he doggedly kept on, prodding himself to greater industry by continually taking on more work. He even charged himself fines, which he gave to charity, when he did not complete the work he had scheduled.

When he found himself lagging in the midst of a history of Ferdinand and Isabella, he gave $1,000 to one of the men who was reading Spanish documents aloud to him. The money was to be forfeit if Prescott did not have 250 pages of the history written within a year. He did not lose the forfeit.

"It is of little moment whether I succeed in this or that thing," he wrote in his diary, "but it is of great moment that I am habitually industrious."

"Be occupied always," Prescott advised. He had every excuse for loafing out his life, yet he took on extra work and made himself one of the world's greatest historical scholars.

PETER PAUL RUBENS

Boston, Brooklyn, Chicago, Cleveland, Detroit, Los Angeles, New York, Sarasota, Toledo—all have museums that display the priceless art creations of another man who made himself get more things done by taking on more work.

That man is our old acquaintance, the amazing Flemish artist, Peter Paul Rubens. He had made a small fortune as an artist by time he was thirty. But he did not rest on his laurels. Instead, he worked more furiously.

Though he had a cavalier's dash and wit, he made himself acquire the work habits of a slave. Summer and winter, he was up by four o'clock. As long as daylight lasted he toiled in his studio at his newest creations. He had classics read aloud to him as he worked, improving his mind as he stood at the easel.

"We visited the very eminent painter Rubens," Otto Sperling wrote, "but he went right on with his painting, listening to a reading from Tacitus, and dictating a letter. We kept silent for fear of disturbing him; but he spoke to us, without stopping his work, the reading, or the dictation, and answered our questions as if to give proof of his powerful faculties."

The visitor might have added that Rubens kept up this furious pace until his death at sixty-three. He also found time to figure in the diplomatic life of Northern and Western Europe. And, while Rubens was diligently at work and taking on more work without cease, his basement was crowded with half a hundred assistant painters who daubed with one eye on the clock and could see no sense in doing more than they had to. Unfortunately, history does not record the names of these men who were diligent only when the boss was at their elbows.

She Started a War

Harriet Beecher Stowe, curly-headed author of "Uncle Tom's Cabin," wrote her most famous book by taking on more work. She started it as a short story for a magazine. Then, on an impulse, she told the editor there was a sequel to the story and promised to send it to him by a definite date. She promised other, as yet unwritten, sequels.

She stuck her dainty neck out by making rash promises. And she fulfilled the promises, though she had to run out of church one Sunday to write the story of Uncle Tom's death, which she had been thinking about during communion. Yet all the while she was taking care of her three young children and feeding a tableful of boarders.

Busy as she was, she was not too busy to take on extra work.

It is an old and true adage that says, "If you want something done, get a busy person to do it." And, we might add, if you want a sluggish person to SHOW MORE LIFE, give him more to do. It can make a new person out of him.

Busy people have to get the extra things done or sink. It is against human nature to sink without making some effort to save oneself.

Taking on extra work transforms the would-be worker into the have-to-be worker. Try it some time; you'll be astonished at how much more you can do if you must.

It is like putting sand on a greased pole.

No man ever had genius who did not aim to do more than he was able.

—SIR HUMPHRY DAVY

Like a postage stamp, a man's value depends on his ability to stick to a thing till he gets there.

—JOSEPH CHAMBERLAIN

When a man has put a limitation on what he will do, he has put a limit on what he can do.

—CHARLES M. SCHWAB

Folks who never do more than they get paid for, never get paid for more than they do.

—ELBERT HUBBARD

20

How to make habit your friend

ANCIENT ATHENS had its mules, too. One Athenian mule, a contemporary of Pericles, made a place for himself in history. Thousands of men and mules combined labors to build the Acropolis, Athens's beautiful civic center. One of the thousands of mules became immortalized in song and story.

This mule had been retired from his job of hauling stone up and down the hillside for old age, sore feet, or some other just and good reason. But despite his retirement he would not stop work. He continued to follow his fellows up and down the trail as they excavated stone for the amphitheater which was to seat 10,000 spectators.

The comic poets of Athens were elated about the mule that would not retire. They joked about him. They pretended the orations of Pericles had so inspired the animal that he wanted to complete the Acropolis no matter what. Actually, of course, it was not orations but habit that kept the superannuated beast moving. He had the habit of work and couldn't quit.

Habit acted too, but differently, in the case of the elephant at an Eastern zoo. For years he was chained to one spot. When his chains were at last removed, he continued to walk aimlessly to and fro in the same path to which the chains had limited him. The keeper tried to tempt him out of it; food was placed just beyond the reach of the path. The hulking creature walked toward the food, but only as near as his chains *used* to allow. There he stood, taut against the imaginary bonds, swaying and trumpeting hungrily. Years of habit had prevented him from taking the one more step necessary to reach the food.

This story illustrates the inertia of habit that can come from long years of doing less than one might.

Some people are like the Athenian mule; they have good work habits. But there are many who have cramped their accomplishments like the metropolitan elephant.

A surprising number of individuals have no more habits of getting things done than Eskimos. Eskimos have progressed to little further than the Stone-age level of civilization. Regularity means nothing to them. They have no regular mealtimes, no regular time for sleeping. They run their lives on a catch-as-catch-can basis. Consistency-making and efficiency-promoting habits are almost absent from their lives. They work as though they were featherheaded.

In sharp contrast to their methods, note those of the blind proprietor of the news-and-candy stand in the lobby of your office building. Ask for your favorite candy or magazine, and without hesitation this blind person will hand it to you. Though his eyes cannot tell him where to locate it, habit does, for each item is consistently placed in the same spot. His good work habits are almost as useful as a pair of eyes to the blind vendor; he has made them his friends for getting things done.

"A place for everything, and everything in its place," is one of the simplest ways of putting habit to work for you to get things done. Consistency is the password.

EXAMPLES OF CONSISTENCY

The watch repairman always sets his tools in the same location; he does not waste time removing the magnifying lens from his eye to hunt for the one he needs next. He works, rather than plays hide-and-seek with his equipment.

The experienced housewife keeps her kitchen and cleaning materials in an habitual arrangement; by so doing, she saves herself the time and annoyance of searching for them.

The executive's desk also shows that he makes habit work for him. Everything on it has a place. He can reach for pen, paper clips, red pencil, rubber stamp, without taking his eyes from his work. He does not need to hunt for things, does the little jobs automatically, without thought. He is not distracted from the big jobs, because habit is on his side of the game.

Such organization for work is the simplest and perhaps the basic habit in getting more things done with less effort. It is ideal for the lazy person who hates to be annoyed by details.

It may be because I qualify as a lazy person, or it may be because I have to be away from home headquarters much of the year, but, whichever the reason, I have learned firsthand the work-facilitating value of keeping organized for work. While I don't carry an office in my hat, I do carry one scattered about my person.

Paper clips and rubber bands I put always in the ticket pocket of my coat. Pencils and memo pad, as well as memos, are set in my left vest or shirt pocket. Extra eyeglasses are in my right vest pocket. Railroad tickets and hotel reservations I place in a special pocket I have tailored in the left side of my coats. Hotel keys go in my right coat pocket, cleansing tissues in the left, lecture notes and details in the inside right pocket, along with post cards for taking care of correspondence. A penknife for clipping newspapers and magazines hangs at the other end of my watch chain.

I work on train, bus, or plane by the hour without ever having to hunt for a thing. Habit instantly produces whatever I need, and habit puts it back in its proper place as soon as I am finished with it. Other passengers may think I am scratching fleas as I reach for and return things to the various sectors of my anatomy.

But I don't mind, because I am getting work done, and done the lazy way by using habits of organization.

According to reports, one high government official, who must remain nameless, will not recommend a man for public office until he has the opportunity to ask him for a match. If the prospective appointee fumbles through his pockets to locate it, he is not appointed. The official believes that a man with good work habits will always know where his matches are kept. Those who pass the match test presumably have the habit of organizing little things so they can save time and thought for bigger ones.

REGULARITY IN BIG WORK HABITS

But one can be systematic in little things and still fail over big work habits. One may have the habit of letting things go or the habit of getting them done.

Many of the world's producers have spurred themselves on to the habit of getting things done by using certain places for work and FOR NOTHING BUT WORK.

William Gladstone, a wealthy Scotchman, ran England off and on for many years. Early in life Gladstone discovered he could produce best when he used a workplace that was habitually associated with the kind of work he wished to do at the time. So he had two desks. One was for business affairs alone. The other, in the same red-and-white room, was for his literary work.

Ex-nurse Mary Roberts Rinehart combined a career with raising a family. She let her physician husband look after all their business details. She accumulated her shopping lists for weeks at a time, went on shopping tours only twice a year. She saved many hours by not going to a store the instant she wanted something new.

She rented an office in downtown Pittsburgh where she could

TO ENJOY WORK,

MAKE IT A HABIT

---

write without family distractions and home associations. That city office meant work and nothing but work to her. At home she concentrated on something different, enjoying her family life. Work attitudes did not handicap her at home or home attitudes check the flow of her thoughts when at work. Years later, after she had completed more than three-dozen books, she tapered off from writing and gave up the city office. But in her home she still used two desks, one for social writing and another, in a different room, for her occasional literary work.

Jane Austen, the English novelist, always used the same little mahogany table for her work. When she was not engaged in writing, the little table was put out of sight and not used for anything else. That table was one of her work habits and always suggested work to her when it was in the room.

"Over the Hill to the Poorhouse" was written by Will Carleton, a poet who kept far, far away from the poorhouse himself. This Michigan-born man made more money from poetry than most Wall Street brokers out of business. The public liked his folksy rhymes of rural life, and broad-shouldered Carleton, who looked more like a banker than a poet, made such a success of both producing and collecting for his poetry that he earned a small fortune.

His workroom was in his brownstone home on Greene Avenue, Brooklyn. "I shut myself in here," he used to say. "At this window is my business desk. At this other window is my composing desk. No papers are ever allowed to stray from one desk to the other."

Robert Southey, whose father ran a small linen shop, became Poet Laureate before he was thirty. He had the habit of scheduling the hours and minutes of each day. And he kept himself hard at it by having different desks for different jobs. When he became tired at one desk, instead of stopping production to rest he merely moved on to another desk and took up another task. He put in a long workday but was still full of zest and vigor when evening fell.

And some people claim poets aren't practical men!

When I was teaching in college I used to recommend to students that they write their love letters at a different table from the one at which they wrote their long papers. This was to keep them from getting things mixed up and writing a theme to their best girls or a mash note to an instructor. Several students confided to me later that the scheme worked, though better for the love letters than the themes. A desk associated mostly with study seemed to cramp their style in writing sweet nothings.

STANDING UP TO THE JOB

A few people engaged in sedentary work have had special desks made so they could stand and thus be more active physically while on the job. Whether the physical activity helped them or not, we may be certain that the special desks did help by always suggesting work.

Oliver Wendell Holmes, Jr., who became a Supreme Court justice, stood at an old schoolmaster's desk to work. He claimed sitting encouraged verbosity.

Round-faced Henry Temple, later Lord Palmerston, who became England's Secretary of War at twenty-five and was for ten years one of her best Prime Ministers, worked standing at a specially constructed desk.

William Lever, who became the world's Soap King and was dignified by the title of Lord Leverhulme, also worked standing up. His work desk resembled an old-fashioned bookkeeper's stand.

Rufus Choate, who was put on his own at nine after his invalid father died, early developed the habit of reading and studying while he walked and ate. In his law office he used a stand-up desk for working. It was more comfortable to sit down, he confessed, but added that it was so comfortable that if he sat he loafed.

David Graham Phillips, the Indiana-born novelist who exposed abuses in government and business. had a special desk built so he could stand while he worked.

Short, nearsighted, badly dressed Brahms composed all his music standing before a high desk.

Eduard Zeller, authority on Greek philosophy, worked standing at a bookkeeper's desk, even when his bones were tired with seventy years of standing.

Heinrich Schliemann made money hand-over-fist in business until he was nearly fifty. Then he married a Greek farm girl thirty-one years younger and left the world of making money behind to start a new and fabulously glorious career. With his bride this amateur scientist—but man of action—excavated the ancient city of Troy, and bedecked his black-eyed bride with the jewels worn by Helen of Troy. A doer, not a theorizer, thin-framed Schliemann worked standing up at high desks. He could be found at the high desk, examining precious relics excavated in their explorations or reading ancient Greek manuscripts, at 3 A.M. in summer, and at 5 A.M. in winter. And when he did sit down, he carefully avoided an easy chair.

And that fiery aviator-poet, Gabriel d'Annunzio, who lost an eye in aerial combat, stood both to read and to write. He used high lecterns which he obtained from old churches and monasteries. Bottles of colored ink were set within his reach, for he not only wrote but underlined much of his reading as well. This was the only monklike thing about his tempestuous life.

Other Work Habits of Producers

The world's producers outstripped other people because they had productive work habits, habits that helped them do superior work easily. Whether or not they were born with genius, they nevertheless worked like geniuses and got geniuses' results. Not many of them stood at their work, but they all had certain essential work habits that are worth reviewing:

1. They had the habit of PLANNING their work not only for tomorrow but also for goals in the future. They worked for a purpose, and that purpose carried them through hardships and over obstacles.

2. They had the habit of working on THINGS THAT COUNTED. They avoided enticing distractions. They knew that the steam that blows the whistle does not turn the wheel. They worked with foresight.

3. They had the habit of saying no to things that would not help them produce. They kept on the main highway, OFF THE DETOURS.

4. They had the habit of reading books and magazines that would help their work. They kept PRIMING THEIR HEADS with ideas, facts, and inspiration.

5. They had the habit of DOING THE UNPLEASANT JOB FIRST.

They did not paralyze present activity by letting past work hang over their heads.

6. They had the habit of MAKING THEMSELVES WORK. They kept their effort alive.

7. They had the habit of DECIDING TRIFLES QUICKLY. They did not putter around trying to make up their minds what to do next.

8. They had the habit of STARTING VIGOROUSLY and promptly, often early in the morning. They did not let the grass grow under their feet.

9. They had the habit of WORKING LIKE CRAFTSMEN. By working for quality, they got more done and received more satisfaction than if they had rushed for quantity.

10. They had the habit of USING THEIR SPARE TIME, the habit of USING BOTH HANDS, the habit of DOING TWO THINGS AT ONCE. They used each minute before it had disappeared forever. Doing nothing was the most annoying thing in the world to them.

11. They had the habit of GETTING OTHERS TO HELP THEM. They TRAINED OTHERS to be extra hands, eyes, and heads for them.

12. They had the habit of WORKING FOR MORE THAN MONEY. Pride in a job well done, in accomplishment, was more rewarding to them than a big bank account.

13. They had the habit of TAKING ON MORE WORK. They kept expanding their abilities and achievements. They caught up on work quickly, could take on more work easily. They kept out of ruts by broadening the highroad. They put pressure on themselves to do or sink.

14. They had the habit of requiring production from themselves, of not accepting their own alibis. They CRACKED THE WHIP OVER THEMSELVES instead of feeling sorry for their lot in life.

And in such ways they made habit their friend in getting things done. They produced enormously and enjoyed life to the full, because all these habits together gave them *the habit of liking work*.

It's foolish just to work. Make work a habit and then play at the job.

The conduct of successful business merely consists of doing things in a very simple way, doing them regularly, and never neglecting to do them.

—LORD LEVERHULME

When you have set yourself a task, finish it!

—OVID

The darkest hour in the history of any young man is when he sits down to figure how to get money without honestly earning it.

—HORACE GREELEY

21

Don't accept your alibis

I RECENTLY received two letters, as different from each other as black from white. The longer one—by far the longest I have ever seen—was written in pencil. For page after page this forty-year-old told me how unfair the world had been to him. He was one of the world's best workers, so he claimed, but the public library, the Catholic bishop, even the Y.M.C.A., whose stationery he was using, were joined in a great conspiracy to keep him from securing a job.

He also maintained he was a splendid fellow to work with but on every job he took other workers made themselves disagreeable, poked fun at him, and poisoned the air he breathed. With all these impossible conditions, he concluded—rather naturally—wasn't he foolish to try to work?

He had written his Congressman about the situation, but Congress had done nothing. So then, having read one of my magazine articles, he had written me to ask what I could do to make the bishop quit blacklisting him.

His conclusion that the world owed him a living was inevitable if all the things he wrote were true. The fact was, of course, that his reasonings were the distortions of a twisted mind. They were excuses which had been developed to the point of abnormality.

He had the best alibis in the world for not working, but the alibis existed only in his thinking, the place where alibis usually start and grow; alibis seldom have any basis in reality.

His instance is extreme, for obviously he had a paranoid type of mental disorder and should have been under treatment for it. His life had become so enmeshed in his alibis that his entire existence was seriously out of gear.

Now look at the other letter. It was a long one, too, but neatly typed on good-quality paper. There was something very like poetry in each of its well-turned sentences. It was from a woman in her thirties, an elevator operator in an apartment building. The letter was written during quiet moments in the elevator.

Evenings this woman took care of children for white families, for this writer was colored. She had so little Negro blood she could pass for white if she wished. She made her own clothes, was the sole support of her aged parents. The burden of caring for them had kept romance from her life, though several white men had showed an interest in her.

Deeply interested in cultural things, her sensitivity about the color line had prevented her from taking part in cultural activities, although she did follow courses of reading, planned for her by professors, in the free library. Now she was writing a novel in what spare time she could make. That is why she wrote me—not to complain about her lot but because she thought I could give her suggestions for a possible publisher.

Could I! Here was a person with many plausible excuses for not doing additional work, yet she was ignoring them and going ahead. I wrote a literary agent about her and also a foundation that specializes in giving opportunities to individuals who have the talent for self-development.

But I wrote to the health officer of the Eastern city where the paranoid lived, suggesting that he look up the alibi expert and give him some psychiatric attention before the latter bombed the Y.M.C.A. or poisoned the bishop. I have never been cordial to alibi artists and must confess that during my twenty years as a college teacher I knew many of these artful dodgers. And, in the business world, too, I have seen a number of people who never gave themselves a fair start because they had the habit of making excuses rather than the habit of making good.

They are the SELF-STOPPERS.

It is easy to find excuses for not doing things. But it is a habit loaded with danger.

It is giving up without even trying.

It undermines the self-confidence.

It encourages a pessimistic attitude.

It is negative thinking about our daily opportunities to do things. And negative thinking is one of the forces that destroys accomplishment.

HE WAS, BRIEFLY, THE RICHEST MAN IN THE WEST

H. A. W. Tabor was a roving, hard-drinking man who became the Midas of the Mountains. He started with nothing and became one of the richest men in the West. But he ended his days broke, prospecting with a pick and shovel, while his daughter died a dope addict in Chicago. From nothing to a hundred million and back to nothing!

High living and low morals helped his downward crash. So did excuses. There was the case of the Minnie Mine, for instance, which Tabor once owned. At his zenith, that mine was too small to interest the Silver King, and anyway, he said, its ore was not especially rich. So he let the Minnie Mine slip away from him.

A stoop-shouldered, gray-haired man from Philadelphia bought the Minnie Mine on installment payments; Tabor, in his tailored broadcloth suit, twirled his black walrus moustaches and smiled when he saw Meyer Guggenheim risk his life savings to reopen the Minnie. But the Dutchman from Philadelphia did not dare let the mine fail. Nor did it. Within six months he had made "second contact" with a rich silver vein. The Guggenheim fortunes were on the way up; "Silver Dollar" Tabor's were on the way down.

Wine, women, and excuses brought Tabor back to below his original starting point. "Haw" Tabor is today just a colorful memory of the West. The House of Guggenheim is world-famous and respected.

The Amateur Crossed the Channel First

From Calais to Dover is only a short distance—twenty-one miles. But twenty-one miles was a long distance in the early days of the airplane. A $5,000 prize awaited the first man to fly the English Channel.

Hubert Latham, rich French playboy and sportsman, decided he would be that man. He had sought adventure in big-game hunting and desert explorations; now he would fly the first plane across the Channel and thus add another adventure to the score about which he bragged in clubs. He prepared for the Channel flight by buying a sleek new monoplane and engaging a mechanic to keep it in perfect condition.

Unexpected competition developed. It amused the wealthy Latham. Look at the plane his competitor, Louis Blériot, was going to use. Homemade. Poorly finished. Ugly. No expert mechanic to keep it in tiptop condition. Latham smiled confi-

---

WE CAN ALL DO MUCH MORE
THAN WE REALIZE

---

dently at his thirty-seven-year-old rival, though he hastened his own preparations—just in case, you know.

One hot Saturday in July, Blériot announced he was ready to try the first air crossing of the Channel the next morning.

So Latham was up before sunrise on Sunday, sleepy-eyed, surveying the weather. "It is not favorable for the flight," he reported and went back to bed.

In a village a few miles away, Blériot pushed out his home-made airplane, consulted his watch. As he warmed up the motor, he turned to some spectators. "Just which way is it to Dover?" he asked them. He crossed the Channel in twenty-five minutes and flew ten miles out of his way before he found Dover.

The amateur won because the wealthy professional could find an alibi to sleep late on Sunday morning.

There is an old French proverb that says, **"He who excuses himself, accuses himself."**

The Great Blizzard No Alibi

James Talcott, leading woolen wholesaler in New York, hired a young office boy. The boy, Joseph P. Day, got up at six o'clock to have the office on Franklin Street swept and tidied up when the clerks arrived at seven-thirty. Several times a day he took a cup of hot water to one of the executives who had chronic indigestion.

When young Day's pay was raised to $5 a week, he boldly asked for a chance to go out and sell woolens. He lacked both age and appearance, but he got the job and soon managed to bring back orders.

Then the Great Blizzard of '88 snarled all New York. The salesmen straggled to Franklin Street late in the forenoon, hugged the stove, and gossiped the rest of the day. "No one will buy on a day like this," they agreed.

But late that afternoon the front door opened, letting in a gust of sharp, arctic air. Young Day staggered in, half-frozen.

"This is a great hour to come to work," an older salesman said.

"Oh, but I've finished a day's work," Day replied. "I always go out on stormy days. You see, I have no competition on those days, so I have plenty of time to show samples. I sold forty-three cases of goods today."

Joe Day was made a junior salesman on the spot, and his pay was doubled.

Joseph P. Day became the world's greatest real-estate salesman. He was an expert at getting things done, not at thinking up plausible alibis. He realized that "not today" was likely to mean "never."

The weather is a perennial excuse for self-stoppers. It is too warm to do that unpleasant task. Too chilly. Too wet. Too stormy. Too threatening. Or it is just too nice a day to be working!

Watch Out for These—They're Alibis!

"I need a better place to work, more equipment" is also a common alibi. But the Curies isolated radium in a rickety shed. The Brashears made their famous astronomical lenses in a shack that was just as rickety and much smaller. Rokitansky founded pathological anatomy in a shed in Vienna. Einstein works in a plain room on a plain kitchen table.

Poor workplaces do not discourage people; they discourage themselves.

"People bother me and prevent me from getting things done," is another of the side-stepper's allegations.

Yet A. Conan Doyle wrote some of his "Adventures of Sherlock Holmes" in the corner of a room where a dozen people were talking and milling about. George Sand scribbled even when surrounded by friends. Concentration is needed for such work, but some people let nothing deter them from getting things done. They do not let grass grow under their feet merely because others are there to distract them.

"I don't know how," whine the Slippery Sams. Perhaps they don't know how. Neither did Westinghouse know how, but he found out. They will never learn by not trying.

"It is too much to undertake," is an often-heard alibi. This, too, is just a negation of one's abilities *before one has made any effort to discover what those abilities may be.*

"My health won't stand it," is the negative thinking of those who would *rather pamper themselves than produce.*

"Someone else can do it better," is the excuse of those who *pass up an opportunity to get credit for themselves.*

"I'm doing too much already," is the alibi of those who *play at being busy.*

"No one will appreciate it, so why do it?" is the pretense of those who *would appreciate themselves more* if they did it.

"They'll expect too much of me if I do it," is the defense of those who unwittingly *admit they have been holding back all the while.*

"I'm already a success and might as well bask in my glory," say some. To those we recommend a quotation from Thomas J. Watson, who created the International Business Machine Corp.: "The minute we say to ourselves that we have succeeded, we have confessed failure. When a man is satisfied that he has succeeded, he means that his striving for success is over, and that marks him as a failure. A man who is doing his best each day is truly alive, but a man who did his best yesterday is starting to die."

"This other work would be more interesting," is the alibi of those who will start off on any detour regardless of whether it ends in a blind alley.

"I am too busy to read," is the alibi of those who *cultivate their own illiteracy* and keep behind the stream of progress.

"I just do today's work and let tomorrow take care of itself," is the excuse of those who fail to plan ahead and so *get hopelessly tangled.*

"I can make enough money as it is," is the alibi of those who imagine people should work for money rather than results.

Enough time and ingenuity are spent in such negative thinking to build the Panama Canal over again each year.

Give yourself a break. Think positively. Don't accept your alibis for not doing things.

The authors know you can do much more than you have been doing. Each of us can. Their sincere hope is that this book helps you tap your fuller abilities and makes you join the ranks of the Achievers.

Whatever else you think, think that YOU CAN. Here's wishing success to you—and the happiness of achievement!

To win without boasting; to lose without excuses.
> —*Motto of*
> A. P. TERHUNE

Better wear out than rust out.
> —*Motto of father of*
> SAMUEL F. B. MORSE

He cannot be called a failure, for he made full use of the talents which had been given him.
> —T. G. WILSON

KEEP ON KEEPING ON!